COST-EFFECTIVENESS ANALYSIS 2ND EDITION

Methods and Applications

HENRY M. LEVIN
PATRICK J. McEWAN

COST-EFFECTIVENESS ANALYSIS 2ND EDITION

Methods and Applications

SAGE Publications
International Educational and Professional Publisher
Thousand Oaks ■ London ■ New Delhi

For information:

Sage Publications, Inc.
2455 Teller Road
Thousand Oaks, California 91320
E-mail: order@sagepub.com

Sage Publications Ltd.
6 Bonhill Street
London EC2A 4PU
United Kingdom

Sage Publications India Pvt. Ltd.
M-32 Market
Greater Kailash I
New Delhi 110 048 India

Printed in the United States of America

Library of Congress Cataloging-in-Publication Data

Levin, Henry M.
    Cost-effectiveness analysis: Methods and applications / by Henry M.
    Levin and Patrick J. McEwan.—2nd ed.
        p.   cm.
    Includes bibliographical referencse and index.
    ISBN 0-7619-1933-3 (cloth: alk. paper)
    ISBN 0-7619-1934-1 (pbk.: alk. paper)
        1. Cost effectiveness.   I. McEwan, Patrick J.   II. Title.
    HD47.4 .L484   2000
    658.15′54—dc21   00-009499

                        05   06   07   7   6   5

Acquiring Editor: C. Deborah Laughton
Editorial Assistant: Eileen Carr
Production Editor: Diana E. Axelsen
Editorial Assistant: Victoria Cheng
Typesetter/Designer: Lynn Miyata
Indexer: Jeanne Busemeyer
Cover Designer: Michelle Lee

Contents

List of Examples

List of Tables

▼

List of Figures

Acknowledgments to the Second Edition

This book benefited greatly from discussions and suggestions over the years about how we might update, expand, and improve the first edition of this book. Over the span of 17 years and 13 printings, we received considerable feedback from scholars, policy analysts, and students that surely improved the content and presentation of the revision. Many researchers, too numerous to mention, have generously shared their work. We want to express our thanks to all of them. We also thank Darrell R. Lewis and Jon S. Eberling for their review of the final manuscript.

Levin wishes to dedicate this edition to the memory of his close friend, Professor Jose Luis Moreno Becerra. Moreno was a professor of Applied Economics at the University of La Laguna in the Canary Islands, Spain. He was a graduate student in the Economics of Education at Stanford some two decades ago and returned to Spain, receiving the highest score in the nation in a competition for a prestigious professorship in Applied Economics. Such a performance gave him the first choice of positions at any Spanish university. He returned to his home in the Canary Islands, and over the years, he became a leading voice of the Economics of Education throughout Spain. He was a founder and the first president of the Economics of

Education Society of Spain, a group with a dynamic agenda and an annual meeting of very high quality. His sudden death in 1999 saddened a wide circle of colleagues and friends, and we cherish our associations with him, both academic and personal. We wish to present this as an homage to Jose Luis for his wife, Tere, and his two children, Ernesto and Elena.

Finally, McEwan wishes to dedicate this edition to the memory of his father. Richard T. McEwan always harbored aspirations of being an academic, but his family was not wealthy and many educational opportunities were unavailable. By working many years at a job that was less than fulfilling, he ensured that both his children would be sufficiently privileged to choose careers that were denied to him. Unfortunately, he did not live long enough to share in their accomplishments. If this book succeeds in its goals, then it is partly due to his curiosity, his intellect, and his encouragement.

Preface to the Second Edition

The first edition of this volume, published in 1983, lamented that "everyone is talking about cost-effectiveness analysis, but none are doing it." Nearly two decades later, is this still a fair assessment?

In education, the use of cost-effectiveness analysis is still rather modest. To our knowledge, this is the only book-length treatment of the subject. Some general textbooks for evaluators devote a section to the topic (Boardman, Greenberg, Vining, & Weimer, 1996; Rossi & Freeman, 1993; Weiss, 1998), yet most provide only a cursory discussion, if any at all. Perhaps unsurprisingly, the number of published cost-effectiveness analyses in education has grown at a slow (albeit steady) pace.[1]

In sharp contrast, cost-effectiveness analysis is rapidly becoming a standard tool of health researchers. There are numerous textbooks and methodological surveys of the field (Drummond, O'Brien, Stoddart, & Torrance, 1997; Gold, Siegel, Russell, & Weinstein, 1996; Johannesson, 1996; Sloan, 1995). Journals of health policy and health economics routinely publish empirical studies—numbering in the hundreds—that compare the cost-effectiveness of different medical interventions. A national panel has even issued recommendations on the proper conduct and interpretation of studies (Weinstein, Siegel, Gold, Kamlet, & Russell, 1996). Most heartening is that cost-effectiveness analysis is increasingly recognized as a useful and necessary tool for choosing among competing health-care investments.

Cost-effectiveness analysis should be more important than ever, particularly in education. At every level of government, administrators are being asked to accomplish more with the same or even fewer resources. At least rhetorically, this is evident in educational debates that emphasize the "cost-effectiveness" or "efficiency" of investments and policies. All too often, however, these claims are not based on solid evidence. At least part of the blame for this situation may reside in the fact that cost evaluation is still not widely understood among policymakers or even among educational evaluators. We hope that an introduction to cost analysis might encourage and enable such individuals to incorporate this approach into their evaluations and decisions. Better training is a necessary—though perhaps not a sufficient—condition for the promotion of cost studies. Thus, the main objective of this volume has remained unchanged since the first edition: to provide school personnel, evaluators, and students with a clear introduction to the rationale and methods of cost analysis.

In other respects, the volume has undergone substantial modification. Throughout the book, we have replaced many of the hypothetical examples from the first edition with actual cost studies from education. We have also rewritten and leavened the text with numerous references to methodological and applied research, in order to reflect new developments in the field. Where progress in education is lacking, we endeavored to reference developments in health cost analysis.

In the first edition, a discussion of effectiveness, benefits, and utility was confined to a single chapter. This edition has expanded the discussion to three completely new chapters (6 through 8) on cost-effectiveness, cost-benefit, and cost-utility analysis. In each case, we review the methods of estimating effectiveness, benefits, and utility and the procedures for interpreting this information in light of costs. We also focus attention on several essential features of a conscientious cost study, such as sensitivity analysis. Chapter 9 is a greatly expanded version of its predecessor, on the use of cost evaluations. For example, it presents a checklist for evaluating cost studies and uses it to evaluate a particular cost-effectiveness study. It also assesses some emergent topics, such as the use of "league tables" to compare the findings of several cost studies. Finally, Appendix B includes an extensive new bibliography of educational cost studies, grouped by their topics.

▶ NOTE

1. Some research bears out these impressions. Between 1985 and 1988, less than 1% of presentations at the Annual Meetings of the American Evaluation Association addressed cost-effectiveness analysis or included it as a component in evaluations. The proportion is even smaller among evaluation studies presented at the Annual Meetings of the American Educational Research Association (Levin, 1991). Monk and King (1993) compared the predominance of cost studies in two journals of public policy: one focused on educational issues and the other of general interest. Seventy-five percent of evaluation studies in the education journal ignored the issue of costs. In contrast, only 20% of articles in the general policy journal omitted a consideration of costs.

CHAPTER 1

Introduction to Cost Analysis

1. Define the objectives of this book.
2. Define "cost analysis."
3. Identify and describe four modes of cost analysis.

A book should begin by tempting the reader with the importance of the subject or the excitement of the story that follows. In our case, this might appear to be a tall order. Yet, consider the size of the education industry in the United States—over $700 billion. Despite this enormous resource base, educational institutions are constantly engaged in a quest for more resources to meet new aspirations or unfulfilled needs. If efficiency were to improve by only 2%, $14 billion would be available for other purposes. At the level of a school district, an improvement of that magnitude would provide an additional $120 per student or about $3,000 per classroom. However, these gains can only be accomplished by identifying ways to use existing resources more efficiently. That is the purpose of cost-effectiveness analysis: to provide a method for choosing among alternatives in order to select those that are able to accomplish a given result most parsimoniously.

Some might say that we ought to be less concerned with the quest for efficiency and more concerned with simply finding more resources, although this is hardly an either/or proposition. For example, imagine that a new state lottery is expected to yield hundreds of millions of dollars in new revenues for public education. Legislators and school administrators have proposed a number of alternative uses, including class size reduction, teacher training, and renovation of aging school facilities. How should the funds be apportioned among these alternatives if our goal is to maximize student learning? Or, on a smaller scale, imagine that each teacher in a school has been given $500 in discretionary funds. How should these funds be invested in the classroom so as to contribute to the greatest improvements in learning?

Lest we become overly optimistic, let us consider a dire scenario. In the wake of an economic recession, the education revenues of a large urban district have declined sharply. The district must eliminate several programs if it is to remain within its budget. If the goal is to minimize the declines that might occur in student learning, which programs should be eliminated?

In all of these cases, we are understandably concerned with obtaining the most "bang" for the "bucks" that are spent on education. Instead of relying upon guesswork or politics to make these hard decisions, we could employ the tools of cost-effectiveness analysis. They would allow us to take account of both the costs and effects of selecting alternatives, making it possible to choose those alternatives that provide the best results for any given resource outlay or that minimize the resource utilization for any given outcome. The standard approaches to evaluation are more limited because they take account only of the effectiveness of alternatives, such as the number of students served, the impact on test scores, and so on.

Consider the approach used in an article that has been cited widely in literature on educational administration and decision making as providing a formula for increasing productivity (Walberg, 1984). The author of this article engaged in what is called meta-analysis by summarizing the literature on many different educational interventions to provide comprehensive tables that compare the estimated results on achievement of many different approaches. Presumably one need just choose those interventions that show large "effect sizes" over those that show low "effect sizes." Even if one agrees that such meta-analyses are useful—and there are important reasons that they ought not be used for this purpose—the absence of cost information means that the results should never be used for decision making in isolation.[1] For example, if one of the interventions is associated with an effect size on achievement of 0.6 and another of 0.4, it does not necessarily follow that the first of the interventions is the superior one. What if the cost of the first intervention is $400 per student and the cost of the second is $200 per student? For any given budget, the overall effect of spending it entirely on the second intervention may improve achievement far more than spending it on the first alternative. By combining cost information with appropriate measures of effectiveness, we are able to create more productive uses of resources and improved educational outcomes with given resources.

Cost analysis of social programs includes a number of broad conceptual and methodological principles that apply equally well to all areas of public endeavor, including education, health, criminal justice, transportation, and other fields. In this volume, we shall focus on the field of education. Education is a particularly amenable topic because it is a subject that is familiar to almost everyone and it is a public activity that has been hit hard by the types of budgetary constraints—and, more recently, unexpected surpluses—that require careful planning and evaluation that takes account of costs. Moreover, it is subject to a constant barrage of criticism that it does not operate in a "cost-effective" or "efficient" manner.

Policy decisions in the public sector must be based increasingly upon a demonstrated consideration of both the costs and effects of such decisions. Tax and expenditure limitation movements, declining enrollments, and recession all have negative impacts on educational budgets, and it is important to take costs into account as well as other aspects of the alternatives. Even in times of relative prosperity, we must decide which investments will produce the greatest educational returns to society. Yet, few evaluators or educational administrators have received training in the nature, development, or use of cost-effectiveness analyses. The standard courses and instructional materials for both evaluators and educational administrators are generally devoid of this subject.

Purpose

The purpose of this volume is to provide a diverse audience—evaluators, educational administrators, and graduate students—with a systematic introduction to the use of cost analysis in educational evaluation. Accordingly, the volume has been written with the intention of familiarizing this audience with the nature and use of cost-analytic tools, as well as showing how to plan and implement a study in this domain. Cost analysis in educational evaluation refers to the use of a broad set of techniques for evaluation and decision making, including cost-effectiveness, cost-benefit, cost-utility, and cost-feasibility. Each type of analysis will be developed separately for consideration, but we will refer to the group of cost techniques taken together as cost analysis in evaluation.

Finally, we should emphasize one purpose for which this volume—and cost analysis in general—are not intended. This book is not meant to train individuals to "audit the books" of programs or organizations, or gauge compliance with expenditure requirements and the like. The set of concepts and methods that we describe are meant to assist individuals in weighing the costs of interventions against their outcomes, and then in choosing the best intervention.

Goals

The general goals of this volume are the following:

1. to provide an understanding of what is meant by cost-effectiveness analysis and its variants;

2. to provide an understanding of the basic problems in constructing and implementing a cost analysis in education;

3. to provide an understanding of the identification and measurement of costs;

4. to provide an understanding of the identification and measurement of effects, benefits, and utility;

5. to provide an understanding of how to usefully combine and interpret information on costs, effects, benefits, and utility; and

6. to provide an understanding of how to use the results of cost-effectiveness studies in decision making.

These are primary objectives and should be accomplishable for all serious readers. An evaluator, an educational administrator, or a student who works his or her way through this volume, doing the various readings and exercises, should be able to accomplish all these goals.

In addition, it is expected that the volume can serve a different need, which will vary among members of our audience. Some educational administrators and evaluators will wish to go beyond learning about the method and its uses to understanding how to actually apply the method to evaluation and administration within their own work settings. For example, an educational administrator may wish to ascertain how to do studies of cost-effectiveness among various alternatives for providing reading instruction, school lunches, or designing budget cuts. An educational evaluator may wish to learn how to augment a standard evaluation of alternatives with information on costs. While this volume is not designed to train such persons to do these tasks in the absence of other training or assistance, it should be considered a necessary step in that direction. By mastering this introduction, an evaluator or administrator should be able to work effectively with a technical specialist on cost-effectiveness analysis or should be able to undertake additional study in mastering the techniques that will be presented.

We have attempted to design the volume so that an individual can utilize it as part of an informal course of self-study or in a formal course on the subject. At various stages, the learner will be introduced to concepts and their applications. These are accompanied by numerous examples drawn from the applied literature on cost analysis, focusing almost entirely on educational examples. Exercises are provided at the end of each chapter to enable the reader to test his or her understanding of the topic that is being covered. Sample answers to these exercises are provided in Appendix A.

The volume will introduce and bring up to date the concepts and methods reflected in earlier works of a coauthor (Levin, 1975, 1981) within an instructional format. Accordingly, a final word on the purpose of the presentation is important. In these days of do-it-yourself instruction, it is appealing to provide a set of mechanical steps that one can simply follow verbatim in order to learn a new skill. Unfortunately, this approach is not appropriate for training in cost analysis and cost-effectiveness analysis. Although one can provide a set of principles that can be used for carrying out the analysis, the actual application in any particular setting will require judgments on the part of the administrator or evaluator. Thus, this volume will not be a substitute for a sensitive and judicious effort by the evaluator in applying his or her craft. Rather, it will provide a new set of concepts and analytic tools that can be incorporated into that activity. Although the guidelines for incorporating these new dimensions will be presented and illustrated, the applications will require careful consideration by the analyst or user.

Importance of Cost-Effectiveness Analysis

Why should educational evaluators or school personnel be concerned with cost-effectiveness analysis? The most superficial answer to this question is that reference to such analysis is often an important source of persuasion as a rhetorical claim. By saying that one has compared the cost-effectiveness of different approaches and found a particular one to be most cost-effective, one can often disarm opponents. Unfortunately, this is the principal way in which the terminology is used in the educational sector. This volume will go beyond such banality. Cost-effectiveness analysis should be a topic of concern because it can lead to a more efficient use of educational resources—it can reduce the costs of reaching particular objectives, and it can expand what can be accomplished for any particular budget or other resource constraint.

This book emphasizes that a proper assessment of both costs and effectiveness is a necessary element of a serious evaluation. All too often, either costs or effects are considered separately, and the resulting conclusions may be misleading. For the most part, educational evaluators attempt to establish whether an intervention is effective is attaining some goal, such as raising academic achievement. Business managers and administrators are often concerned with lowering educational costs in order to fit school or district expenditures within a fixed budget.

Nevertheless, both parties share a common goal: They wish to attain maximal school effectiveness for a given budget, or conversely, they wish to attain a given level of effectiveness at a minimal cost. They are unlikely to accomplish this goal if higher effectiveness and lower costs are pursued as independent goals. To illustrate this point, it is useful to consider two examples.

EXAMPLE 1.1. The Perils of Ignoring Costs

Reducing class size is among the most popular and intuitively appealing options for improving schools. It seems to provide a rare instance of agreement among parents, teachers, administrators, and politicians of every stripe. Recent years have witnessed a number of initiatives to reduce class size, especially in the primary grades (Brewer, Krop, Gill, & Reichardt, 1999). At least 19 U.S. states have considered class size reduction plans. In one of the largest initiatives, California sought in 1996 to reduce class sizes in the early primary grades to 20 students. In 1998, President Clinton proposed a federal initiative that would reduce class sizes in grades 1 through 3 to 18 students.

Much of the support for class size reduction is based on the promising results of a single educational experiment: Project STAR in Tennessee (Krueger, 1999; Mosteller, 1995). Commissioned by the Tennessee legislature, the experiment compared the achievement of students who were assigned to three kinds of classes: (1) students in regular classes (22 to 25 students) without teacher aides, (2) students in regular classes with teacher aides, and (3) students in small classes (13 to 17 students). In participating schools, the cohort of students who entered kindergarten in the 1985-86 school year was randomly assigned to each of the three classroom types. Their progress on achievement tests was followed until the third grade. The results from one evaluation suggested that performance on standardized tests increases by about 4 percentile points during the first year in which students were assigned to smaller classes (Krueger). Effects tended to be relatively larger among minority and lower-income students. Each subsequent year of participation in a smaller class further increased achievement by about 1 percentile. In contrast, teacher aides were found to have little effect on student achievement.

Overall, the results provided strong evidence that reducing primary class sizes has important effects on student achievement. On this basis alone, many feel that it is a worthwhile investment. But reducing class size requires substantial resource investments (Brewer et al., 1999). New teachers must be hired and—if school space is unavailable—classrooms must be built and furnished (on the costs of class size reduction, see Example 1.6). These same resources could be spent on any number of educational interventions: more computers for the classroom, additional teacher training, longer school days or years, different curriculum and textbooks, higher teacher salaries, and so on. Perhaps investments in one of these alternatives would yield similar effects on student achievement at an even lower cost than class size reduction. If so, the savings could be devoted to other educational investments or returned to the taxpayers.

(continued)

EXAMPLE 1.1. The Perils of Ignoring Costs *(continued)*

Some years ago, Levin and his colleagues Glass and Meister (1987) explored this issue. The authors compared the costs and effectiveness of four different educational reforms. They concluded that reducing class size was one of the more costly options for obtaining a fixed gain in student achievement. In contrast, peer tutoring was found to be among the most cost-effective in terms of achievement gains per unit of cost (see Example 6.3 for a detailed description of this study). In a study of junior-secondary education in Botswana, Fuller, Hua, and Snyder (1994) compared the costs and effects of three educational interventions. Reducing class size proved to be an effective means of raising mathematics achievement, as did the provision of additional teacher in-service training in mathematics pedagogy. The authors then calculated the size of the investment in either intervention that would be required to achieve the same 1-year achievement gain. The investment in class size reduction would have proven nearly 30 times larger.

Although these findings are suggestive, this is a fertile area for research. There is regrettably limited evidence on the relative cost-effectiveness of educational interventions such as class size reduction (Brewer et al., 1999; Grissmer, 1999).

EXAMPLE 1.2. The Perils of Ignoring Effectiveness

Declining enrollments in schools often force administrators to make difficult decisions about school closure. Should numerous smaller schools be maintained, or should their enrollments be consolidated into a single larger school? On the surface, the decision might seem to be related exclusively to costs. The accountant or business manager should merely calculate the cost of each alternative and implement the least costly.

Indeed, costs may be lower in larger schools due to economies of scale (Bray, 1987; Lee & Smith, 1997). Schools may benefit from lower prices on bulk purchases of school supplies or furnishings. Perhaps most important is that the fixed costs of operating a school can be spread over a larger number of pupils. For example, a larger school needs to maintain only one playground and cafeteria, pay one electricity bill, support one library, and so forth. Numerous smaller schools would be forced to duplicate these fixed expenditures, and per-pupil costs could rise. In rural areas of developing countries, isolated schools may not enroll enough students to fill even a standard classroom. Since even five students require a teacher, per-pupil costs may turn out to be quite high.

EXAMPLE 1.2. continued

Nevertheless, it is not a foregone conclusion that larger schools are less costly. In consolidating schools, there may be new costs of transporting students greater distances (Chambers, 1981; Kenny, 1982). If large schools are sufficiently distant (as in many rural areas), then boarding facilities may need to be provided (Bray, 1987). Small schools that are physically close to their communities may be better poised to generate donated resources from local parents and citizens.

Let us presume, however, that the overall cost per student declines in larger school units. Does school size alter the effectiveness of schools? There is some evidence that larger schools have lower educational effectiveness (Chambers, 1981; Lee & Smith, 1997). Precisely why this is so is unclear. It may be that larger schools are more depersonalized and provide both students and educational professionals with less of a feeling of individual importance and involvement (Barker & Gump, 1964; Lee & Smith, 1997). Or it might be traced to the presence of a core curriculum in smaller high schools that emphasizes academic excellence for all students, regardless of their abilities or aspirations (Lee & Smith, 1997). In areas of low population density, students may be forced to travel long distances to reach a larger school. Their resulting fatigue could reduce their learning once they arrive or even deter attendance in the first place (Bray, 1987).

Despite the cost savings of larger, consolidated schools, they may entail sacrifices in effectiveness, though this obviously needs to be analyzed on a case-by-case basis. Thus, larger schools that are less costly may ultimately prove to be less cost-effective. Administrators might consider other means of cutting educational costs that will not undermine effectiveness. For example, smaller schools can reduce costs by sharing teachers and administrators and, in the case of secondary schools, by drawing on such community resources as courses offered by community colleges. They can also lease unused classroom space for child care, senior citizen centers, and private educational endeavors such as computer schools or tutoring centers. The key point is that each of these alternatives should be clearly established, so that the relative costs *and* effects of each alternative can be evaluated.

Each example illustrates the pitfalls of concentrating exclusively on either effectiveness or costs. If evaluators intend the results of their studies to be used for decision making, the information on effects of alternatives (such as class size reduction) is not adequate in itself to make a choice. If educational administrators wish to provide suggestions for cutting expenditures, the cost consequences of the alternatives (such as school consolidation) are not adequate in themselves for making an informed decision. In short, information on both costs and effects is necessary to adequately inform the decision. The rest of this chapter elaborates several frameworks for organizing the decision-making process.

Cost-Analysis Approaches in Evaluation and Decision Making

One of the more confusing aspects of incorporating cost analysis into evaluation and decision making is that a number of different, but related, terms are often used interchangeably. These include cost-effectiveness, cost-benefit, cost-utility, and cost-feasibility. Although each is related to and can be considered to be a member in good standing of the cost-analysis family, each is characterized by important differences that make it appropriate to specific applications (Levin, 1975). The purpose of this section is to describe these differences. Each approach will be illustrated with a concrete example of a study from the educational literature, with the exception of cost-utility analysis. Because cost-utility analysis is still rare in education, we shall use a hypothetical example.

Cost-Effectiveness Analysis

Cost-effectiveness (CE) analysis refers to the evaluation of alternatives according to both their costs and their effects with regard to producing some outcome. Typically, educational evaluation and decision making must focus on the choice of an educational intervention or alternative for meeting a particular objective, such as increasing test scores in basic skills or reducing the number of students who drop out. In these cases, the results of alternative interventions can be assessed according to their effects on improving test scores or on the number of potential school dropouts who stay in school.

When costs are combined with measures of effectiveness and all alternatives can be evaluated according to their costs and their contribution to meeting the same effectiveness criterion, we have the ingredients for a CE analysis. For example, alternatives can be evaluated on the basis of their cost for raising student test scores by a given amount or the cost for each potential dropout averted. From a decision-oriented perspective, the most preferable alternatives would be those that show the lowest cost for any given increase in test scores or per averted dropout. By choosing the most cost-effective alternative, we free up resources that can be invested in other aspects of education (or in another endeavor).

It is assumed that (a) only programs with similar or identical goals can be compared and (b) a common measure of effectiveness can be used to assess them. These effectiveness data can be combined with costs in order to provide a cost-effectiveness evaluation that will enable the selection of those approaches that provide the maximum effectiveness per level of cost or that require the least cost per level of effectiveness.

Example 1.3 reflects a situation that is all too common in actual evaluations, in which the most effective approach is not always the most cost-effective. Yet, without an analysis of costs, it would be impossible to know this. Further, the adoption of the most effective alternative can actually cost many times as much as the most cost-effective one.

The cost-effectiveness approach has a number of strengths. Most important is that it merely requires combining cost data with the effectiveness data that are ordinarily available from an educational evaluation to create a cost-effectiveness comparison. Further, it lends itself well to an evaluation of alternatives that are being considered for accomplishing a particular educational goal. Its one major disadvantage is that one can compare the CE ratios only among alternatives with a similar goal. One cannot compare alternatives with different goals (e.g., reading vs. mathematics or education vs. health) nor can one make an overall determination of whether a program is worthwhile in an absolute sense. That is, we can state whether a given alternative is *relatively* more cost-effective than other alternatives, but we cannot state whether its total benefits exceed its total costs. That can only be ascertained through a cost-benefit analysis.

Cost-Benefit Analysis

Cost-benefit (CB) analysis refers to the evaluation of alternatives according to their costs and benefits when each is measured in monetary terms. Since each alternative is assessed in terms of its monetary costs and

EXAMPLE 1.3. A Cost-Effectiveness Analysis of Primary School Investments in Northeast Brazil

The states that form northeast Brazil are among the poorest areas in the world. Not surprisingly, the situation of their primary schools in the early 1980s was correspondingly bleak. Many children did not even attend primary school and were functionally illiterate. Those children who did attend were confronted with schools that were deprived of many basic resources, including infrastructure, classroom materials such as textbooks, and well-trained teachers. In an environment of low student achievement and resource scarcity, determining the cost-effectiveness of school investments becomes particularly important. How can the limited funds available to the school system be spent in order to maximize the academic achievement of students?

The first step is to clearly delineate a range of possible educational interventions. The first column in Table 1.1 lists several, grouped into categories. The first category, infrastructure, lists three investments: the provision of potable water, the provision of a variety of school furniture (including desks and bookcases), and the provision of additional school facilities (including offices and a bathroom). A fourth intervention, "hardware," is a combination of the previous three. The second category, material inputs, includes two interventions: the provision of student textbooks and the provision of writing materials. "Software" is a combination of both of these. The final category, teachers, includes two separate in-service teacher training programs that were available at the time (*curso de qualificação* and *Logos II*), either 4 or 3 years of additional formal schooling, and an increase in the teacher salary.

The next step is to determine the costs that result from applying additional units of each intervention. The additional costs are presented in column 2. To derive these costs, the authors used the "ingredients" method described in Chapters 3 through 5 of this volume. The ingredients of each intervention, such as materials and personnel time, were exhaustively listed, and an annual per-student cost was derived for each ingredient. The authors took care to "annualize" the costs of durable inputs, such as infrastructure, which last for more than a single year (the methods for annualizing costs are presented in Chapter 4). Thus, the additional annual cost per student of providing a basic package of school facilities was estimated as $8.80 (bear in mind that costs in this highly impoverished area are considerably lower than in industrialized countries). Note that "hardware" investments, as one might expect, tend to be more costly than "software" investments.

EXAMPLE 1.3. continued

The next step is to estimate the effectiveness of each intervention. The measure of effectiveness that is utilized is a test of Portuguese language achievement among second graders in 1983.[2] To estimate effectiveness, the authors use nonexperimental methods, namely a statistical technique called multiple regression analysis. In essence, the method allows one to compare the relative achievement of students using greater and lesser quantities of each intervention, while holding constant other determinants of achievement such as a student's socioeconomic status. A general description of experimental and nonexperimental methods of establishing effectiveness will be given in Chapter 6. According to the results in column 3, for example, the provision of "Logos II" training to teachers caused the average second grader's Portuguese score to rise by 3.59 points. Some interventions showed no apparent effect on achievement or even a negative effect; these are marked by "—."

The final step is to combine the data on costs and effectiveness by calculating a cost-effectiveness ratio. The ratio indicates the cost required to attain a 1-point increase in achievement. (Some studies use a different convention by estimating effectiveness-cost ratios, or the points of effect that result from a $1 investment in a given intervention.) Clearly, we should be most interested in investing in those interventions that exhibit the lowest cost per unit of effect. A simple examination of the ratios in column 4 suggests that material inputs have among the lowest cost-effectiveness ratios. By providing more textbooks, for example, policymakers can attain 1 point of effectiveness at a cost of $0.26 per student. In contrast, other interventions exhibit much higher cost-effectiveness ratios. Increasing teacher salaries costs $6.50 per unit of effect, while investing in a general package of "hardware" costs $1.79 per unit of effect.

How would our decisions have been different if costs had been excluded from the analysis? We might have been tempted to invest heavily in school facilities and hardware, which exhibit the highest effectiveness. But they are also among the most costly inputs and, consequently, somewhat less cost-effective. The authors conducted a similar cost-effectiveness analysis using another measure of effectiveness (mathematics achievement) as well as data from other years and grade levels. Although their additional results are largely consistent with these conclusions, the limited results we present in the accompanying table should be considered only illustrative.

SOURCE: Harbison and Hanushek (1992).

TABLE 1.1 Costs, Effects, and Cost-Effectiveness Ratios for Primary School Investments

Intervention	Cost Per Student Per Year	Effect on Portuguese Score (points)[a]	Cost/Effectiveness Ratio (cost per unit of effectiveness)
Infrastructure			
Water	$ 1.81	3.51	$0.52
School furniture	$ 5.45	—	—
School facilities	$ 8.80	7.23	$1.22
"Hardware"	$16.06	8.97	$1.79
Material inputs			
Textbook usage	$ 1.65	6.40	$0.26
Writing material	$ 1.76	4.70	$0.37
"Software"	$ 3.41	4.86	$0.70
Teachers			
Curso de qualificação	$ 2.50	—	—
Logos II	$ 1.84	3.59	$0.51
4 years primary school	$ 2.21	3.18	$0.70
3 years secondary school	$ 5.55	2.38	$2.33
Increasing teacher salary	$ 0.39	0.06	$6.50

SOURCE: Adapted from Harbison and Hanushek (1992, Table C6-1).

NOTE: The original table presents effectiveness-cost ratios, rather than the cost-effectiveness ratios presented above. For an explanation of the difference, see Chapter 6 of this volume.

a. "—" indicates no evidence of positive effect.

the monetary values of its benefits, each alternative can be examined on its own merits to see if it is worthwhile. In order to be considered for selection, any alternative must show benefits in excess of costs. In selecting from among several alternatives, one would choose that particular one that had the highest benefit-cost ratio (or, conversely, the lowest ratio of costs to benefits).

Because CB analysis assesses all alternatives in terms of the monetary values of costs and benefits, one can ascertain (a) if any particular alternative has benefits exceeding its costs, (b) which of a set of educational alternatives with different objectives has the highest ratio of benefits to costs, and (c) which of a set of alternatives among different programs areas (e.g., health, education, transportation, police) shows the highest benefit-cost ratios for an overall social analysis of where the public should invest. The latter is a particularly attractive feature of CB analysis because we can compare many programs with widely disparate objectives, as long as their costs and benefits can be expressed in monetary terms. In contrast, the alternatives that are compared in a CE analysis are limited to a common objective.

Example 1.4 shows both the potential value of CB analysis and its potential difficulties. On the advantage side of the ledger, it can be a useful way to gauge the overall worth of a program or policy. It should not be implemented if its costs are greater than its benefits. We can also judge a project by the overall size of the net benefits—that is, by how much benefits exceed costs. Further, to the degree that other educational endeavors and those in other areas of public expenditure (such as health, transportation, environmental improvement, criminal justice, and income maintenance) are evaluated by the cost-benefit method, it is possible to compare any particular educational alternative with projects in other areas that compete for resources.

The disadvantage of this method is that benefits and costs must be assessed in pecuniary terms. It is not often possible to do this in a systematic and rigorous manner. For example, while the gains in earnings attributed to lower levels of dropping out might be assessed according to their pecuniary worth, how does one assess benefits such as improvement in self-esteem of the educated adults or their enhanced appreciation of reading materials? This shortcoming suggests that only under certain circumstances would one wish to use cost-benefit analysis. Those situations would obtain when the preponderance of benefits could be readily converted into pecuniary values or when those that cannot be converted tend to be unimportant or can be shown to be similar among the alternatives that are being considered. That is, if the decision alternatives differ only on the basis of those benefit factors that can be converted to pecuniary values, the other aspects

EXAMPLE 1.4. A Cost-Benefit Analysis of Drop-Out Prevention in California

The problem of high school dropouts is of substantial concern to educators, policymakers, and society at large. It is well-known that dropouts tend to earn lower wages than high school graduates. Indeed, the wage gap between dropouts and graduates widened extensively during the 1980s. This suggests that benefits to preventing dropouts, as measured by their additional wages over a lifetime, may be extensive. Of course, programs or reforms that encourage students to remain in school are also costly. We can only determine whether it is worthwhile to undertake these programs by carefully weighing the costs against the benefits.

In the early 1980s, the state of California instituted a dropout prevention program in the San Francisco peninsula. A number of "Peninsula Academies" were created that functioned as small schools within existing public high schools. Academy students in grades 10 through 12 took classes together that were jointly coordinated by academy teachers. Each academy, in concert with local employers, provided vocational training in a single occupational area such as the health industry or computers.

An evaluation first estimated the additional costs of each academy, beyond what would have been spent on a traditional high school education. Column 2 in Table 1.2 gives the total costs for the 3-year (grades 10 through 12) program that was provided to the cohort of students entering in 1985-86. Several categories of cost ingredients were considered: personnel such as teachers, aides, and administrators; facilities and equipment; and the cost of time donated by local employers. Academy costs tended to be higher because of their relatively smaller class sizes and extra preparation periods that were given to some teachers. Note that local employers were not directly remunerated for the time they donated to counseling. Nonetheless, the time spent on these activities could have been devoted to other worthwhile activities, and it represents a cost from society's point of view.

The evaluators then estimated the benefits produced by lowering the number of high school dropouts. To do so, the authors employed a quasi-experimental design. Prior to initiating the program, a comparison group of students attending the traditional high school was selected for each academy. Care was taken to ensure that students in the comparison group had

EXAMPLE 1.4. continued

approximately the same characteristics as academy students. After 3 years, the number of actual academy dropouts was compared with the number that would have occurred if they had dropped out at the same rate as the academy's comparison group. In most schools, evidence suggested that the academies prevented dropouts (indicated by a positive number of "dropouts saved"). In a few schools, however, the dropout rate was higher in academy schools (indicated by a negative number). To monetize these benefits, the authors calculated the lifetime income difference between a high school graduate and a high school dropout. Their estimate of $86,000 is a present value, discounted to reflect for the differential timing of the benefits received (a complete discussion of discounting is given in Chapter 5). Multiplied by the number of dropouts saved, the authors calculate each academy's total benefit (again, benefits turn out to be costs in a few cases because some academies actually increased the number of dropouts).

The final step is to subtract costs from benefits. The net benefits column suggests that the program is worthwhile in academies C, E, F, G, and K (i.e., the benefits are greater than the costs). In academies A, H, and J, however, the costs outweigh the benefits. Considering all eight academies, the overall benefits of the program exceed the costs. Another way of comparing benefits and costs is to calculate a benefit-cost ratio. Ratios that are greater than 1 suggest that benefits are greater than costs (note that we have not bothered calculating ratios for the two academies that did not produce any benefits). Despite the favorable results, the final results are heavily influenced by a single academy (C).

The previous analysis assumes that we have exhaustively catalogued the relevant costs and benefits. However, it is likely that we have excluded important benefits (e.g., the savings incurred because more-educated adults are less likely to be incarcerated). The authors also present evidence that academy schools are effective at producing other outcomes such as a higher GPA. Some of these measures of effectiveness may be difficult to monetize and include in a CB analysis. However, they might be usefully included in an accompanying CE analysis.

SOURCE: Stern, Dayton, Paik, and Weisberg (1989).

TABLE 1.2 Costs, Benefits, and Cost-Benefit Ratios of a Drop-Out Prevention Strategy

Academy	Costs	Dropouts Saved		Benefit Per Dropout Saved		Benefits	Net Benefit (total benefits– total costs)	Benefit-Cost Ratio
A	$ 89,424	-3.4	×	$86,000	=	-$ 292,400	-$ 381,824	—
C	$ 174,600	21.5	×	$86,000	=	$ 1,849,000	$ 1,674,400	10.59
E	$ 106,998	1.8	×	$86,000	=	$ 154,800	$ 47,802	1.45
F	$ 35,280	2.0	×	$86,000	=	$ 172,000	$ 136,720	4.88
G	$ 382,830	5.8	×	$86,000	=	$ 498,800	$ 115,970	1.30
H	$ 57,534	-2.0	×	$86,000	=	-$ 172,000	-$ 229,534	—
J	$ 136,572	0.2	×	$86,000	=	$ 17,200	-$ 119,372	0.13
K	$ 218,226	3.4	×	$86,000	=	$ 292,400	$ 74,174	1.34
Total	$ 1,201,464	29.3		$86,000	=	$ 2,519,800	$ 1,318,336	2.10

SOURCE: Adapted from Stern, Dayton, Paik, and Weisberg (1989, Table 6).

can be ignored in the cost-benefit calculations. Or, if those dimensions of benefits that cannot be assessed in pecuniary terms are considered to be trivial, one can limit the CB comparison to the factors that can be evaluated with monetary measures.

However, in those cases in which the major benefits are difficult to assess in pecuniary terms, some other mechanism for assessment must be found. Both cost-effectiveness and cost-utility analyses represent analytical frameworks that do not depend on the ability to represent benefits in pecuniary terms.

Cost-Utility Analysis

Cost-utility (CU) analysis is a close cousin of CE analysis. It refers to the evaluation of alternatives according to a comparison of their costs and their utility or value. "Utility" is a term frequently employed by economists to express the satisfaction derived by individuals from one or more outcomes. Unlike CE analysis, which relies upon a single measure of effectiveness (e.g., a test score, the number of dropouts averted), CU analysis uses information on the preferences of individuals in order to express their overall satisfaction with a single measure or multiple measures of effectiveness. Data on individual preferences can be derived in many ways, either through highly subjective estimates by the researcher or through more rigorous methods designed to carefully elicit the opinions of individuals (we describe a number of these methods in Chapter 8). Once overall measures of utility have been obtained, however, we proceed in much the same way as a CE analysis. We choose the interventions that provide a given level of utility at the lowest cost or those which provide the greatest amount of utility for a given cost.

To date, CU analysis has been most frequently employed by health researchers. One of the most common measures of effectiveness for health interventions is life years gained. Two medical interventions are considered equally effective if they both extend life by the same amount. Despite their equal effectiveness, each may yield a different quality of life. For example, one medical intervention could leave individuals significantly impaired in their ability to function on a daily basis. In this case, it would be desirable to adjust the measure of effectiveness for each intervention (life-years

EXAMPLE 1.5. A Cost-Utility Analysis of Alternative Reading Programs

Assume that a school board decides that reading is a high priority for the next year. The school administration is asked to select new curricula to improve the teaching of reading. Different curricula are sought by the administration from both commercial publishers and other sources. For each alternative, the administration requests information on the nature of the curriculum, its strategy, and evidence of its success.

Fortunately, the administration is able to locate a number of high-quality, experimental evaluations that were conducted on each of the five curricula. These evaluations estimated the percentile gain of the average student on four measures of effectiveness: reading speed, reading comprehension, word knowledge, and student satisfaction with reading. The results are presented in Table 1.3. In addition, the marginal, or additional, cost per student was estimated through a standard "ingredients" approach (see Chapters 3 through 5).

If there was a single alternative that consistently scored highest on all measures of effectiveness and was the least costly, then the decision would be obvious. However, that is not the case. The five alternatives vary widely both in

gained) in order to more accurately reflect individual preferences for the varying health states that are produced. A common practice is to weight life-years gained by estimates of utility; this adjusted measure is referred to as Quality-Adjusted Life-Years (QALYs).

CU analysis is often used to combine multiple measures of effectiveness into a single estimate of utility. Educational interventions yield effects in many areas: mathematics achievement, reading achievement, self-esteem, behavior, attitudes, and so on. A CE analysis necessarily focuses on one measure of effectiveness at a time. It would be convenient to produce an overall measure of the desirability, or utility, of a given intervention, which encompasses information on all the measures of effectiveness. One method of doing so is to weight each measure of effectiveness by an "importance weight." The weights should reflect the contribution of each measure of effectiveness to the overall utility of the decision maker. Weighted estimates can then be summed in an overall utility measure. For example, decision makers (or another group of individuals) may feel that mathematics achievement is relatively more important than another effect,

EXAMPLE 1.5. continued

their measured effectiveness and costs. It would be quite helpful to construct a summary measure of utility, which reflects the overall satisfaction that is derived from each alternative.

We require an explicit rule for combining the four measures of effectiveness. One possibility would be to take a simple average of all measures of effectiveness for each alternative. So, for example, the average for Alternative A would be $(8 + 6 + 6 + 7) \div 4 = 6.75$. This implicitly gives equal weight to each measure, suggesting that each contributes equally to the overall satisfaction that is produced by an alternative. However, this may not reflect the true preference structure of administrators, teachers, or parents. It is possible that reading comprehension is valued more highly than student satisfaction and, therefore, it should receive a proportionally larger weight.

Thus, in consultation with a small group of parents and school personnel, the administration derived a set of four utility weights (using some of the simple methods that are described in Chapter 8). These are often called

(continued)

and therefore choose to weight it more heavily than other measures of effectiveness.

The advantages of the CU approach are that it makes careful attempts to consider individual preferences and that a large number of potential outcomes can be included in the evaluation. Furthermore, a CU analysis often contributes to a process of consensus building and participatory decision-making, as stakeholders are called upon to assess their preferences for diverse outcomes. The major disadvantage is the fact that the results are often difficult to reproduce among different evaluators because of the numerous and sometimes conflicting methodologies that are used to estimate importance weights. Two evaluators who are studying similar alternatives may derive drastically different results by using a different method to elicit the preferences of individuals or by surveying the preferences of a different sample of individuals.

Example 1.5 provides a hypothetical example of a cost-utility study in education. To date, there are very instances in which these methods have been applied in education. We shall review a few of these in Chapter 8.

EXAMPLE 1.5. A Cost-Utility Analysis of Alternative Reading
Programs *(continued)*

"importance weights," because they reflect the relative contribution of each
measure of effectiveness to overall utility. In this case, the weight of reading
comprehension is 0.40, which suggests that it is twice as important as word
knowledge, with a weight of 0.20 (see the final row of the table).

A new measure of utility was constructed for each alternative. After
weighting each measure of effectiveness by the corresponding importance
weight, the results are summed. For alternative A, the overall utility is 6.7, given
by the following expression:

$$0.25 \times 8 + 0.40 \times 6 + 0.20 \times 6 + 0.15 \times 7 = 6.7$$

The final columns of the table show cost–utility ratios that were derived by
dividing the cost per student by the appropriate utility score. The lowest CU ratios imply the lowest cost for obtaining a given level of utility, and the highest
CU ratios imply the highest cost. On this basis, alternative A appears to be the
most preferable one as evidenced by the lowest CU ratio, and alternative E appears to be the least preferable one because of its very high cost relative to its
utility scores. Alternatives C and D appear to be about equal in terms of CU ratings, and alternative B is next to the bottom in terms of CU attractiveness. Before choosing an alternative, the administration should temper these results
with a discussion of their meaning and an exploration of factors (such as ease
of implementation) that may not have been included in the analysis. That is, the
CU findings ought to enter the discussion prominently, but the choice should
not be mechanically based on the CU ratings without considering other pertinent factors. If choices are made that are at odds with the CU recommendations, the reasons for not accepting the CU priorities ought to be explicit.

Cost-Feasibility Analysis

CB, CE, and CU analyses all share a number of properties. They all enable a choice among alternative strategies by obtaining some measure of
both costs and results for each potential strategy, so that one can choose the
approach that has the lowest cost for any particular result or the best result
for any particular cost. However, there is one situation in which estimates
of costs alone are important. Cost-feasibility (CF) analysis refers to the
method of estimating only the costs of an alternative in order to ascertain

TABLE 1.3 Costs, Utilities, and Cost–Utility Ratios of Strategies for Improving Reading

Alternative	Cost Per Student	Measure of Effectiveness				Overall Utility (weighted sum)	Cost/Utility Ratio
		Speed	Comprehension	Word Knowledge	Student Satisfaction		
A	$168	8	6	6	7	6.7	$25.26
B	$153	5	4	6	3	4.5	$34.00
C	$210	6	9	7	7	7.6	$27.81
D	$195	4	9	9	5	7.2	$27.27
E	$279	9	6	4	6	6.4	$43.94
Importance weight		0.25	0.40	0.20	0.15		

EXAMPLE 1.6. A Cost-Feasibility Analysis of National Class Size Reduction

We observed in Example 1.1 that class size reduction is an increasingly popular policy for improving education. In addition to the many U.S. states that are pursuing smaller class sizes, a 1998 federal proposal of President Clinton's would have reduced classes in the early grades to no more than 18 students. Ultimately, we should be interested in weighing the overall pecuniary benefits of class size reduction against the costs. Or, if monetizing the important benefits proved too difficult, we could compare the relative cost-effectiveness of several interventions (including class size reduction) in accomplishing a given educational goal such as improving achievement. But even before such an analysis is undertaken, a much simpler question is whether such a sweeping plan could be feasibly implemented in light of current and future budget constraints. Would the costs associated with a national class size reduction be prohibitive?

A 1999 study by Dominic Brewer and his colleagues attempted to estimate the costs of different approaches to national class size reduction in grades 1 through 3. The authors were obliged to make a number of assumptions about the scope and design of the policy to be implemented; these were used to arrive at a set of "baseline" cost estimates. Upon arriving at their baseline estimates, they varied several key assumptions in order to observe the sensitivity of cost estimates. Their baseline estimates relied on some of the following assumptions:

▷ There are three possible targets for class size reduction: 20, 18, and 15.

▷ Class size reduction is implemented on a districtwide basis. That is, the average class size in each school district is required to meet a target level, although individual classes in the district might be larger or smaller.

▷ The policy applies uniformly to all students in all schools. That is, there is no targeting of the policy towards specific groups such as high-poverty schools or districts.

whether or not it can be considered. That is, if the cost of any alternative exceeds the budget and other resources that are available, there is no point in doing any further analysis. As a concrete illustration, one might view the situation of compensatory education, in which a specified amount is available for augmenting the education of each disadvantaged child. If this

EXAMPLE 1.6. continued

▷ Only operational costs are considered, such as salaries and benefits of teachers, aides, and administrators as well as instructional materials and supplies. No consideration is given to the costs of facilities and infrastructure.

As Table 1.4 shows, the total operational costs of lowering class size to 20 in the program's first year would be roughly $2.1 billion, a per-pupil cost of $189. Lowering class size to 15 would result in substantially higher total and per-pupil operational costs of $11.0 billion and $981, respectively. The first alternative (20) is much less costly than the others because many states, such as California, have already reduced class sizes to 20 in early elementary grades. The last alternative (15) is vastly more expensive because no U.S. state has reduced average class size in grades 1 through 3 to 15 students.

The preceding estimates reflect only one policy design among many alternatives. The authors estimate the costs of several alternative policies by varying some of the previous assumptions. For example, class size reduction is less costly if the targeted levels of class size must only be met on average across the entire state, rather than across districts. On the other hand, it is more costly if average class sizes in each school must meet targeted levels. Moreover, the policy is much less costly if it is targeted only at schools with large numbers of high-poverty students, gauged by the number of students eligible for free or reduced lunch.

To reiterate, the preceding estimates cannot inform decision makers whether investing in class size reduction is a socially desirable investment in absolute terms or whether it is relatively more desirable than another investment. This can only be accomplished by weighing the costs of class size reduction against its benefits or effectiveness. Nevertheless, the cost estimates can tell decision makers whether national class size reduction is feasible within the current set of budget constraints.

SOURCE: Brewer et al. (1999).

amount is $400 per child, then any alternative that violates this constraint would not be feasible. Cost-feasibility represents a limited form of analysis that can determine only whether or not alternatives are within the boundaries of consideration. It cannot be used to determine which ones should actually be selected.

TABLE 1.4 Costs of National Class Size Reduction

Maximum Class Size	Total Operational Costs, 1998-99 (in millions of dollars)	Per-Pupil Operational Costs, 1998-99
20	$ 2,127	$189
18	$ 5,049	$448
15	$ 11,047	$981

SOURCE: Brewer et al. (1999, Table 2).

Summary of Cost-Analysis Approaches

In this section we have defined and illustrated a number of cost-analysis approaches that are used to evaluate educational alternatives. Table 1.5 provides a brief summary of each of the four approaches, including the key analytical questions addressed by each, as well as the strengths and weaknesses already outlined. After reading the subsequent chapters, you may find it helpful to return to the table, in order to solidify your understanding.

Outline of Volume

The remainder of the book will be devoted to a presentation and discussion of the use of cost analyses as well as a description of the principles and techniques for developing such analyses. The next chapter will discuss the decision context, audience, and particular issues that are pertinent to the choice of analysis, its implementation, and its presentation. Chapters 3 through 5 will address the nature of costs and their identification, measurement, and distribution. The reader should be aware that the discussion in these chapters applies equally well to all modes of cost analysis. That is, the differences among the modes are primarily on the outcomes side rather than the cost side.

Chapters 6 through 8 will focus on the particular concerns associated with conducting CE, CB, and CU analyses, respectively. In each chapter, we

TABLE 1.5 A Summary of Four Approaches to Cost Analysis

Type of Analysis	Analytical Question(s)	Measure of Cost	Measure of Outcomes	Strengths of Approach	Weaknesses of Approach
Cost-effectiveness	◆ Which alternative yields a given level of effectiveness for the lowest cost (or the highest level of effectiveness for a given cost)?	Monetary value of resources	Units of effectiveness	◆ Easy to incorporate standard evaluations of effectiveness ◆ Useful for alternatives with a single or small number of objectives	◆ Difficult to interpret results when there are multiple measures of effectiveness ◆ Cannot judge overall worth of a single alternative; only useful for comparing two or more alternatives
Cost-benefit	◆ Which alternative yields a given level of benefits for the lowest cost (or the highest level of benefits for a given cost)? ◆ Are the benefits of a single alternative larger than its costs?	Monetary value of resources	Monetary value of benefits	◆ Can be used to judge absolute worth of a project (in contrast to CE and CU analyses) ◆ Can compare CB results across a wide variety of projects in education or other areas (e.g, health, infrastructure)	◆ Often difficult to place monetary values on all relevant educational benefits

(continued)

TABLE 1.5 A Summary of Four Approaches to Cost Analysis (*continued*)

Type of Analysis	Analytical Question(s)	Measure of Cost	Measure of Outcomes	Strengths of Approach	Weaknesses of Approach
Cost-utility	◆ Which alternative yields a given level of utility at the lowest cost (or the highest level of utility at a given cost)?	Monetary value of resources	Units of utility	◆ Incorporates individual preferences for units of effectiveness ◆ Can incorporate multiple measures of effectiveness into single measure of utility ◆ Promotes stakeholder participation in decision making	◆ Sometimes difficult to arrive at consistent and accurate measures of individual preferences ◆ Cannot judge overall worth of a single alternative; only useful for comparing two or more alternatives
Cost-feasibility	◆ Can a single alternative be carried out within the existing budget?	Monetary value of resources	None	◆ Permits alternatives that are not feasible to be immediately ruled out, before evaluating outcomes	◆ Cannot judge overall worth of project, because it does not incorporate outcome measures

will discuss the general approaches to measuring effectiveness, utility, and benefits. In addition, we will discuss how to combine that information with costs and analyze the results. Finally, Chapter 9 reviews the challenges to incorporating cost evaluations in the decision making process. Appendix A gives sample answers to the exercises at the end of each chapter. Appendix B provides a comprehensive bibliography of methodological sources on cost analysis and educational cost studies.

Exercises

1. Typical educational evaluations look only at the effects of alternative interventions on student outcomes without considering the cost consequences. Under what circumstances would adopting the "most effective" alternative actually increase overall costs to the school district for any specific educational result relative to choosing a "less effective" alternative? Provide a hypothetical illustration.

2. There have been many studies of the relation between enrollment levels in schools and school districts and the cost per student. These studies purport to show how cost varies with school size, and they attempt to determine the enrollment ranges in which costs are lowest. Do these studies meet the criteria for cost-effectiveness analysis? Explain your answer.

3. What are the fundamental differences among cost-effectiveness, cost-benefit, cost-utility, and cost-feasibility analysis? When should each be used?

4. For each of the following situations, determine which type of cost analysis is most appropriate among the following four modes: cost-effectiveness, cost-benefit, cost-utility, cost-feasibility.

   a. A school district wishes to increase the employability of students who terminate their formal education at high school graduation. Accordingly, it seeks an answer to the question of whether it should expand vocational educational offerings for students who are presently in the general education program.

   b. The school board wishes to accommodate budget cuts by reducing some of the elective course offerings in the high school. A reduction in the budget of $60,000 has been targeted.

c. A university must decide if it is desirable to establish a new department in computer science.

d. The state legislature wishes to consider the introduction of computers into every high school in the state. However, it is not clear that the school budget is adequate.

e. A school district is seeking approaches to improving the writing of its students. Advice is sought from the English department on alternatives. Proposed solutions include (a) smaller class sizes with more stress on writing and more writing assignments, (b) hiring college students with excellent writing skills to assist teachers in grading writing assignments, and (c) developing special writing courses for students in addition to their regular English classes.

f. A community college must reduce its course offerings in the next academic year to accommodate a dismal budgetary situation. The college offers over 1,400 courses in some 38 departments and programs. Enough courses must be cut to achieve savings of $500,000.

g. Both computer-assisted instruction and smaller class sizes are being discussed as ways to improve the mathematics competencies of youngsters in a particular school district. The administration wishes to ascertain which alternative is preferable.

▶ NOTES

1. See Chapter 6 for a critique of the use of meta-analysis for decision-making and for cost-effectiveness analysis. Consider that a summary of all studies of a particular intervention provides an average of good and poor studies and effective and ineffective applications and versions of the intervention. For example, good and poor versions of computer-assisted instruction are averaged to get an effect size of computers on achievement. But, decision makers do not choose among averages of good and bad. Rather, they need to select from among the most successful versions of particular intervention families. The "average" is not a decision variable.

2. The original study analyzes Portuguese and mathematics achievement in second and fourth grade, using several years of data; the reader is encouraged to consult the original study for further details (Harbison & Hanushek, 1992).

CHAPTER 2

Establishing an Analytic Framework

► OBJECTIVES

1. Identify the evaluation problem.
2. Establish the alternatives.
3. Determine the audience for the evaluation.
4. Select the appropriate type of cost analysis.
5. Ascertain the needs for expertise and other resources.
6. Decide whether a cost analysis is worth doing.

Before beginning a cost analysis, it is important to establish the analytical framework that will be utilized. This framework consists of identifying the nature of the problem, clarifying the specific alternatives that should be considered in the analysis, establishing the identity of the primary and secondary audiences for the analysis, and selecting the type of cost analysis to use. In this chapter, we will discuss each of these issues.

Identification of the Problem

One of the most neglected areas of evaluation generally is proper identification of the problem. By proper identification, we mean that the problem should be posed in such a way that the analytic response is an appropriate one. To take an example that was discussed in Chapter 1, the problem that is often posed by school districts facing financial exigencies because of declining enrollments is, "Which school or schools do we close?" The real problem that must be faced, however, is how to cut the budget in a way that does the least damage to the educational program. The alternatives to consider include the possibilities of school closure, but they also include the options of reducing personnel, cutting specific offerings, increasing class size, leasing excess space in existing schools, and a variety of other potential routes to cutting the budget or raising school revenues. Narrowing the question to which schools are to be closed is to rule out options that may be more appropriate when cost-effectiveness criteria are used. That is, there can obviously be no cost-effectiveness analysis among alternatives that are not considered.

Identification of the problem must begin with the specific origins of the problem. For example, the origins may be that certain groups of children are not learning to read at an appropriate level. In that case, one might wish to ascertain the reasons that they are not learning to read at that level. One possibility is that they need special attention because of learning difficulties.

Another is that they have entered school with reading deficiencies that are not accommodated by the beginning level and pace of instruction. Another is that the curriculum and teaching methods are inappropriate. Each of these causes would require a different response.

Before one begins to address the problem, one must attempt to specify with great clarity and insight the nature of the problem that ought to be addressed. One process for doing this effectively is the inquiry approach used by the Accelerated Schools Project, described in Hopfenberg et al. (1993, pp. 95-137). This may begin with a general question of a learning deficiency, budgetary squeeze, high drop-out rates among particular groups, school vandalism issues, and so on. Once the general issue is identified, however, it must be pursued in greater detail to ascertain the probable causes of the problem. For example, student misbehavior that is caused by inappropriate rules and selective enforcement represents a different problem than student misbehavior that is a result of racial conflict, a chaotic school program, or serious learning deficiencies within particular populations. It is important to investigate a range of probable causes by discussing what seems to be happening with those persons who have contact with the phenomenon. Only after a careful and sensitive investigation can one identify the problem in such a way that a range of alternative responses can be posited for analysis.

What Are the Alternatives?

The alternatives for addressing particular problems are those potential interventions that might respond to the problem and improve the situation being addressed. It is important to ask whether all the pertinent alternatives have been placed on the agenda for consideration. Obviously, the classes of alternatives that ought to be considered are those that are most responsive to the problem. Again, this will require a sensitive search for ways of meeting the challenge that has been posed. Although one may wish to draw upon traditional responses as well as those that other entities have used in facing similar problematic situations, one should not be limited to these. In fact, often they may not be the most responsive approaches.

For example, the traditional approach to solving problems of fiscal exigencies has been to rule out of consideration the cutting of administrative and teaching positions. Instead, the emphasis has been on cuts in non-personnel areas such as maintenance and supplies. When reductions in personnel costs have been considered, attempts have been made to restrict them to service workers and paraprofessionals rather than professionals. Consider, however, that 80% or more of school district expenditures are vested in the salaries and other benefits provided to personnel. Further, 70% or more is generally attributable to the costs of teachers, administrators, and other professional personnel. Accordingly, any substantial cut or restriction of expenditures must inevitably reach these categories. It is unrealistic to believe that major cuts can be accomplished without affecting personnel.

By ruling out cuts of administrative and professional personnel, the possibilities for budgetary reduction become unduly limited or distorted. For example, a functioning school system needs supplies and maintenance, and a heavy impact on these areas can harm profoundly the educational productivity of a school. It is true that cutting jobs should be avoided when possible because of the human suffering that is created by such dislocations, but such actions can be taken in ways that will minimize harm to the present staff through capitalizing on normal attrition, early retirements, and other voluntary reductions in the workforce. When financial straits are extremely dire, reductions in personnel must be considered.

A similar concern is raised when one augments the criterion of responsiveness with that of comprehensiveness. That is, one must ask not only whether the alternatives that will be considered are responsive to the problem, but also whether all the "responsive" ones have been brought into the policy arena. Often, both administrators and evaluators will rule out alternatives before analyzing them when such options are politically sensitive. That is, the pragmatic aspects of daily life suggest that one avoid pitched political battles by keeping politically sensitive issues off the agenda if at all possible. While one can appreciate the pressures on both evaluators and administrators in this regard, there are two reasons that all of the relevant alternatives should be analyzed.

First, it is a matter of professional integrity to provide information on all of the pertinent alternatives, while letting the decision-making and political processes eventually determine the choice among them. If those processes are not adequately informed about possible responses, they can never consider the costs and impacts of many of the pertinent alternatives. There is an appropriate place for analysis and one for decision making. If certain alternatives are precluded from consideration by their political sensitivity, then the political and decision-making processes have taken place before the information and analyses have been derived. Clearly, the two stages are interrelated, but good decision making should be based upon informed choices rather than ones that eliminate potential options before they are ever analyzed and considered.

A second reason for considering even those alternatives that are politically sensitive is that such sensitivity or opposition may be dependent upon circumstances. That is, while some alternatives are indeed "untouchable" in the normal course of events, they may become salient for consideration under more dire circumstances. If a school district is facing serious budgetary problems, it must consider all possibilities that would reduce the budget. If student proficiencies in certain academic areas are woefully inadequate, then a wide range of programs for improvement begins to enter the realm of consideration. It is important to consider the strengths and weaknesses or the costs and effects of selecting from all of the pertinent alternatives. It should also be borne in mind that the retention of existing practices is always an alternative.

Indeed, this leads to a final comment on alternatives. Cost analysis is premised on the view that decision makers have choices. The objective is to make the best selection from competing alternatives. Cost-effectiveness analysis and other forms of cost evaluations are done in order to choose among alternatives. If there are no alternatives, there is no point in doing an analysis. That is, no matter how competent the evaluation, it will simply lack usefulness if one cannot do anything with what is learned.

Who Is the Audience?

In addition to identifying the problem and the alternatives that might address the problem, it is important to be clear about the audience or audiences for whom the analysis will be done. The audiences include one or more groups of stakeholders—that is, individuals or institutions with an interest in the outcomes of the evaluation process. It is helpful to think of a primary audience and a secondary audience. The primary audience is generally the decision maker (and the clientele whom he or she represents) who has requested the analysis. The secondary audience consists of those persons and groups who will also draw upon the analysis.

Since the analysis is being prepared explicitly for the primary audience, it is important that it meet the specifications of that audience. For example, if one is requested to do a cost-feasibility study of using educational television in the school curriculum, it is important to ascertain exactly what is behind the request. Is there a specific technological or curriculum approach that the decision maker has in mind, or is the charge to be concerned with the costs of a wide variety of approaches, from selected courses to full curriculum coverage? These details can be worked out through dialogue and specification of the issues, and the analysis and report should be written with the needs of the primary audience in mind. They may still result in tension if the decision maker places certain alternatives beyond consideration even though the alternatives may be in the best interests of the constituents represented by that decision maker. Under such conditions, an evaluator or administrator will face a dilemma that is not easily reconcilable. This is a subject about which little more will be said, but it is central to the politics of evaluation (Cohen, 1970; Weiss, 1975).

Often, however, cost-effectiveness or even cost-feasibility reports are read by secondary audiences who wish to use the information and study provided in one setting to inform decisions in another setting. If a study will be restricted to its primary audience, one need not be concerned about secondary audiences. However, if a secondary audience is likely to utilize the study, it is important to be clear about what is possibly generalizable to other settings and what is not. An important example is that in reviewing the costs of instructional programs, a school district may generate many cost analyses that do not include the value of resources that are contributed by the state or other levels of government or by volunteers. Quite logically, they include only those resources that are underwritten by local school funds.

For purposes of decision making in the district under scrutiny, the omission of "contributed" resources in calculating costs is understandable. But what if the cost analyses are used by other school districts to choose among potential programs and decision makers in those districts are unaware of what the real required resources are because the report includes only those that were paid for out of local financial sources? Clearly, the analyses may be misleading, since not every other school district in that secondary audience will necessarily have equal access to volunteers and other contributed inputs. Therefore, it is incumbent upon those districts to know the "costs" of all the resources that are required for any alternative, not just those paid for out of the local district in which the study is done and which represent the primary audience.

The importance of determining which audiences one is addressing and for what purposes is that these data guide the level and nature of the presentation and the types of information and analysis that should be forthcoming. However, given limited resources or conflicts between the needs of different audiences, the top priority should always be given to the requirements of the primary audience. In cases in which the report is not appropriate for other audiences with different needs or in different situations and settings, the authors should be explicit about these limitations, so that the results are not misused.

What Type of Analysis to Use?

Once one has established the problem, the alternatives to be considered in addressing it, and the audiences, it is necessary to select the type of analytic framework that will be used. In the previous chapter, we identified four such approaches that use cost analysis:

1. cost-effectiveness (CE)

2. cost-benefit (CB)

3. cost-utility (CU)

4. cost-feasibility (CF)

Each approach has different strengths and weaknesses, as described in Chapter 1. In this section, we will provide criteria that are helpful in considering which of these analytic tools is appropriate. The criteria include the nature of the analytic task, the receptivity of the audience to different techniques, the time available to carry it out, and the expertise and resources that are available to the evaluator. Each will be discussed in turn.

Nature of the Analytic Task

The nature of the analytic task refers to the characteristics of the problem, the alternatives, and whether the specific type of analysis that is being considered is appropriate. A bit of attention was already devoted to this issue in the previous chapter. What is important to consider in this context is the fact that some of the modes of cost analysis are inappropriate for particular problems, while others are appropriate but difficult to implement without substantial resources. To take a major example, cost-feasibility analysis cannot be used to determine the overall desirability of particular alternatives; it can only establish whether they fit within resource constraints.

Likewise, cost-benefit analysis requires that both costs and benefits be measured in monetary terms. While the value of additional earnings and employment from an educational investment might be measured in this way, it is not likely that higher test scores or positive feelings toward learning can be meaningfully converted into monetary units. That is, for many potential educational interventions, the use of cost-benefit analysis will be impossible or problematic. Thus, like CF analysis, CB analysis can be used only when the conditions are appropriate, and those conditions tend to be fairly stringent.

In contrast, cost-effectiveness and cost-utility analyses can be applied under a wide variety of situations. For example, both can be easily incorporated into standard educational evaluations that focus on the measurement of nonmonetary outcomes such as academic achievement.

EXAMPLE 2.1. Assessing Primary and Secondary Audiences

The Wilson School District has a large component of Hispanic enrollments. Since many of the students come from homes in which English is not spoken or is not the primary language, it is not surprising that reading scores are low. The state has provided Wilson with special funding for improving the reading proficiencies of Hispanics, but the district must provide an annual report on how it is using the funds and the results of the program. The district wishes to do an evaluation of different approaches to teaching English and reading to students from non-English-speaking backgrounds. Among the alternatives are English as a Second Language (ESL), bilingual instruction, and total immersion in English. The Wilson School District has asked you to do a cost-effectiveness analysis of these programs to make a recommendation on which should be adopted. Before undertaking this task, you need to analyze the potential primary and secondary audiences.

The primary audiences are those who must use the results directly for their own decision making. These would include the school board, the district administrators, the state education agency, and the pertinent curriculum specialists and teachers. If there is a bilingual advisory council, it would also qualify as a primary audience. An attempt should be made to design the evaluation and report to meet the needs of these audiences. The state will likely set out standards for meeting its needs. For the other audiences, it may be useful to interview representatives to ascertain the types of information that they would like to obtain from the evaluation. Since you may have to choose the types of information that will be provided from among numerous requests, you might also attempt to ask each audience to set priorities among its concerns.

The secondary audiences include those who are likely to read the evaluation and who have an interest in its results. These might include the Hispanic population in the school district, educational personnel who are not directly involved in the interventions, employers and residents of the district, and other school districts that may have an interest in the analysis for informing their own decisions. In these cases, it is important to provide enough information that the report can serve their needs. Again, setting priorities is important, since no evaluation endeavor is likely to meet all the needs of every potential primary and secondary audience.

Receptivity of the Audience

Audiences may be more or less willing to accept certain kinds of analyses that nonetheless yield similar conclusions. For example, CB analysis is less palatable to some audiences because it requires placing a monetary value on certain kinds of outcomes. In the health field, CE and CU analysis are frequently used, even in situations where CB could also be fruitfully applied. In part, this stems from uneasiness among many researchers and decision makers about monetizing health benefits such as life expectancy (Garber & Phelps, 1997; Garber, Weinstein, Torrance, & Kamlet, 1996).

A similar discomfort with monetizing outcomes seems to exist in the field of education, though perhaps to a lesser extent. One could imagine a program that is aimed at reducing high school dropouts (such as the program described in Example 1.4). Since the program is designed to reduce the number of high school dropouts, an obvious measure of effectiveness is the number of dropouts averted. Eventually, of course, staying in high school might yield monetary benefits in the form of additional wages. We can conduct either a CE or a CB analysis, depending on the outcome measure that is chosen (dropouts averted or increased wages). It is conceivable that the CE analysis will be more warmly received by some audiences, because it does not attempt to describe the outcomes of the program in pecuniary terms.

If CE and CB analyses do produce similar conclusions, it seems prudent to choose the analytical technique that is most likely to be well received by the primary audience. In many circumstances, however, it may be that CE and CB analyses produce different conclusions. A CB analysis can treat a number of outcomes at once—presuming that all of them can be expressed in pecuniary terms—but a CE analysis can treat only one at a time. Thus, choosing to conduct a CE analysis might entail sacrifices in terms of the depth of analysis, and results might even be misleading. In these cases, the researcher is best advised to allow the demands of the analytical task to guide the choice of analytical technique rather than the demands of the audience.

Time Constraints

Any approach that requires a considerable investment of time to design the study, collect the data, and analyze the data must be contrasted with the time that is available before the decision must be made. For example, if one wishes to evaluate the cost-effectiveness of different instructional programs for teaching reading to second graders, it may take a year just to obtain the test score results from the pretest to the posttest. When one adds to that the time required to design the study, analyze the data, and prepare the report, one is probably facing a total time commitment of 2 years. Clearly, if a decision must be made in 6 weeks, such an approach is not within the realm of consideration; and, without concrete data on the effects of an intervention, this type of cost-effectiveness study is not possible.

An alternative is to do a cost-utility analysis in which the outcomes will be assessed by a systematic, but subjective, evaluation of what is known about each alternative. Such a study may be possible within a relatively short time span, such as 6 to 12 weeks. Even so, the more time that is made available, the more likely it is that a full and careful analysis will be possible. The main point here is that the time constraint can have a profound impact on what type of analysis is possible.

Available Expertise

The expertise that is available for carrying out a study is another factor that must be considered in selecting a method of analysis and study design. CE analysis can often be done by taking the normal evaluation design and integrating it with a cost component. This means that if competent evaluators are available to contribute to the study, the addition of the cost dimension is all that will be required. Of course, one should bear in mind that the certification of evaluation specialists is problematic, so it should not be assumed that anyone with some training in that area is competent to do both effectiveness and cost sides of the analysis. Many evaluators do not have that expertise, and it is only by scrutinizing previous work of evaluation personnel that one can ascertain their competencies. The training programs and career backgrounds that prepare evaluators are too varied in their content and rigor, regardless of the similarities in titles and courses or descriptions of work experiences, to ensure quality control.

Assuming a competent evaluator for the effectiveness portion of the design, the addition of the cost component by someone familiar with that aspect can be done through a team approach. In contrast, CB analysis requires a fairly intricate understanding of the workings of economic markets as well as other mechanisms. Whether that expertise is available will have a great bearing on the feasibility of using the CB approach, assuming that the evaluation can be cast in the CB framework in the first place. CU analysis also has its own expertise requirements, although these probably are closer to those of CE analysis than CB analysis in their content.

Other resources become pertinent to consideration of which approach to use. If a particular approach requires a large survey of students and schools with a massive statistical analysis, it is important to ensure that not only are the time and expertise available, but also that the budget and expertise for the survey and computations are available. All the resources required for implementation, such as time and expertise, must be considered when you compare particular approaches and study designs.

Is a Cost Analysis Needed?

Thus far, it has been assumed that in most cases a cost analysis should be done; however, this is not necessarily the case. We have already suggested that if there are no alternatives, the entire evaluative situation becomes moot for purposes of decision making. Surely, cost analysis does not alter this conclusion. Further, if sufficient time or other resources are lacking or if cost-effectiveness types of data will not alter decisions, there is probably not a strong case for doing a cost analysis. However, even when all the prerequisites for implementing and using a cost analysis are present, it is important that such an evaluation be worth doing in the first place.

Michael Scriven (1974, pp. 85-93) has developed the notion of cost-free evaluation. In considering the choice of an analytic approach and supportive design for implementation, one must ask what will be gained by finding a better alternative. If the gains will be relatively small, only a small investment in evaluation would be merited. Indeed, if the potential gains of a good decision are minuscule, it is possible that no formal analytic study should be undertaken. That is, intuition and present knowledge should suffice, given that little will be gained from a more formal and extended evaluation. However, when the value of selecting a new alternative can be very great, it may be worth making a large investment in evaluation and analysis. Scriven would say that this situation meets the cost-free evaluation criterion if the probable gains from the evaluation will be in excess of the costs of the evaluation. It is cost free in that more is saved by a good and appropriate evaluation than is expended in resources on that evaluation.

In summary, before selecting a particular analytic technique, it is important to go through a set of procedures that might be summarized by the following checklist:

1. formal identification and understanding of the problem
2. consideration and selection of alternatives to be evaluated
3. recognition of audiences and their needs
4. selection of appropriate mode of analysis
5. consideration of feasibility of conducting evaluation
6. assessing whether an evaluation is likely to be worthwhile

Given these decisions, it is possible to proceed to the next stage of the analysis—the design of the study to obtain measures of costs and outcomes.

Exercises

1. How would you seek to identify the problem in the following cases?

a. Student test scores at the high school level have been declining for the past five years.

b. The physics department of a college is having little success in placing its graduates.

c. A school district faces an anticipated budget deficit for the next year of $200,000.

d. A university wishes to consider replacing its old mainframe computer.

2. Identify a potential problem associated with each of the four situations set out in the previous question. Describe at least two alternatives that might be considered for addressing each problem.

3. Suggest the hypothetical primary and secondary audiences for the evaluations that would follow in each of the four cases above.

4. What types of cost analysis (CE, CB, CU, CF) would seem appropriate for each?

5. How would you determine whether a formal cost analysis would be worthwhile?

CHAPTER 3

The Concept and Measurement of Costs

1. Describe the concept of costs.
2. Show the inadequacy of budgets for cost analysis.
3. Present a methodology for measuring costs.
4. Identify categories of cost ingredients.
5. Describe sources of cost information.

The Concept of Costs

To most of us, the notion of cost is something that is both as obvious as the price of a good or service and as mysterious as the columns of data on an accounting statement or budget. In this chapter, we will introduce a concept of costs that will differ somewhat from both of these, and we will present a straightforward method that can be used by evaluators to estimate costs. Any social intervention or program has both an outcome and a cost. The outcome refers to the result of the intervention. Outcomes of educational interventions include such common indicators as higher student achievement, lower dropouts, improved attitudes, greater employability, and so on. But why are all interventions associated with costs, and what is meant by costs?

Every intervention uses resources that can be utilized for other valued alternatives. For example, a program for raising student achievement will require personnel, facilities, and materials that can be applied to other educational and noneducational endeavors. If these resources are used in one way, they cannot be used in some other way that may also provide useful outcomes. The human time and energy, the buildings, materials, and other resources used in one endeavor have other valuable uses. By devoting them to a particular activity, we are sacrificing the gains that could be obtained from using them for some other purpose.

The value of what is given up or sacrificed represents the cost of an alternative. Accordingly, the "cost" of pursuing the intervention is what we must give up by not using these resources in some other way. Technically, then, the cost of a specific intervention will be defined as the value of all the resources that it utilizes had they been assigned to their most valuable alternative use. In this sense, all costs represent the sacrifice of an opportunity that has been forgone. It is this notion of opportunity cost that lies at the base of cost analysis in evaluation. By using resources in one way, we are giving up the ability to use them in another way, so a cost has been incurred.

Although this may appear to be a peculiar way to view costs, it is probably more familiar to each of us than it appears at first glance. It is usually true that when we refer to costs, we refer to the expenditure that we must make to purchase a particular good or service, as reflected in the statement, "The cost of the meal was $15." In cases in which the only cost is the expenditure of funds that could have been used for other goods and services, the sacrifice or cost can be stated in terms of expenditure. However, in daily usage, we also make statements like, "It cost me a full day to prepare for my vacation," or "It cost me two lucrative sales," in the case of a salesperson who missed two sales appointments because he or she was tied up in a traffic jam. In some cases we may even find that the pursuit of an activity "cost us a friendship."

In each of these cases, a loss was incurred, which was viewed as the value of opportunities that were sacrificed. Thus, the cost of a particular activity was viewed as its "opportunity cost." Of course, this does not mean that we can always easily place a dollar value on that cost. In the case of losing a day of work, one can probably say that the sacrifice or opportunity cost was equal to what could have been earned. In the case of the missed appointments, one can probably make some estimate of what the sales and commissions would have been had the appointments been kept. However, in the case of the lost friendship, it is clearly much more difficult to make a monetary assessment of costs.

In cost analysis, a similar approach is taken, in that we wish to ascertain the cost of an intervention in terms of the value of the resources that were used or lost by applying them in one way rather than in another. To do this, we will construct a logical and straightforward approach called the "ingredients" model. Basically, the ingredients model will require that we specify all the ingredients that are required for any particular intervention. Once these ingredients are specified, a value is placed on each of them. When the values of all the ingredients are added, the total cost of the intervention is established. Subsequent analyses can divide costs according to who pays them and how they are paid as well as by other distinctions. In the evaluation setting, the cost of each alternative can be determined by applying the ingredients method.

Inadequacy of Budgets for Cost Analysis

A very common question that often arises is, Why should we go to all this trouble to estimate costs? Almost all social programs have budgets and expenditure statements, which presumably contain expenditure data that can be used to address the cost issues. Although the existence of budgets is universal, the assumption that they will contain all the cost information that is needed is usually erroneous.[1] First, budgets often do not include cost information on all the ingredients that are used in the intervention, since contributed resources such as volunteers, donated equipment and services, and other "unpaid" inputs are not included in budgets.

Second, when resources have already been paid for or are included in some other agency's budget, they will not be discernible. For example, a building that is provided to a school district by some other unit of government or one that is fully paid for will not be found in the budget of a school district.

Third, the standard budget practices may distort the true costs of an ingredient. Typical public budgets and expenditure statements charge the cost of major rehabilitation only to the year in which the cost was incurred. Thus, when the roof or heating system of a school is replaced, the expenditures are found in the budget for the year in which the repairs were made.

Yet, a new roof or heating system may have a 30-year life, so that only about one-thirtieth of it should be charged to the cost of programs in any given year. Budgetary conventions would typically charge the costs of such capital investments to a single budgetary year, overstating the true costs for that year and understating the costs of operating the program for the 29 subsequent years.

Fourth, the costs of any particular intervention are often embedded in a budget or expenditure statement that covers a much larger unit of operation. Accordingly, it may be difficult to isolate the unique costs of a new reading program in a school district budget, since the budget is not constructed according to the costs of particular interventions or activities. In fact, most educational budgets are "line item" classifications of expenditures according to functions and objects. Examples of functions include administration, instruction, and maintenance. Examples of "objects" include teachers, supplies, clericals, and administrators. Not only is it difficult to tie such budget listings to particular activities or interventions, but it is often impossible even to ascertain what the costs are for a given school or broad instructional program such as a language program, since no such breakdowns are usually provided.

Finally, most budgetary documents represent plans for how resources will be allocated rather than classifying expenditures after they have taken place. This means that, at best, they refer to planned disbursements rather than actual ones. Accordingly, beyond all their other limitations for cost analysis, budgets may not provide precise figures for actual resource use. Actual statements of expenditures may be more accurate, but they are still subject to the shortcomings mentioned before.

For these reasons, cost analysis cannot place primary reliance on budgetary or expenditure documents to ascertain the costs of interventions. Of course, these documents may still provide data that will be very useful. However, they cannot serve as a principal source for constructing cost estimates, but only as a supplementary source of information.

The Ingredients Method

The ingredients method represents a straightforward approach to estimating costs. It has been especially designed to assist the evaluator.[2] Basically, the idea behind this approach is that every intervention uses ingredients that have a value or cost. If the ingredients can be identified and their costs can be ascertained, we can estimate the total costs of the intervention as well as the cost per unit of effectiveness, benefit, or utility. We can also ascertain how the cost burden is distributed among the sponsoring agency, funding agencies, donors, and clients.

The reader should be aware that the approach goes by other names in the literature on cost analysis. For example, it is often referred to as the resource cost model (for a methodological exposition, see Chambers & Parrish, 1994a, 1994b). At their core, the ingredients and resource cost approaches are very similar. Both require that each intervention be exhaustively described in terms of the ingredients or resources that are required to produce the outcomes that will be observed. All these ingredients must be carefully identified for purposes of placing a value or cost on them.

The remainder of this chapter will be used to present the methodology for identifying and specifying ingredients. The next chapter will show how to place a value on ingredients to ascertain their costs. Subsequent chapters will consider how to measure the costs of multiyear projects, how to allocate costs to different constituencies, how to use cost information in evaluations, and how to plan the mechanics of a cost analysis.

Identifying Ingredients

The first step in applying the ingredients method is to identify the ingredients that are used. This entails the determination of what ingredients are required to create or replicate the interventions that are being evaluated. Presumably, the evaluation of outcomes among alternative interventions will provide estimates of what those interventions accomplish in terms of particular criteria. Accordingly, the ingredients method starts with a simple question. In order to obtain the effects that will be observed, certain resources are required for each intervention. What are they? Every ingredient that is used to produce the effects that will be captured in the evaluation must be identified and included. Essentially, we are concerned with identifying all the resources that it takes to produce the effect that will be observed. It is obvious that even contributed or donated resources such as volunteers must be included as ingredients according to such an approach, for such resources will contribute to the outcome of the intervention, even if they are not included in budgetary expenditures.

In order to identify the ingredients that are necessary for cost estimation, it is important to be clear about the scope of the intervention. One type of confusion that sometimes arises is the difficulty of separating the ingredients of a specific intervention from the ingredients required for the more general program that contains the intervention. This might be illustrated by the following situation. Two programs for reducing school dropouts are being considered by a school district. The first program emphasizes the use of providing additional counselors for dropout-prone youngsters. The second program is based upon the provision of tutorial instruction by other students for potential dropouts as well as special enrichment courses to stimulate interest in further education. The question that arises is whether one should include all school resources in the analysis as well as those required for the interventions or just the ingredients that constitute the interventions.

In this case, the ingredients that should be evaluated for purposes of cost analysis should include only those additional ones that are required for the intervention. This is what we will refer to in Chapter 5 as a marginal cost analysis. That is, both alternatives assume that students will continue receiving the standard schooling services, so these need not enter the analysis. What we are concerned with is the additional or incremental services that will be needed in order to provide the alternative dropout-reduction programs. Thus, one should consider only the incremental ingredients that are required for the interventions that are being evaluated.

Familiarity With the Interventions

In order to identify ingredients, it is first necessary to familiarize oneself with the interventions that will be evaluated. The importance of obtaining familiarity with the alternative interventions cannot be overstated in cost analysis. In order to know which ingredients are utilized, one must know well the interventions that are under consideration, for it will be necessary to provide considerable detail on the resources that are required. We return to this issue in the final section of the chapter.

Specification of Ingredients

The identification and specification of ingredients is often facilitated by dividing ingredients into four or five main categories that have common properties. A typical breakdown would include (1) personnel, (2) facilities, (3) equipment and materials, (4) other program inputs, and (5) required client inputs.

Personnel

Personnel ingredients include all the human resources required for each of the alternatives that will be evaluated. This category includes not only full-time personnel, but also part-time employees, consultants, and volunteers. All personnel should be listed according to their roles, qualifications, and time commitments. Roles refer to their responsibilities, such as administration, coordination, teaching, teacher training, curriculum design, secretarial services, and so on. Qualifications refer to the nature of training, experience, and specialized skills required for the positions. Time inputs refer to the amount of time that each person devotes to the intervention in terms of percentage of a full-time position. In the latter case, there may be certain employees, consultants, and volunteers who allocate only a portion of a full workweek or work year to the intervention.

Facilities

Facilities refer to the physical space required for the intervention. This category includes any classroom space, offices, storage areas, play or recreational facilities, and other building requirements, whether paid for by the project or not. Even donated facilities must be specified. All such requirements must be listed according to their dimensions and characteristics, along with other information that is important for identifying their value. For example, facilities that are air-conditioned have a different value than those that are not. Any facilities that are jointly used with other programs should be identified according to the portion of use that is allocated to the intervention.

EXAMPLE 3.1. Why Should Volunteers Be Considered a
Cost Ingredient?

There are many instances in which schools are the recipients of volunteer services. To illustrate this point, let us compare two hypothetical public school districts: Springfield and Middletown. They are similar in most every respect (e.g., per-pupil spending and the socioeconomic mix of their students). However, Springfield has proven quite adept at marshaling the services of a broad array of volunteers.

First, the district is located next to large private university, where a group of motivated students has taken it upon themselves to organize a homework tutoring program. Every Tuesday and Thursday after class, university students arrive at elementary schools to assist low-achieving students with their homework. Second, the Parent-Teacher Association (PTA) in Springfield is quite dynamic. Because most teachers do not have classroom aides, the PTA has assisted the district in locating regular classroom volunteers among parents and other community members. Some of these volunteers have even received permission from their employers to leave work early in order to participate. Third, the Springfield district is located next to a large biotechnology firm. The firm's CEO is very concerned about the quality of science education in public schools. Thus, he has arranged for several research scientists to take off two Fridays a month in order to assist high school teachers in designing new curricular units and to participate in class presentations.

Regrettably, the Middletown school district has not been able to take advantage of similar volunteer services. Given this state of affairs, how should we compare the average cost of public education in the two districts? Our immediate instinct might be to simply compare per-pupil expenditures in each district. At first glance, their costs might appear to be quite similar. After all, Springfield may have more volunteers, but these individuals do not receive salaries, so where is the cost incurred? The notion of including the donated time of volunteers as a program "cost" could strike many as counter-intuitive.

Equipment and Materials

These refer to furnishings, instructional equipment, and materials that are used for the intervention, whether covered by project expenditures or donated by other entities. Specifically, they would include classroom and

EXAMPLE 3.1. continued

However, we need to remember how we are conceptualizing costs. Whenever a resource (or ingredient) is employed in an educational program, it can no longer be employed in alternative ways. This represents a clear sacrifice to some members of society. For example, the university students who volunteer to be tutors are sacrificing valuable time that could be devoted to their own studies or leisure activities. Similarly, the parents, community members, and scientists who participate in classroom activities may be less productive at work or enjoy less free time. The cost of volunteerism is what society must give up by not using the time of volunteers in its most valuable alternative use. Of course, this presents knotty problems of how to place a monetary value on the time of volunteers (we will return to this issue in Chapter 4). Clearly, however, volunteers in the Springfield community are making sacrifices that should be weighed as costs.

Employing this definition of costs enriches the potential of a cost analysis in many ways. First, we can analyze how costs are distributed among various groups of stakeholders in society: the school district, parents, local businesses, and so on. In some cases, such as the previous one, significant costs may be borne by entities other than the district. By understanding the distribution of costs, we are in a better position to analyze how stakeholders might support or oppose an educational program. Later on, in Chapter 5, we will describe methods for analyzing the distribution of costs among stakeholders, using a cost worksheet.

Second, a consideration of volunteer costs might provide a better guide to policy. Let's say that a particular tutoring program relies heavily on unpaid volunteers. Another school district is planning to implement the same program, although circumstances obligate it to use paid tutors at a considerable monetary cost. If the cost analysis of the original tutoring program did not include volunteer costs, it would have provided a misleading portrait of the costs of replicating the program.

office furniture as well as such instructional equipment as computers, audiovisual equipment, scientific apparatus, books and other printed materials, office machines, paper, commercial tests, and other supplies. Both the specific equipment and materials solely allocated to the intervention and those that are shared with other activities should be noted.

Other Inputs

This category refers to all other ingredients that do not fit readily into the categories set out above. For example, it might include any extra liability or theft insurance that is required beyond that provided by the sponsoring agency, or it might include the cost of training sessions at a local college or university. Other possible ingredients might include telephone service, electricity, heating, regular Internet access fees, and so forth. Any ingredients that are included in this category should be specified clearly with a statement of their purpose.

Required Client Inputs

This category of ingredients includes any contributions that are required of the clients or their families. For example, if an educational alternative requires the family to provide transportation, books, uniforms, equipment, food, or other student services, these should be included under this classification. The purpose of including such inputs is that the success of some interventions will depend crucially on such resources, whereas the success of others will not. To provide an accurate picture of the resources required to replicate any intervention that requires client inputs, it is important to include these inputs in the analysis.

General Considerations in Listing Ingredients

Three overriding considerations should be recognized in identifying and specifying ingredients. First, the ingredients should be specified in sufficient detail that their value can be ascertained in the next stage of the analysis. Thus, it is important that the qualifications of staff, characteristics of physical facilities, types of equipment, and other inputs be specified with enough precision that it is possible to place reasonably accurate cost values on them.

Second, the categories into which ingredients are placed should be consistent, but there is no single approach to categorization that will be suitable in all cases. The one that was set out above is a general classification scheme that is rather typical. It is possible, however, that there need be no "other inputs" category if all ingredients can be assigned to other classifications. For example, insurance coverage can be included with facilities and equipment to the degree that it is associated with the costs of those categories. Likewise, if parents are required to provide volunteer time, that ingredient can be placed under client inputs rather than under personnel. The categories are designed to be functionally useful rather than orthodox distinctions that should never be violated.

Finally, the degree of specificity and accuracy in listing ingredients should depend upon their overall contribution to the total cost of the intervention. Personnel inputs often represent three quarters or more of the costs of educational and social service interventions. Accordingly, they should be given the most attention. Facilities and equipment may also be important. However, supplies can often be estimated with much less attention to detail, since they do not weigh heavily in overall costs. The important point is that an eventual error of 10% in estimating personnel costs will have a relatively large impact on the total cost estimate because of the importance of personnel in the overall picture. However, a 100% error in office supplies will create an imperceptible distortion, because office supplies are usually an inconsequential contributor to overall costs. In general, the most effort in identifying and specifying ingredients should be devoted to those ingredients that are likely to dominate the cost picture.

Sources of Ingredients Information

We have already mentioned that it is important to obtain a familiarity with the intervention that is being subjected to cost analysis. Only by doing so can the evaluator identify the ingredients used by the intervention in sufficient detail (and, subsequently, attach values to those ingredients). Normally, this familiarity can be gained in at least three ways: (1) through a review of program documents, (2) through discussions with individuals involved in the intervention, and (3) through direct observation of the intervention.

An essential starting point is the examination of program documents. These documents may include general descriptions of the program prepared by program staff or outsiders, budgets and expenditure statements, Web sites, reports by previous evaluators of the program, internal memos

EXAMPLE 3.2. A Cost Analysis of the Perry Preschool Program (Part 1)

In the 1960s, a well-known experiment was conducted among a small group of at-risk children in Ypsilanti, Michigan. Some children were randomly assigned to participate in the Perry Preschool Program, while others were designated as the control group. The program was designed to provide a high-quality preschool environment for at-risk children, including 2-hour classes on weekday mornings and weekly 90-minute home visits by teachers. A series of cost-benefit analyses by Steven Barnett have sought to weigh the costs of the program against its benefits (later on, in Example 7.1, we discuss the full results of these evaluations).

The cost analysis was based upon the ingredients method. The list of ingredients was derived from a thorough examination of program publications and from interviews with former teachers and administrators. The main categories of cost ingredients include the following:

▸ *Instructional staff.* Four teachers were employed in each year of the program; in addition to their salaries, it is important to consider the fringe benefits that they received (e.g., retirement contributions) and employer contributions to the Social Security tax.

▸ *Administrative and support staff.* Teachers were not the only personnel involved in the program. Other program staff managed the special education program, including a Special Services Director.

▸ *Facilities.* The program was held in the facilities of the Ypsilanti Public School District. Thus, an important cost ingredient is the existing physical plant of the school district that was utilized by the program, including classroom space.

▸ *Equipment.* To set up and furnish the preschool classroom, some equipment was purchased especially for the program.

▸ *Classroom supplies.* These include several subcategories of ingredients, including the food that was used for the children's daily snacks and other nondurable educational materials that were used by the children.

▸ *Developmental screening.* Prior to initiating the program, a large number of children were tested and interviewed. The screening process was used to decide which children were eligible to participate in the program, based upon family incomes and risk of educational failure.

EXAMPLE 3.2. continued

▶ *School district overhead.* The program was operated within the Ypsilanti Public School District. As might be expected, the district assumed many program expenses. These include maintenance, utilities, and the costs of providing the support of general administrative and nonteaching staff.

▶ *Client inputs.* The client inputs used in the program were judged to be negligible. No fees were charged to parents, and all supplies were given to parents (and thus accounted for by previous ingredient categories). Parents lived within walking distance of the school, so there were no additional transportation costs borne by them. The only possible ingredient supplied by clients is the time that parents spent with teachers in occasional home visits. However, these visits were strictly voluntary and some parents chose not to participate.

The prior list provides an essential starting point, but it is important to specify in greater detail the exact nature and quantity of each ingredient (of course, Barnett followed this procedure in carrying out his cost study). For example, what are the qualifications of the teaching staff (e.g., experience, formal education, and training)? What kinds of equipment were used to furnish the classroom (e.g., desks)? How many of each kind were used to furnish the classroom? When conducting a cost analysis, we can generally save ourselves a great deal of trouble by exhaustively detailing the ingredients ahead of time. As we will see in Chapter 4, it is difficult to place a reliable value on an ingredient that is only vaguely specified. Of course, one should also keep in mind the admonitions of the last section. One should focus the greatest attention on the ingredients that are likely to occupy the greatest weight in the final cost estimates—instructional staff being the most obvious).

In the next chapter, Example 4.2 describes the values that were attached to the preceding ingredients.

SOURCE: Barnett (1996, pp. 19-25).

or e-mails, and countless other sources of information. The evaluator must approach this task as a good detective might, attempting to turn up every bit of potentially useful documentary evidence. In some cases, this initial search might produce a veritable mountain of paper that is rather daunting to the cost analyst; in others, the evaluator might be stymied by an unfortunate lack of documentation or perhaps even cooperation from program staff. In sifting through the available information, one should not view it as necessarily reflective of the actual ingredients used in the program. Indeed, a program description may ignore significant categories of ingredients (such as client inputs or volunteers) or provide an overly optimistic discussion of how some ingredients are used (such as teacher training sessions). However, a thorough review will provide the evaluator with sufficient background to ask the right questions during subsequent interviews.

A second source of information may include interviews with individuals involved in the intervention. These individuals might include the program designers; program directors and administrative staff; school personnel such as principals, teachers, and aides; and parents. In some cases, particularly when adults or older children are participants, it may be helpful to interview the program recipients directly. In conducting interviews, the evaluator should seek to confirm or contradict the impressions left by documentary evidence. For example, does the program actually use three full-time teachers, or is that not the case? Do training sessions occur every Friday as stated on the program Web site, or do they occur less frequently? In every case, we should be concerned with identifying the ingredients that are *actually* used in the intervention, rather than the ingredients that were supposed to have been used in the ideal case.

Even after reviewing documents and conducting interviews, it is often helpful to conduct direct observations of the intervention. In a reading program, for example, the evaluator might sit in on several classes. Again, the purpose of doing so is to ascertain the ingredients that are actually being used. If the program designer mentioned that students should have individual workbooks, is it the case that all students in the class have workbooks? If program documents state that 50 minutes of classroom time is devoted to instruction, is this revealed during classroom observations?

In reading, interviewing, and observing, it is important to search for agreement and disagreement across sources. Ultimately, we hope that various sources of information will aid in triangulating upon a reasonable set of cost ingredients. (In fact, the issue of triangulation is important throughout the process of cost evaluation. Whenever multiple sources of information can be used to confirm a result, it strengthens our confidence in the findings.) Where there are significant disagreements, we might be inspired to probe more carefully. Often, however, disagreements cannot be easily resolved. For example, it may be that a particular intervention was implemented in two substantially different ways across a series of program sites; each version of the program used a different set of cost ingredients. In cases such as these, we should be upfront in our evaluation about the uncertainty. A helpful procedure is to present results from several variants of a cost analysis, using different sets of assumptions about the specific cost ingredients that are employed.

Exercises

1. What is meant by the term "cost" when used in cost analysis?

2. What are the "costs" associated with the following situations?

   a. It takes a full day at the passport office to renew your passport.

   b. Your failure to keep records results in an inability to take certain deductions on your income tax.

   c. The school sponsors an outdoor party for the student body that destroys a major portion of the lawns and shrubbery.

   d. A rise in school crime and vandalism requires that some teachers be used to patrol the campus rather than teach.

   e. The birth of a child places heavy demands on your family schedule so that you must defer the completion of courses for a master's degree.

3. What characteristics of budgets make them inappropriate sources for estimating costs?

4. What is the ingredients approach to estimating costs?

5. Indicate the types of ingredients that are likely to be required for the following programs. Provide as much detail as you are able.

a. A peer tutoring program will be established in which sixth graders will spend 2 hours a week tutoring third graders who are not making adequate progress in reading or mathematics. The school will set aside a special room for this purpose and will use parent volunteers to coordinate the tutors and set a tutoring schedule. Tutors will be trained in a 10-hour course that will take place over the first 2 weeks of school. A teacher with experience in peer tutoring will do the training.

b. A high school is considering the establishment of a fencing team for both males and females that will undertake a full schedule of interscholastic competition.

c. A school district is considering the establishment of its own program for the education of children with speech and hearing impairments. Previously, such students were sent to classes sponsored by the county.

d. A principal is dissatisfied with the quality of mathematics instruction in her school. She has discussed the matter with the teachers, and they believe that a combination of a new curriculum and in-service training for teachers will improve matters.

► NOTES

1. For an additional perspective on this issue, see Chambers (1999). He compares and contrasts two different models for cost estimation. One is based on an accounting model developed by the accounting firm of Coopers & Lybrand; the second is based on an economic approach, referred to as the resource cost model (the latter is quite similar in its approach to the ingredients method).

2. For similar descriptions of the ingredients method, see Levin (1975, 1988, 1995).

Placing Values on Ingredients

OBJECTIVES

1. Describe the purpose and principles for determining the values of ingredients.
2. Present methods for placing values on specific types of ingredients.

The previous chapter reviewed the overall notion of costs and the reasons that the types of cost data that are required are not readily available from budget statements. We also introduced the ingredients approach to constructing cost estimates and set out the principles and procedures for identifying and specifying ingredients. In this chapter, we wish to place cost values on each of the ingredients in order to obtain an estimate for total costs and for cost components of interventions.

Purpose and Principles of Cost Valuation

At this point, we presumably know the resources, or ingredients, that are required for each intervention. However, the fact that we know which

59

ingredients are required does not enable us to estimate costs. Once again, we must turn to the definition of costs as a sacrifice equal to the value of something that is given up by using resources in a particular way. By using the ingredients for a specific intervention, we sacrifice their potential use for something else. The cost to us is the value of what we must give up by using the ingredients in this way rather than in their best alternative use. Accordingly, a monetary measure of costs represents the monetary value of all of the ingredients when used in their best alternative use. In essence, it tells us the value of the sacrifice that we must make to use all the ingredients for this intervention by providing a summary measure in dollars of the value of the ingredients in other uses.

Market Prices

The most common method for placing monetary values on ingredients is that of using their market prices. According to economic theory, when markets for a particular good or service are perfectly competitive, the equilibrium price established by that market will represent the value of that good (Dorfman, 1967). The method of using market prices has two attractive features, availability and simplicity. First, since there are reasonably competitive markets for many of the ingredients (e.g., personnel, facilities, and equipment) used in educational interventions, there will be a set of prices readily available that can be used to determine the costs of those inputs. Second, using the market price of ingredients is a simple way to derive cost data.

Shadow Prices

Unfortunately, competitive markets are not always the only source of ingredients. In some cases, there is a market for a particular ingredient, but the market does not meet the criteria for perfect competition. There are relatively few buyers or sellers, or other market imperfections exist. In these cases the existing market price may be an inaccurate reflection of the cost of obtaining additional units of an ingredient, and adjustments must be made to provide a more appropriate cost measure. For example, assume that a talented program director is presently receiving salary and other benefits valued at $60,000 a year, but there are very few persons who possess such talents. If one wished to ascertain the cost of using such talent to replicate an intervention at many new sites, one would have to take account of the fact that the scarcity of such talent may generate a considerably higher cost for additional qualified persons as demand for such talent increases.

Alternatively, there may be no obvious market for a particular ingredient. For example, a school district may decide to lend an old facility to a new program. There is no financial transaction, because the building was purchased and paid for a long time ago. Moreover, no market exists for this type of facility. In these cases, it is necessary to ascertain what the value of the ingredient would be if there were a market. When attempts are made to ascertain the value of a good that does not have a competitive market price, the estimated value is called a shadow price.[1] Both market and shadow prices can be used to ascertain the values of the ingredients for purposes of cost estimation.

Methods for Valuing Ingredients

When ingredients have market prices, the best measure of cost is usually that price. The market price is a measure of what must be sacrificed in terms of the value of other commodities to provide the ingredient for the intervention. Market prices exist wherever goods or services can be offered for sale and purchased openly by buyers and sellers. At any particular time, one can purchase those goods and services at that price. Thus, if one can obtain teachers of a given quality at a given price (salary plus fringe benefits) in the open market, one can use that price to evaluate the cost of a teacher with those characteristics. The same is true of everything purchased in the marketplace—facilities, equipment, materials, supplies, and other personnel. In all of these cases, one seeks the market price for obtaining those goods and services.

In those cases in which market prices are inaccurate reflections of the true cost, one must adjust the market price appropriately. In the case mentioned above of the use of scarce talent, an increase in demand will result in a higher price. Accordingly, some effort must be made to ascertain how demand will increase for such ingredients as a result of the intervention as well as what the consequences such a shift in demand will have on the market price. Most cost analysis in education will not require this adjustment if one is dealing with a single intervention rather than an attempt to replicate it numerous times. In the single intervention case, the use of an ingredient will generally not affect the market; however, in the case of numerous duplications of the intervention, demand for the ingredient may increase enough to raise its price.

When market prices are not available, one must use some estimate of what those prices would be, or shadow prices. For example, there may be no specific market for an old school building, but there are various ways that we could ascertain what the market price would be if there were a market. There may be no market for the services of sixth graders who are asked to tutor first graders. But there may be a way of measuring the social sacrifice or cost of using the time of sixth graders to tutor first graders by asking, What is the value of the sixth graders' time in other uses, such as learning? For example, what if it were found that sixth graders who spend their time tutoring learn less than similar sixth graders who do not tutor? One way of ascertaining the shadow price of their time in tutoring is to estimate what it would cost to maintain their learning achievements at the level of their nontutoring peers. Each case in which shadow prices must be estimated presents a different challenge that must be analyzed idiosyncratically. Fortunately, the problem is rare enough in educational cost analysis that one will not encounter it very frequently.

Given these overall principles, it is possible to set out methods for ascertaining the value of ingredients for each of the categories stipulated in the previous chapters. Since costs always have a time dimension, one should be specific about the period for which one will evaluate costs. In this chapter, we will limit the analysis to an evaluation of annual costs. In Chapter 5, however, we will show how to estimate costs when a project must be evaluated on a multiyear basis.

Personnel

Since personnel account for about three quarters of the total costs of typical educational interventions, it is important to devote considerable effort to obtaining accurate estimates of their costs. The services of most personnel are purchased in the marketplace, so it is data derived from such market transactions that we should consider first. When a personnel position can be filled by attracting persons with the appropriate education, experience, and other characteristics at the prevailing salary and fringe benefits generally paid for such talent in the marketplace, the cost of such a person is considered to be the monetary value of the salary and fringe benefits. This determination presumes that a market exists in that there are many employers seeking such personnel, and there are many people seeking such positions. At any one time, these dynamics will result in a prevailing salary and fringe benefits that must be paid to obtain persons for any given position, and that expenditure on salaries and fringe benefits represents their costs. It is important to point out that the price of obtaining personnel in different school districts or teaching situations is also affected by working conditions and other factors (Chambers, 1980). Thus, even though there may exist a general market for particular types of personnel, any specific analysis should take account of observed differences in the employment situation.

The salary and fringe benefits for each person can usually be obtained from normal payroll or expenditure data. It is important to add to each salary all the fringe benefits, including employer contributions to social security, other pension plans, health and life insurance, and perquisites that benefit the employee, such as the use of a car for private purposes. In many cases, fringe benefits packages are expressed as an overall percentage of salaries, since some fixed percentage of salaries is allocated to these benefits. For example, 23% of salaries might be allocated to fringe benefits. In such a case, one need only obtain salary data and add the fringe benefits based upon the percentage allocation for that purpose.

In situations in which one has data on actual expenditures for particular categories of personnel, personnel costs can be readily ascertained. In other cases, such as new interventions that are being proposed or the use of volunteers, expenditure data that can be used to assess costs are not as obvious. In these cases, it is necessary to estimate the market value of the personnel services that are provided. For example, in the case of estimating the costs of a proposed program, one can use data from other existing interventions or the marketplace to calculate the expected costs for each type of personnel. Likewise, the value of a volunteer can be determined by estimating the market value of the services that the volunteer will provide. Thus, if the volunteer has the qualifications for and will serve as a teacher's aide, one can use the salary and fringe benefits of a teacher's aide to set the value of the volunteer to the program.

EXAMPLE 4.1. The Perils of Using "Shortcuts" Instead of the Ingredients Method

The identification and valuation of ingredients is not always an easy task. The evaluator must identify all the main ingredients of a program, and this can only be accomplished through time-intensive site visits, interviews, and examination of program documents. Then, values must be placed on each of the ingredients. This often requires equal amounts of creativity and legwork on the part of evaluators.

When time is limited or data are scarce, we are often tempted to bypass the ingredients method and use a "shortcut" method of our own devising. A prominent example is the comparison of the costs of public and private schools in the United States. Many have argued that private schools have lower per-pupil costs than public schools and hence are able to produce educational services more efficiently (e.g., Hoxby, 1998). However, there is no definitive cost comparison that uses the ingredients method.[2] Instead, it is commonplace to make "shortcut" comparisons on this subject. In one study, the authors compare per-pupil expenditures in public schools to the per-pupil tuition that is charged by private schools (Boaz & Barrett, 1996). The notion is that private school tuition, or revenues, provides a reasonable estimate of costs.

How accurate are these cost estimates likely to be? Unfortunately, they are probably afflicted by a number of important errors and omissions. Private schools may receive additional resources from several sources, including parents who pay special fees, donate time, purchase school materials or uniforms, participate in fund-raising events, or provide direct donations.[3] For example, Tsang and Taoklam's (1992) careful cost accounting in Thailand shows that private school tuition accounts for only 40% of direct and indirect family contributions.[4] Even public schools—especially in developing countries—depend heavily on private contributions.[5]

In summary, most personnel costs can be obtained by ascertaining the expenditures on salaries and fringe benefits for each of the personnel ingredients. When such data are not available, costs can usually be estimated by considering the market value of the services that will be utilized.

Facilities

In the case of facilities, there are two possibilities. The first is that the intervention will utilize rented or leased space so that its market value is

EXAMPLE 4.1. continued

Religious private schools may also receive direct subsidies from churches, the services of clergy working at below-market wages, and the donated use of land and buildings (Bartell, 1968). Estimates from the 1990s, based on a random sample of U.S. Catholic elementary schools, show that the average school receives 28% of its revenue from parish subsidies (Kealey, 1996). Besides monetary subsidies, many personnel in private schools are members of religious orders and their salaries understate their true market value. In 1995, for example, 47% of Catholic elementary principals were priests or members of a religious community (Kealey, 1996). Their average salary was $20,274 per year, compared with an average salary of $34,520 for principals who were laymen or laywomen.

Even when all ingredients are measured correctly, a different service mix between public and private schools complicates a straightforward comparison of per-pupil costs. For example, public schools often receive greater numbers of children that require special education or vocational education, both of which are more costly than standard instruction (Levin, 1998). Furthermore, public schools often serve greater numbers of students who come from families with lower incomes and parental education. Some empirical research in the United States finds that such students are more costly, on average, to provide with a given set of school outcomes (Downes & Pogue, 1994; Duncombe, Ruggiero, & Yinger, 1996).

By pursuing a shortcut method, we may arrive at substantially misleading estimates of private and public school costs. The best way of avoiding these pitfalls would be to conscientiously apply the ingredients method.

evident from expenditures. In that situation, the annual cost is the expenditure on such facilities. When a portion of a leased facility is used for the intervention, the cost value can be determined by ascertaining the portion of the lease cost that should be allocated to the intervention. For example, if 25% of a building is being used for the intervention, then about one quarter of the annual cost of that space should be allocated to the intervention.

In many cases, however, the facilities are owned rather than leased by the sponsoring agency. That is, they were purchased or constructed in the past by the school district or university that is sponsoring the intervention. Since there is no financial transaction, how can one determine what the value of the facility is for a given year? The simplest way to estimate that cost is to ask what the cost would be for similar space. That is, although a market for leased school facilities does not necessarily exist, it is possible to ascertain what space in similar types of buildings might cost to lease.

Usually, one will need the assistance of a local real estate agent to make this estimate. In that case, one needs to have an overall picture of the amount of space that is being used for the intervention and of such features as its age, construction, improvements, and amenities. These can be conveyed to a person who is knowledgeable about the local real estate market to get an estimate of the lease cost for such space.

An alternative way of estimating the value of a facility is to compute its annual cost by taking account of depreciation and the interest on the remaining, or undepreciated, value. This procedure requires knowledge of three factors: the replacement cost of the facility, the life span of the facility, and the rate of interest that is forgone by investing in a building rather than in another investment.

The replacement cost of the building represents the amount that it would take to construct a similar facility. If only a part of the facility is being used for the intervention, one should estimate that portion of the overall facility and its cost that should be allocated to the intervention. Alternatively, one can get estimates of facility costs on the basis of the cost per square foot and multiply this amount by the square footage used for the intervention. Depreciation refers to the amount of the facility that is "consumed" in a year. Essentially, depreciation costs are estimated by determining the life of the facility and dividing the total replacement cost by the number of years of use. For example, if a building has a useful life of 30 years, about one thirtieth of the facility is "used up" each year. Thus, the depreciation cost would be equal to one thirtieth of the replacement value of the building.

However, depreciation is not the only cost involved. The undepreciated portion of the facility represents an investment in resources that could have been used in some other way. By using those resources to construct the facility, alternative investment possibilities and their potential income and services have been forgone. These forgone income opportunities can be reflected by asking, "What interest rate could have been earned had the investment been made in the best alternative project?" That is, alternative ways of using those resources would have yielded a financial return that is approximated by multiplying an interest rate by the undepreciated portion of the facility investment.

This is the second component of costs: The forgone income on an investment that could have been realized if the resources had been used for some other alternative. For example, consider that had an amount equal to the undepreciated portion of the facility been invested in a bank account and lent out by the bank for some other purpose, a rate of interest would have been paid on this investment. Because of the forgone opportunities represented by the sunken investment in the undepreciated portion of the facility, we calculate the cost to us of that investment. Accordingly, the second part of the annual cost of a facility is determined by applying a rate of interest to the undepreciated portion of the facility—that is, the value of the facility that remains after taking account of its past depreciation.

In sum, the method of determining the annual value of an "owned" facility is to take the following steps:

1. Determine the replacement value of the facility.

2. Determine the life of the facility.

3. Divide the replacement value by the number of years of life to obtain the cost of depreciation for each year of use.

4. Multiply the undepreciated portion by an appropriate interest rate to obtain the opportunity cost of having resources invested in the undepreciated portion of the facility.

5. Add the annual cost of depreciation and the annual interest forgone on the remaining investment to obtain an annual cost.

Although this procedure is a valid one and is used by businesses to estimate the annual cost of facilities and equipment, it suffers from a serious problem with respect to social investments. Clearly, such a cost estimate will depend crucially upon the age of the facilities in that the greater the undepreciated portion, the higher the opportunity costs. Yet, the value of the services received in any one year may not differ substantially from that of other years, regardless of the age of the building. For this reason, attempts have been made to "annualize" costs by estimating an average of the combination of depreciation and interest on the undepreciated portion over the life of the facility.

Although there is a formula for annualizing the cost of a facility, Table 4.1 provides a much simpler method that can be used by the analyst. Table 4.1 shows annualization factors for facilities with different lifetimes

TABLE 4.1 Annualization Factors for Determining Annual Cost of Facilities and Equipment for Different Periods of Depreciation and Interest Rates

Lifetime of Assets (n)	Interest Rate (r)							
	1%	2%	3%	4%	5%	7%	10%	15%
1								
2	0.5075	0.5150	0.5226	0.5302	0.5378	0.5531	0.5762	0.6151
3	0.3400	0.3468	0.3535	0.3603	0.3672	0.3811	0.4021	0.4380
4	0.2563	0.2626	0.2690	0.2755	0.2820	0.2952	0.3155	0.3503
5	0.2060	0.2122	0.2184	0.2246	0.2310	0.2439	0.2638	0.2983
6	0.1725	0.1785	0.1846	0.1908	0.1970	0.2098	0.2296	0.2642
7	0.1486	0.1545	0.1605	0.1666	0.1728	0.1856	0.2054	0.2404
8	0.1307	0.1365	0.1425	0.1485	0.1547	0.1675	0.1874	0.2229
9	0.1167	0.1225	0.1284	0.1345	0.1407	0.1535	0.1736	0.2096
10	0.1056	0.1113	0.1172	0.1233	0.1295	0.1424	0.1627	0.1993
11	0.0965	0.1022	0.1081	0.1141	0.1204	0.1334	0.1540	0.1911
12	0.0888	0.0946	0.1005	0.1066	0.1128	0.1259	0.1468	0.1845
13	0.0824	0.0881	0.0940	0.1001	0.1065	0.1197	0.1408	0.1791
14	0.0769	0.0826	0.0885	0.0947	0.1010	0.1143	0.1357	0.1747
15	0.0721	0.0778	0.0838	0.0899	0.0963	0.1098	0.1315	0.1710
16	0.0679	0.0737	0.0796	0.0858	0.0923	0.1059	0.1278	0.1679

17	0.0643	0.0700	0.0760	0.0822	0.0887	0.1024	0.1247	0.1654
18	0.0610	0.0667	0.0727	0.0790	0.0855	0.0994	0.1219	0.1632
19	0.0581	0.0638	0.0698	0.0761	0.0827	0.0968	0.1195	0.1613
20	0.0554	0.0612	0.0672	0.0736	0.0802	0.0944	0.1175	0.1598
21	0.0530	0.0588	0.0649	0.0713	0.0780	0.0923	0.1156	0.1584
22	0.0509	0.0566	0.0627	0.0692	0.0760	0.0904	0.1140	0.1573
23	0.0489	0.0547	0.0608	0.0673	0.0741	0.0887	0.1126	0.1563
24	0.0471	0.0529	0.0590	0.0656	0.0725	0.0872	0.1113	0.1554
25	0.0454	0.0512	0.0574	0.0640	0.0710	0.0858	0.1102	0.1547
26	0.0439	0.0497	0.0559	0.0626	0.0696	0.0846	0.1092	0.1541
27	0.0424	0.0483	0.0546	0.0612	0.0683	0.0834	0.1083	0.1535
28	0.0411	0.0470	0.0533	0.0600	0.0671	0.0824	0.1075	0.1531
29	0.0399	0.0458	0.0521	0.0589	0.0660	0.0814	0.1067	0.1527
30	0.0387	0.0446	0.0510	0.0578	0.0651	0.0806	0.1061	0.1523
40	0.0305	0.0366	0.0433	0.0505	0.0583	0.0750	0.1023	0.1506
50	0.0255	0.0318	0.0389	0.0466	0.0548	0.0725	0.1009	0.1501

NOTE: The annualization formula is:

$$a(r,n) = \frac{r(1+r)^n}{\left((1+r)^n - 1\right)}$$

where r = interest rate and n = lifetime of asset for depreciation.

at a variety of interest rates. For example, if a facility has a 20-year life and the appropriate interest rate is 5%, the annualization factor is 0.0802. One need only multiply this factor by the replacement cost of the facility to obtain an annual cost. For instance, if the replacement cost of the facility is $100,000, the annual cost would be about $8,020. This table can also be applied to a portion of facilities by determining what proportion of the total facility is used for the intervention. It is that proportion of the replacement cost that would subsequently be used for the calculation.

Assuming that the replacement cost and life of the facility can be estimated, it is only necessary to choose the interest rate. The basic problem in choosing this rate is that economists themselves are not able to agree upon an exact number. Economists have made strong arguments that interest rates should range between 0% and 11%, with a range of 3% to 7% as perhaps the most plausible (Barnett, 1996). We shall return to this discussion in Chapter 5.

In summary, the annual cost of facilities can be estimated from using their annual leasing cost or rental value or estimating their annual value by considering depreciation and opportunity costs of the undepreciated investment. Table 4.1 can be of great assistance in making the latter calculation.

Equipment

The rules for estimating the costs of equipment are quite similar to those for estimating the costs of facilities. The annual cost of all leased equipment can be easily established. One can also use the rental or lease value to obtain estimates of the cost value of equipment that is donated or borrowed. In the absence of such information, one can use the replacement cost of a piece of equipment to estimate the annual cost by applying the annualization factors in Table 4.1. For example, if a piece of equipment has a replacement cost of $10,000 and a 10-year life, the annualization factor for a 5% interest rate is 0.1295 and the annual cost is about $1,295. This figure reflects both the cost of equipment depreciation and the cost of income that was forgone because funds were unavailable for alternative uses. In general, these principles can be used quite readily to set annual values on equipment.

Supplies

The costs of supplies are often difficult to estimate using the ingredients method because it is too arduous to set out their composition and price in detail. For example, office supplies may consist of paper, pens, pencils, toner cartridges, paper clips, calendars, and so on. It would take enormous resources to list each of these and determine market prices. Also, such supplies typically account for less than 5% of the total cost of educational interventions, so errors in estimating their costs do not create very much distortion in the total cost figure. For example, a 20% error in the cost of a category that makes up only 5% of the total cost estimate will result in only a 1% distortion. But a 20% error in the cost of a category that makes up 75% of total costs, such as personnel, will create a 15% distortion, or a distortion that is 15 times as great.

Accordingly, one might estimate the cost of supplies by simply adding the total expenditures on supplies to the estimated value of those that are contributed. Only in the case in which supplies are a large part of the intervention would one wish to devote greater effort to the details of this category.

Required Client Inputs

The method for determining the cost of client inputs will depend upon the types of inputs under consideration. Here, we are referring only to ingredients that must be provided by clients, such as transportation. We are not referring to fees that are charged to clients, since these represent a payment mechanism that will be addressed in Chapter 5. Some educational programs may provide their own transportation, and it is important to take account of the value of this ingredient regardless of who is supplying it.

The usual approach to ascertaining the costs of transportation is to include the total expense. For example, if parents must purchase bicycles, protective headgear, and other equipment for their children for getting to school, this can be assessed according to the method for costing out equipment. The replacement value for the equipment can be converted into an annualized cost through the use of Table 4.1. If the bicycle (or other equip-

EXAMPLE 4.2. A Cost Analysis of the Perry Preschool Program (Part 2)

In the last chapter, Example 3.2 described several categories of cost ingredients in the Perry Preschool Program. Once ingredients are identified, values need to be attached to each of these ingredients. The cost analysis of the program incorporated a variety of methods and data in order to calculate the program costs in 5 separate academic years (1962-63 to 1966-67). The overall cost estimates for a single year (1962-63) are summarized in Table 4.2. They are briefly described below.

> ▷ *Instructional staff.* The salaries of teachers were obtained directly from the accounting files of the Ypsilanti School District. At the time, contributions to social security and retirement accounts were an administratively determined percentage of salaries. Thus, the appropriate percentages were applied in order to obtain the cost of fringe benefits.

> ▷ *Administrative and support staff.* The costs of administrative and support staff were obtained from the annual audit reports and budgets of

ment) will only be used 10% of the time for going to school, then we might estimate the cost as 10% of the annualized value.

If the parents transport their children to school in a carpool, it is possible to calculate the annual cost based upon estimated mileage and the value of parental time. The major car rental companies make estimates of the cost per mile for operating a car. Since the car is not likely to be purchased solely for this purpose, one should probably consider only the operating cost of the additional mileage (gas, oil, tires, maintenance) rather than a part of the "fixed" cost (depreciation, interest, insurance). One might check with local businesses to determine the amount that is reimbursed for each mile of auto travel (e.g., 25 cents or 30 cents per mile). The value of parental time can be estimated by considering what it would cost to hire someone (such as a school bus driver) to provide this service. That cost in wages and fringe benefits can be applied to the number of hours a year required for parental driving.

If the child takes public transportation, it is the average cost per passenger of the transportation system that can provide the most reasonable

EXAMPLE 4.2. continued

the Ypsilanti Public School District. These costs could only be obtained for a single year (1968-69). Thus, these figures were applied to each of the previous years for which a cost estimate was needed after making adjustments for inflation.

▶ *Facilities.* The facilities belonged to the school district and were in use before (and after) the Perry Preschool Program. Therefore, it would be misleading to use their overall value to calculate an annual facilities cost. Instead, the evaluator calculated the annualized cost of interest and depreciation, following the methods that were described earlier in the chapter. The interest rate was set at 3.5% and the facilities were assumed to lose 3% of their total value in each year due to depreciation.[6] (The study author also obtained cost estimates using several other interest rates; later on, in Chapter 5, we address the issue of how to choose an interest rate.)

(continued)

cost estimate. Each public transportation system has an estimate of such a cost. Of course, the rider pays only a portion of that cost, and taxpayers pay the remainder. However, it is the overall cost that is required for cost estimation, and the allocation of cost can be made at a subsequent stage.

Summary of Cost Valuation of Ingredients

The valuation of ingredients requires taking each category and using appropriate methods to ascertain their cost values. All ingredients must be evaluated for their costs, even those that are contributed or provided in-kind. Particular costing methods for each category are used in order to obtain an annual cost. Once these costs are determined, they can be added to obtain the total cost of the intervention. This can be divided by the number of students or clients to obtain a per-student cost for the intervention.

EXAMPLE 4.2. A Cost Analysis of the Perry Preschool Program (Part 2) *(continued)*

▷ *Equipment.* The program used a variety of equipment. Like facilities, this equipment lasts for more than 1 year, and it is necessary to calculate an annualized cost. Again, the interest rate was set at 3.5%; equipment was assumed to lose 10% of its total value in each year due to depreciation.

▷ *Classroom supplies.* In each year of the program, $480 was allocated to classroom supplies; this figure was used as the annual cost of classroom supplies.

▷ *Developmental screening.* Children who participated in the program received developmental screening prior to their entry. The ingredients of this screening were estimated at $234 in 1962-63.

▷ *School district overhead.* The Ypsilanti Public School District provided services that benefited the preschool students, including maintenance, utilities, and general administrative support. To calculate the costs of overhead, the evaluator divided the total annual expenditures of the district on these services—obtained from annual audit reports—by the total number of students enrolled in district schools. This produced a per-student overhead cost that was multiplied by the number of students participating in the Perry Preschool Program.

An interesting feature of the estimates in Table 4.2 is that instructional staff accounted for 91% of costs in 1962-63. This is often the case in educational programs that rely heavily on the services of teachers. When identifying and valuing ingredients, the evaluator is often pressed for time and money. Thus, it would be wise to follow the advice of Chapter 3 and focus one's efforts on the categories of ingredients that are likely to weigh most heavily in the final estimates, such as personnel.

SOURCE: Barnett (1996, pp. 19-25).

TABLE 4.2 Ingredient Costs of the Perry Preschool Program

	Cost in 1962-63 (nominal dollars)
Instructional staff	$28,853
Administrative and support staff	$ 1,134
Facilities and equipment (annualized depreciation and interest)	$ 2,337
Classroom supplies	$ 480
Developmental screening	$ 234
School district overhead	$ 1,722
Total	$ 31,760
Number of children	21
Cost per child	$ 1,512

SOURCE: Adapted from Barnett (1996, Table 4).

Exercises

1. What are market prices, and when should they be used to determine costs of ingredients? Give an example.

2. What are shadow prices, and when should they be used to estimate the costs of ingredients? Give an example.

3. When a given ingredient is scarce or will be needed in rather large quantities, what is the problem in using its market price to estimate its cost for employing the ingredient in future replications?

4. State briefly how the costs of personnel should be ascertained for both paid personnel and volunteers.

5. How should the costs of facilities be ascertained?

6. Calculate the annualized value of a building that would cost $1 million to replace and has a life of 25 years. Use interest rates of 5%, 10%, and 15%.

7. Make the same calculation for a 20-year life at an interest rate of 7.5%.

8. Give two methods for estimating the costs of equipment.

9. Assume that a piece of equipment has a replacement cost of $10,000 and an 8-year life. What is its annualized cost at an interest rate of 15%?

▶ NOTES

1. For a more technical discussion of shadow prices, in the context of cost-benefit analysis, see Boardman, Greenberg, Vining, and Weimer (1996, pp. 52-53, 70-76).

2. This conclusion is echoed by Rouse (1998).

3. See Tsang (1988, 1995) for a general discussion.

4. In Tsang and Taoklam's (1992) study of primary education in Thailand, the authors found—using the ingredients method—that private school costs were 78% of the cost of public schools. Jimenez et al. (1995) used a "shortcut" method to estimate the costs of private and public secondary schools in Thailand. They found that private school costs were 39% of the costs of public schools. A comparison of the two studies suggests that substantial biases may be introduced by not applying the ingredients method.

5. Bray (1996) surveys educational cost studies in nine East Asian countries. He finds that direct private costs as a percentage of total costs in public primary schools range from less than 10% in Laos to over 70% in Cambodia. Most hover around 20%. Evidence in McEwan (1999) suggests that direct private costs account for around 44% of total costs of public primary schools in Honduras. Case studies of several African and Asian countries show that families assume between 40% and 81% of public school costs (Mehrotra & Delamonica, 1998).

6. This is true for building facilities. In the case of land, there is no depreciation cost (that is, the land is assumed to maintain a constant value); however, there is an interest cost, because funds tied up in land are unavailable to earn interest in alternative investments.

CHAPTER **5**

Analyzing Costs

> ### OBJECTIVES
>
> 1. Summarize the application of cost methodology with the use of a cost worksheet.
> 2. Show how to analyze the distribution of cost burdens among different stakeholders.
> 3. Address cost estimation for multiyear projects.
> 4. Illustrate the estimation of costs under uncertainty.
> 5. Present different ways of using costs for decisions.

The previous two chapters explored the definition of costs and the ingredients method for estimating them. We also discussed the identification and specification of ingredients and methods for determining the costs attached to each of them. The purpose of this chapter is to analyze the cost estimates that are derived from this exercise and to place them in a decision-oriented framework.

Using a Cost Worksheet

Table 5.1 shows a cost worksheet that can be used to set out and analyze costs using the ingredients method. This format enables you to first list

77

TABLE 5.1 Worksheet for Estimating Costs

Column 1: *Cost Ingredients*	Column 2: *Total Cost*	Column 3: *Cost to Program Sponsor*	Column 4: *Cost to Other Government Agencies*	Column 5: *Cost to Other Private Organizations*	Column 6: *Cost to Students and Parents*
Personnel					
...					
Facilities					
...					
Materials and equipment					
...					
Other inputs					
...					
Required client inputs					
...					
Total ingredients cost					
User fees		−( )			+( )
Cash subsidies		−( )	+( )	+( )	
Net costs					

78

ingredients, according to the categories set out in the previous two chapters, as well as their costs. It is based on the procedures that were set out in Chapters 3 and 4. It also adds a new dimension to the analysis by enabling us to ascertain who is paying the costs for each alternative. The importance of this feature will be described below.

Corresponding with the procedures delineated in Chapter 3, the first column provides for a listing of ingredients. In similar fashion, column 2 permits a listing of the costs of each ingredient as formulated in Chapter 4, and the sum of that column can be thought of as the total cost of the intervention. Thus, these two columns enable you to list ingredients and estimate their overall costs.

Total costs are defined as the total value of all the resources required for any particular intervention. Given our definition of cost, this can be thought of as the value of the sacrifices made by society—the value of what must be given up—to undertake the intervention. Thus, the total cost is the opportunity cost to society of undertaking the intervention rather than using the ingredients for their most productive alternative use.

A school district may need to choose among competing approaches to improving reading scores or upgrading analytical skills or providing students with "computer literacy." The total costs of each of the alternatives for addressing any of these objectives can be estimated by following the procedures reflected in filling out the first and second columns of Table 5.1. In many cases, however, all the ingredients will not be provided by the school district. For example, some alternatives may be eligible for support from federal and state agencies. It may be possible to obtain volunteers to staff some interventions, and various costs might be met through contributions of services.

It is important to know not only the total cost of each alternative but also who will pay it among such constituencies as the school district, parents, the state government, the federal government, private agencies, and so on. If the school district will be making the decision, it is likely to consider only its share of the cost burden rather than the overall costs in ranking alternatives. In contrast, the other constituencies that are sharing the costs will be most concerned about the costs to them. Indeed, both costs and effects should be viewed from the perspective of different constituencies or groups that have a stake in the outcome (Bryk, 1983). The ranking of alternatives by each constituency will largely reflect the perceived benefits and costs, broadly speaking, to that constituency rather than the larger societal perspective. For this reason, we must estimate not only the total ingredients cost of an intervention, but also the cost of that intervention for each constituency or "stakeholder."

Before showing how to use the worksheet to distribute costs among those paying for them, it is necessary to emphasize the importance of the total cost estimate. An estimate of total costs provides an overall summary of the cost of an intervention. For this reason, it includes a specification and costing of all the ingredients. When a cost-effectiveness study is disseminated beyond the initial site where it has been used for decisions, it is crucial that all the ingredients be included. In this way, any decision maker considering the alternative can determine what ingredients are necessary and what their costs are.

If the study were to be limited to only those costs that were paid for by the initial sponsor, they will give a misleading picture of the true overall costs. Since we can never know in advance which ingredients other constituencies will pay for, we should include a complete accounting in the overall statement of costs. For example, some local school districts have no difficulties in finding volunteers, while others have to pay all personnel (we already described a scenario such as this in Example 3.1). If a former district were to leave out of its cost analysis all volunteer staff, it would not be apparent to a second district what the true ingredients requirements and costs would be in a situation in which all personnel must be paid. Accordingly, it should be left to the secondary user of the data to ascertain which of the total ingredients must be paid for and which can be obtained through contributions and volunteers.

Allocating Costs Among Constituencies

The worksheet in Table 5.1 has been designed to accomplish two major tasks. As shown above, it can be used to determine the total ingredients cost for an intervention. In addition, it can be used to show how the costs of each proposed or actual intervention are distributed among different constituencies or stakeholders. The distribution of costs takes two forms: ingredients costs and financial costs. In this section we will review the use of the worksheet to allocate both types of costs to ascertain the net total costs borne by each constituency.

Columns 3 through 6 on the worksheet in Table 5.1 are used to list the costs that will be shared by each of several different constituencies or stakeholders. Column 3 represents the cost to the sponsor. For example, if the sponsor of the prospective intervention were a school district, we would write in the name of the district. Column 4 provides a listing of costs that will be paid by another government agency, and column 5 would include costs paid from private sources such as volunteers, charitable foundations, churches, and private contributions. Additional columns can be provided for subgroups such as different levels of government or different government agencies. This should be determined separately for each cost analysis. Finally, column 6 refers to those costs that must be borne by students and their families. For example, some programs require students and their families to provide books, equipment, and transportation in order to participate.

Distributing Ingredients Costs

The first step in ascertaining the costs that will be paid by each constituency is to determine which ingredients will be provided by each. In this way, the cost for each ingredient in the first column can be entered in the appropriate column 3 through 6 that represents the entity that will provide that ingredient. Again, more columns can be provided if needed for other constituencies that are pertinent to the analysis. Bear in mind that in distributing the estimated costs among constituencies, we are not estimating any additional costs. We are merely allocating the existing costs to the constituencies who will be paying them. This is analogous to first estimating the cost of a piece of property to an investment partnership and then distributing the cost to the different partners. The questions of what an intervention costs and who pays for it are analytically separate issues. By accounting for the value of all the ingredients, column 2 already includes the total costs of the intervention.

As an illustration of this procedure, we can refer to personnel costs. Personnel costs that are paid by the school district would be entered in column 3. Those that would be paid by the state or federal government would be entered in column 4. The cost of community volunteers would be entered in column 5, and so on. A similar procedure would be followed for facilities, materials and equipment, and other inputs. A check on the accuracy of these entries can be made by making sure that the sum of the entries for each ingredient in columns 3 through 6 are equal to the cost entry for that ingredient in column 2.

In summary, all the ingredients can be allocated to the different constituencies providing them. Once these distributions are made, one can calculate the total ingredients cost for each constituency. That is, the value of the ingredients provided by each constituency can be calculated by adding the entries in each of the columns.

Distributing Cash Subsidies

There is one final calculation that we will need in order to ascertain the net cost for each constituency. In addition to providing ingredients, the various constituencies may provide cash contributions and payments that subsidize the purchase of ingredients provided by other constituencies. For example, students and their families may be charged user fees to participate. In addition, various constituencies may provide cash contributions or subsidies to the sponsoring school district. These transactions—shown in Table 5.1 under the headings "user fees" and "cash subsidies"—serve to create subsidies or cash transfers from some constituencies to the sponsoring school district. Such subsidies will reduce the net costs to the school district and increase the costs to the other constituencies. It's important to note that they do not affect the total costs, but only who pays for them.

User fees are any cash charges that must be paid by participants in order to have access to the proposed program. In this case, we would add the total amount of user charges to the total amount of ingredients costs at the bottom of column 6, as indicated in Table 5.1. Since these would be transferred to the sponsoring school district, we subtract an identical amount at the bottom of column 3 to reflect a reduction in the net cost that will be borne by the school district. The total costs represented by their ingredient or resource values have not changed; only the apportionment of those costs among constituencies has changed.

In like manner, we take the cash subsidies, grants, and contributions from other government agencies and add those to the total ingredients costs under column 4 and do the same for cash contributions from private sources under column 5, as indicated in Table 5.1. Obviously, since these cash disbursements increase the cost commitments of these constituencies, they will increase the net costs to those groups. Since these are also transferred to the sponsoring school district, they should be deducted from the ingredients cost for the district. That is, they reduce the costs to the school district as reflected in a net total cost for that entity that is lower than the direct ingredients provided by the sponsoring district.

Calculating Net Costs to Each Constituency

After these cash transfers are noted, we can calculate the net cost to the school district and to the other constituencies or stakeholders. These totals are shown at the bottom of Table 5.1 and are literally the "bottom line" in terms of cost burdens for the various constituencies. The net cost for each constituency is the total ingredients cost for that constituency less cash payments received from other constituencies or plus cash payments made to other constituencies. In this way, we can not only derive the total ingredients cost of the intervention, which is the overall social cost, but we can also divide that into the costs paid by each of several constituencies.

Of course, Table 5.1 is designed to be illustrative. That is, it is possible to do this analysis for any set of constituencies, such as advantaged and disadvantaged families or different government agencies within a level of government. The most important factor in determining which constituencies to evaluate is to ask which ones have a stake in the decision and will be sharing the costs by providing ingredients or cash subsidies.

In summary, it is important to know not only the total costs of an intervention, but also how those costs are distributed among different constituencies or stakeholders. A worksheet like that in Table 5.1 will enable you to specify ingredients and estimate their costs and the total cost of the intervention. It will also enable you to distribute those costs among the major constituencies so that each of the stakeholders can evaluate its own cost burden for each alternative. Of course, this type of cost analysis should be done for each of the alternatives under consideration. When combined with the effectiveness of each alternative, it can be used to ascertain the relative desirability for each stakeholder of the various proposed interventions.

In practice, the easiest method of constructing and analyzing a cost worksheet is to use spreadsheet software, such as Microsoft Excel. Each of the ingredients and ingredient costs from Table 5.1 can be entered in the corresponding cells of a computer spreadsheet. Formulas can be entered in each row of column 2 that sum the costs of each ingredient in columns 3 through 6. At the bottom of columns 2 through 6, formulas can be entered

EXAMPLE 5.1. Determining Who Pays the Costs

To provide a concrete illustration of the previous topic, we will consider a cost worksheet for a hypothetical education program. Let's say that a local school district recently implemented a program called "Saturday Science Scholars," in which a group of students gathers for roughly two Saturdays a month during the school year (16 meetings in all). The purpose of the program is to bring together high school science teachers, students, and professors from a prestigious local university in order to pique student interest in scientific careers and expose them to cutting-edge research. Fortunately, the local school district encountered a broad range of support in carrying out the program from the state government, a private university, and parents.

Our immediate goal is to estimate the annual program costs and assess how they are distributed among the different constituencies. The program ingredients are listed in the first column of Table 5.2. To best implement the program, it requires the services of two high school teachers, two university professors, and two parent volunteers on each Saturday. They will use the existing high school science lab and classroom facilities. However, they will further require the use of advanced laboratory equipment that the high school does not own, as well as a variety of chemicals and other materials for experiments. The school facilities would not normally be in use on a Saturday, so the program will require janitorial services, energy, and insurance. Finally, the usual school bus services are not available on Saturdays, so many parents will be required to transport their children in the family car.

Let us assume that we followed the methods of Chapters 3 and 4 in attaching values to these ingredients (of course, this would require specifying in greater detail the exact quantity and nature of many of the ingredients, such as the lab facilities). Even when some ingredients were apparently "free," such as parental volunteers, we attempted to ascertain their cost by using the prevailing salaries for teacher aides in the school district. In several cases, we used the techniques provided in Chapter 4 to annualize the costs of durable goods. For example, we estimated the annual interest and depreciation costs for the high school science lab. We also estimated the annualized costs of the science lab equipment, because such equipment lasts for a number of years. The total cost of each ingredient is provided in column 2.

that sum the total ingredients costs and the net costs to each constituency. There are many advantages to analyzing costs in a computer spreadsheet. For example, small features of the analysis can be varied—such as the cost

EXAMPLE 5.1. continued

In columns 3 through 6, these ingredient costs are distributed among four constituencies: the local school district, the state government, the private university, and parents. Column 2, "Total Cost," provides the cost of ingredients assumed by each constituency. Most ingredient costs are borne by the local district and the private university. For example, the district will assume the costs of teacher salaries and benefits, whereas the university will pay salaries and benefits of the professors. Parents bear some costs, in the form of donated time or transportation services.

We next consider the issues of user fees and cash subsidies. Parents are obligated to pay the school district some user fees, totaling $1,000. Moreover, the district applied for and received a cash grant from the state government in the amount of $7,500. These do not affect the total program costs because they merely transfer resources from one set of hands to another. However, they do have the effect of altering the distribution of the cost burden among constituencies. As the final row in Table 5.2 shows, the net costs to the school district are reduced (by $8,500), whereas they increase for the state government and for parents.

Although the total value of ingredients is estimated at $35,225, the school district will underwrite only about 21% of this, or $7,350. The state government assumes a similar proportion of costs. The private university actually pays the largest proportion, about 43%, mainly because of the high costs of the university professors. Finally, parents assume a fairly substantial portion of costs, about 15%, in the form of user fees or donated services.

This particular example should illustrate the perils of focusing exclusively on the costs to the local school district (column 3). By doing so, we would arrive at a deeply misleading picture of the total resource costs of the program. Moreover, it is not clear that all school districts would be able to obtain the grants and donations that were obtained in this case. For example, state grants may not be available, or district parents may be unable to provide the same level of volunteerism. For districts that are considering a replication of the science program, it is particularly important to have a good estimate of what the total resource costs are and how they are distributed among constituencies.

of an ingredient to a particular constituency—and the spreadsheet will use the formulas to automatically calculate the new total costs. This is extremely helpful when conducting a sensitivity analysis (described later in

TABLE 5.2 Annualized Costs for a Hypothetical Program

Column 1: Cost Ingredients	Column 2: Total Cost	Column 3: Cost to Local School District	Column 4: Cost to State Government	Column 5: Cost to Private University	Column 6: Cost to Students and Parents
Personnel					
2 high school teachers	$ 9,000	$ 9,000			
2 university professors	$14,400			$14,400	
2 parent aides (volunteers)	$ 3,600				$3,600
Facilities					
High school science lab and classroom	$ 2,000	$ 2,000			
Materials and equipment					
Photocopies	$ 400	$ 400			

	A	B	C	D	E
Materials for science experiments	$ 500	$ 250			$ 250
Laboratory equipment	$ 500				$ 500
Other					
Maintenance and janitorial services	$ 1,500	$ 1,500			
Insurance	$ 1,800	$ 1,800			
Energy	$ 900	$ 900			
Required client inputs					
Transportation (time, vehicle costs)	$ 625				$ 625
Total ingredients cost	$35,225	$15,850	$ 0	$15,150	$ 4,225
User fees		-$ 1,000			$ 1,000
Other cash subsidies		-$ 7,500	$ 7,500		
Net costs	$35,225	$ 7,350	$ 7,500	$15,150	$ 5,225

this chapter). Moreover, the worksheet can be easily expanded to include new categories of ingredients (rows) or new constituencies (columns).

Costs Over Multiple Years

We have stressed that any cost analysis must be referenced to a time period. That is, we are concerned with what the costs—and benefits, effects, or utility—of an intervention are for a particular period of time. Since educational programs are typically planned on an annual basis, a period of a year is often used as the basis for estimating costs. Indeed, we emphasized the procedure of annualizing the cost of facilities and equipment in Chapter 4.

In many cases, however, educational programs occur over a period of 2 or more years. When costs extend over 2 or more years, the analysis should consider two issues: inflation and discounting. We shall discuss each of these in turn.

Adjusting Costs for Inflation

For each year of a multiyear project, it is possible to undertake an ingredients analysis and to estimate the costs of each ingredient. However, this analysis will not reflect the fact that costs may be higher in future years because of price inflation. To account for inflation, the costs from each year should be adjusted to the price level of a single year. The choice of this year is arbitrary, although once chosen it should be used consistently. When costs are not adjusted for inflation, they are said to be expressed in "nominal" or "current" terms. After adjustments are made, they are said to be expressed in "real" terms. If, for example, the nominal costs in 1996 are adjusted to the prevailing level of prices in 1999, the costs are expressed in "real 1999" terms.

Information on the overall rate of inflation can generally be derived from state and federal government agencies such as the U.S. Departments of Labor and Commerce. The price changes due to inflation are summarized in an index (e.g., the consumer price index) that reflects the changing prices of a standard "basket" of goods and services.[1] To illustrate how to account for inflation, Table 5.3 provides a small example. A hypothetical consumer price index (CPI) is presented over a period of years. It is equal to

TABLE 5.3 Using a Hypothetical Consumer Price Index (CPI) to Adjust Costs

	1993	1994	1995	1996	1997	1998	1999	2000
CPI	91.8	94.9	97.2	100.0	102.4	105.8	110.1	112.5
Nominal dollars	$85.00	$90.00	$95.00	$100.00	$105.00	$110.00	$115.00	$120.00
Real 1996 dollars	$92.59	$94.84	$97.74	$100.00	$102.54	$103.97	$104.45	$106.67
Real 2000 dollars	$104.17	$106.69	$109.95	$112.50	$115.36	$116.97	$117.51	$120.00

100 in 1996, which is designated as the base year. The CPI is 102.4 in 1997; this indicates that a typical basket of consumer goods and services rose in price between 1996 and 1997 from $100 to $102.40.

In the next row, there is a stream of nominal costs that are not adjusted for inflation. Let's say that we wish to adjust the nominal cost of $85 in 1993 to the price levels of 1996 (i.e., real 1996 dollars). The CPI for 1996 is divided by the CPI for 1993, which is then multiplied by the nominal cost of $85:

$$\$85 \times \frac{100.0}{91.8} = \$92.59$$

What if we wanted to convert the nominal cost of $85 in 1993 to real 2000 dollars? This is accomplished by the following:

$$\$85 \times \frac{112.5}{91.8} = \$104.17$$

A more complex way of adjusting costs for inflation is to use different price indexes for different ingredients, rather than using a single index. For example, although personnel and facilities costs may rise over time, they often rise at different rates. There are separate price indexes published for different categories of goods and services. In general, however, the consumer price index (CPI) is probably sufficient for obtaining a good approximation.

Discounting Costs

We must also adjust costs for their time value, a procedure that is referred to as "discounting." The basic idea is that costs occurring in the future are less of a burden than costs occurring in the present. Thus, we need to discount future costs to properly compare them with present costs. Unfortunately, discounting is frequently confused with adjusting for inflation, even though the two are completely distinct. Even in the absence of inflation, there is still a need to discount costs for their distribution across time.

Let us imagine two different projects. The first incurs a cost of $1,000 in the first year, while the second project incurs a cost of $1,000 in the second year. Which project is less costly? Our immediate instinct might be to assume that both cost exactly the same, but this would be a mistake. Since the costs of the second project are deferred by a year, we could invest the $1,000 elsewhere, perhaps placing it in a bank account that earns interest.

TABLE 5.4 Three Alternative Expenditure Patterns

Year	Individual A	Individual B	Individual C
1	$1000	$ 200	0
2	0	$ 200	0
3	0	$ 200	0
4	0	$ 200	0
5	0	$ 200	$1000
Total (undiscounted)	$1000	$1000	$1000
Present value (discount rate of 5%)	$1000	$ 909	$ 823

Thus, the second project is less costly, because it does not tie up funds that can be profitably employed elsewhere. Stated differently, incurring costs in the future is preferable to incurring them now. To reflect this in our analysis, we should discount costs that occur in the future. In the following section, we describe a simple procedure for doing so.

Procedure for Discounting

The underlying issues can be seen more clearly if we take a simple example of three expenditure patterns over a 5-year period. As shown in Table 5.4, where these patterns are illustrated, the total expenditure in all three cases is $1,000. However, in the case of Individual A, the entire amount is spent in the first year, whereas in the case of Individual B, the amount is divided into equal annual payments of $200. In the case of Individual C, the entire amount is spent in the last year. From the perspective of the sacrifice principle of costs, Individual B has incurred a lower cost than Individual A, because he has the use of some of his money for almost all of the 5-year period. Individual C has the lowest cost of all, since her expenditure pattern permits her to use the entire amount in the first 4 years—perhaps held in an interest-bearing savings account—sacrificing it only in the final year of the period. In contrast, Individual A must give up all of his $1,000 in the first year. The result is that Individual A must sacrifice more value in alternative opportunities than does Individuals B or C, even though the total outlay of each over a 5-year period is $1,000.

This can be seen more clearly if we look at Year 2. Individual A has relinquished $1,000 and must sacrifice $1,000 in alternatives. However, Individual B has relinquished only $200 and can use the other $800. For example, if Individual B were to put the $800 into a 1-year investment at an interest rate of 5%, he would realize an additional $40 in income for that year. Clearly, the expenditure pattern represented for Individual B would leave him better off than Individual A. In the case of C, she could earn the 5% for each of the first 4 years and receive $50 of additional income each year. Thus, even though each person is making an outlay of $1,000 over the 5-year period, the value of the outlay is most costly to A and least costly to C.

The principle embedded in this example also holds when we ascertain the costs of multiyear projects for social entities. In general, the more that we are able to defer costs until the latter part of the investment period, the lower the sacrifice, or "real" costs, to the entity. The method for doing this is to compare alternative investment patterns by calculating their present values in a way that reduces the impact of future expenditures relative to current ones. This procedure takes account of the fact that deferring costs enables one to have access to resources for a longer period. Thus, the present value tends to neutralize differences in the time pattern of allocations when adding up the cost outlays for a multiyear project.

The calculation of present value uses an interest rate (or "discount" rate) to discount future costs relative to current ones. The formula for estimating the present value of a future cost outlay is:

$$PV = \frac{C_t}{(1+r)^{t-1}}$$

In this formulation, PV stands for present value; C denotes the cost; r denotes the discount rate; and t is the year in which the cost outlay will be made, where t is equal to 1 for this year, 2 for next year, 3 for the following year, and so on. To show how to use the formula, we can take as an example the outlay of $1,000 in Year 5, as reflected in the expenditure pattern of Individual C in Table 5.4, and use a discount rate of 5%:

$$PV = \frac{\$1000}{(1.05)^4} = \frac{\$1000}{1.216} = \$823$$

On the basis of this calculation, it appears that the present value of a $1,000 disbursement made 5 years hence at a discount rate of 5% is about $823. If a higher discount rate were used, such as 10%, the present value would be $683, reflecting the higher opportunity cost attached to using the resources. Later on, we provide a discussion of the criteria for choosing a discount rate. More generally, the present value of any time pattern of expenditure can be found by using the expression:

$$PV = \sum_{t=1}^{n} \frac{C_t}{(1+r)^{t-1}}$$

When this expression is applied to the 5-year expenditure patterns of Individuals A, B, and C with a 5% discount rate, one finds that the present value of the cost for A is $1,000, for B it is $909, and for C it is $823. That is, C has the lowest sacrifice in costs, even though she, too, spends $1,000 over the 5-year period.

There is consensus that discounting should be applied in this manner to reflect the preference by individuals and society for having resources sooner rather than later. Most textbooks on cost-benefit analysis provide a thorough discussion of the procedures for discounting (e.g., Boardman, Greenberg, Vining, & Weimer, 1996, pp. 119-158). Note that the concepts and methods of discounting are also applicable to patterns of benefits, effects, and utility over time. In subsequent chapters, we return to a discussion of discounting in these specific contexts.

Choosing a Discount Rate

Although there is widespread agreement on the need to discount future costs, there is less agreement on the specific discount rate that should be used in the analysis. Part of the controversy stems from the fact that there are a number of conceptual approaches to determining the discount rate. In one approach, the discount rate is reflected by the returns to consumer savings options (e.g., the interest rate on treasury bills). That is, what returns are being sacrificed by consumers in order to consume resources now instead of saving them? Another approach suggests that the discount rate should reflect the average returns to investments that are made by entrepreneurs in the private sector. That is, what are entrepreneurs sacrificing by investing resources in a particular project instead of other profitable endeavors? Yet another approach advocates using a weighted average of the two preceding rates. For an excellent discussion of these and other views, see Chapter 5 in Boardman et al. (1996).

In practice, analysts have utilized a variety of discount rates, ranging between 0% and 11% (Barnett, 1996). The ambiguity is perhaps encouraged by the different standards that are often set by government offices. The U.S. Office of Management and Budget, the Congressional Budget Office, and the General Accounting Office have all set different standards for the discount rates that should be used in project evaluations (Boardman et al., 1996). At least one author feels that the most credible range of estimates of the discount rate varies between 3% and 7%, with the true discount rate probably at the lower end of that range (Barnett, 1996). In health, a recent set of national guidelines suggests that a discount rate of 3% is probably most reasonable, although good arguments can be made for a somewhat larger range (Lipscomb, Weinstein, & Torrance, 1996).

The disagreement in the literature suggests that evaluators should choose an initial discount rate of 3% to 5%, but then calculate their estimates of costs using a wider range of discount rates, perhaps from 0% to 10%. By following this procedure—referred to as a sensitivity analysis—one can assess whether the key findings about costs are substantially altered by employing different assumptions. Later in this chapter, and again in Chapter 6, we shall provide a discussion of sensitivity analysis.

Cost Distribution Over Multiple Years

A final concern about multiyear programs is that the cost distribution might change over time. That is, in the early years, the sponsor might receive grants from foundations or government in order to provide an incentive for a new approach. At some future time, however, this assistance might be withdrawn as the contributing agency turns its attentions in other directions. For this reason, it is important to review carefully the allocation of ingredients and cash subsidies provided by other constituencies to the sponsoring one to see if they hold for the period of analysis. If it is likely that some of them may be reduced or increased in subsequent years, these changes should be taken into account in considering the costs to each stakeholder or constituency and in using that information to assess priorities among competing alternatives.

Accounting for Uncertainty

At this stage, the overall method for estimating costs and distributing them to different constituencies or stakeholders has been presented. Now it is necessary to discuss certain issues that arise in cost estimation and utilization. The first issue is that of estimating costs under uncertainty. Although we provided a number of techniques for estimating costs, there are two circumstances when special analysis is warranted to account for uncertainty. The first case is that in which there simply is no reliable standard on which to base a cost estimate. The second is one in which there is a range of cost estimates for a particular ingredient.

When No Cost Information Is Readily Available

In the first case, the intervention may require an input for which there is no information on costs. For example, the project may require the preparation of a manual to instruct teachers. What will the manual cost? The best way to address this type of problem is to try to divide the manual itself into subingredients for producing it. In so doing, it will be possible to focus on the process and the ingredients for creating the manual, and the costs of each of these ingredients can be estimated with greater precision than the more abstract task of estimating the overall cost of a manual.

A more difficult example is that of estimating the cost of ingredients that are not readily available at the time that an intervention is being planned. A project that uses future technology will face this type of problem. For example, although the cost of computer hardware may not pose a problem for cost estimation, the school district may need to develop its own instructional software. Such development is not always predictable in terms of the time and other resources that will be required to design it and make it operational. In this case, it is best to obtain several independent opinions from experts on the probable costs. Of course, this may lead to the second case, in which there is a variety of different cost estimates.

One of the most challenging issues that might face an evaluator occurs when the program itself has not been implemented or even clearly defined. This is discussed further in Example 5.2.

EXAMPLE 5.2. Estimating Program Costs When a Program
Does Not Exist

The discussion thus far has assumed that a well-defined educational program exists and that the evaluator is familiar with its operations. When this is not the case, it turns out to be rather difficult to apply the ingredients method. If the "program" is ill defined or changes greatly from one site to another, then the evaluator is hard-pressed to catalog the specific ingredients used and attach values to them. In such cases, it is difficult to carry out and interpret the results of a cost analysis.

Even so, there are cases in which a program has yet to be implemented or even fully designed, but decision makers still require good information about its potential costs. A prominent example is the controversial policy of educational vouchers. Vouchers are government-funded tuition coupons that parents can redeem at the public or private school of their choice. Small-scale programs have been implemented in U.S. cities such as Milwaukee and Cleveland, in which relatively small numbers of students were eligible to receive vouchers (e.g., see Levin, 1998; Witte, 1998). However, there is great interest in the potential effectiveness and costs of schools under a large-scale application of vouchers, in which a great majority of public and private students would be eligible to participate.

Henry Levin and Cyrus Driver (1996, 1997) attempted to gauge the costs of implementing a nationwide voucher plan in the United States. They were hampered in many respects—particularly in that there is no universally agreed-upon notion of what a "voucher" plan constitutes. For example, some students may or may not be eligible to receive larger vouchers (e.g., high school, special education, or low-income students). Some schools may or may not be eligible to accept vouchers (e.g., religious schools). The voucher system may or may not be supported by information gathering and dissemination services (e.g., national achievement tests). With these and other uncertainties, the authors sought to provide a range of cost estimates that could account for several types of voucher policies.

They considered five categories of cost ingredients. First, there are costs of accommodating additional students. Many of the students who are currently enrolled in private schools would be eligible to receive vouchers (even though they already opted out of the public system). To estimate costs, the authors used several assumptions about the size of the voucher and the proportion of private school students who would be eligible to receive vouchers.

Second, there are costs of record keeping and monitoring. Although there are already costs of information collection in the current system, a voucher plan would require extensive and ongoing monitoring of students, in order to determine their eligibility. In a simple plan, this would merely involve knowing the

EXAMPLE 5.2. continued

age of each student. In a more complex plan—one that adjusted the amount of the voucher according to several variables—information might be required on student income, eligibility for special educational services, and so on. To estimate the costs of record keeping and monitoring, the authors relied upon a cost study of the federal Social Security Administration, which administers a similar monitoring system. They estimated a range of costs, depending on assumptions about the amount of student information that would be collected.

Third, a voucher plan would lead to student mobility across schools, thus producing additional transportation costs. To estimate the costs of transportation, the authors used a wide variety of assumptions and data sources. These included the costs of existing school transportation systems in California and St. Louis. They also assessed the potential transportation costs that might be incurred under alternatives transportation systems, such as local trains or shuttle services.

Fourth, a voucher plan may provide for the collection and dissemination of data about schools and student performance, thus ensuring that the best-quality schools are chosen by parents. To estimate these costs, the authors relied upon an existing cost study of Parent Information Centers (PICs) in Massachusetts. PICs were implemented in order to provide parents with greater information about their schooling options.

Fifth, a voucher plan may involve additional costs if disputes arise among parents and school personnel. This might occur if some students wish to transfer schools in the middle of year or are ruled ineligible to receive vouchers. To estimate the costs of adjudicating disputes, the authors used an existing cost study of special education in California. When parents disagree with school decisions regarding special education, the law provides for mediation and other mechanisms of dispute resolution. The cost of adjudication in the California system might be similar to those under a voucher plan.

Of course, a cost study such as this is never definitive, and great care must be taken in presenting its results. First, it should clearly state its assumptions about the characteristics and ingredients of the hypothetical program. Second, it should describe the methods and data that were used to construct the estimates in sufficient detail so that others can replicate the results. Third, it should estimate program costs under a range of assumptions. For example, do program costs change substantially when the voucher is available to only a certain group of students?

SOURCE: Levin and Driver (1996, 1997).

When There Are Different Cost Estimates

A variety of cost estimates can arise when there is no previous experience on what a particular ingredient may cost. The uncertainty of a new technology is obvious, but the problem can arise even when estimating personnel or facilities costs. For example, a proposal to hire science and mathematics teachers at their market salaries to overcome shortages in the schools would be immediately beset by the challenge of knowing what salary level would be required to attract adequate numbers of such personnel into teaching. A proposal to build a new facility might face uncertainty about some of the structural requirements, a dilemma that can be resolved only after extensive and costly testing of the subsoil. In these cases, it is important to take into consideration a range of cost estimates.

One of the most common techniques for doing so is known as sensitivity analysis. The purpose of sensitivity analysis is to estimate costs under a range of assumptions in order to assess whether the conclusions drawn from the analysis are appreciably altered. The simplest method is to ascertain a range of plausible values—high, medium, and low—for each parameter of the analysis that is characterized by uncertainty. The medium value can be thought of as the most probable result, which can be the midpoint between the two extremes or some middle estimate that is based upon the most probable assumptions. The parameters that are varied might include the prices or quantities of specific cost ingredients or, perhaps, the discount rate.

Once a range of values is established for a given parameter, the analyst calculates the overall costs under each assumption. The general idea of the procedure is illustrated in Figure 5.1. In this hypothetical case, there is uncertainty about the annual salary that will be paid to teachers in a particular education program. Thus, the analyst establishes a plausible range of salaries, including low, medium, and high estimates. The three estimates of the teacher salary are used to calculate three different estimates of the total costs of the educational program.

Figure 5.1 presents the three estimates of total costs, each corresponding to a different assumption about the level of teacher salaries. As we might expect, total costs rise as we use a higher estimate of teacher salaries. Our motivation in conducting this procedure is to assess whether the initial conclusions about total costs (using the "medium" estimate of teacher salaries) stand up to alternative assumptions. If they do not, then we might be

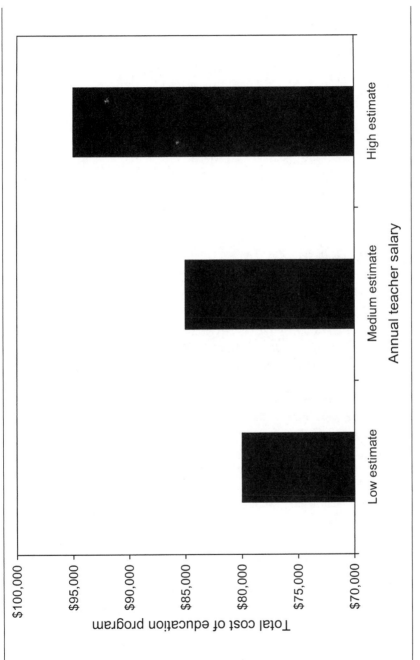

FIGURE 5.1. An Application of Sensitivity Analysis

99

encouraged to pursue more accurate sources of information or to interpret our results with greater caution. In fact, the estimates of total costs appear rather sensitive to the teacher salary (most likely because instructional staff is an important category of cost ingredients).

Sensitivity analysis is a useful tool that should be applied at every stage of a cost-effectiveness analysis. Even if the results of a sensitivity analysis are not reported in exhaustive detail, they serve as a powerful reminder to the evaluator that uncertainty often stands to alter the fundamental conclusions of a cost analysis. In Chapter 6, we will return to the topic once again, in addition to discussing some alternative methods of accounting for uncertainty.

Costs and Decisions

A final set of issues relating to the use of costs in decisions is how to integrate cost analysis and cost-effectiveness analysis with the decision framework. As demonstrated above, it is possible to determine overall social costs of an intervention as well as the costs to the sponsor and to other constituencies. In general, the type of decision that will be made as well as who will make it will determine which cost figure will be pertinent. For example, if we do a national study to ascertain the most efficient way to raise computer literacy, we may wish to rely on the total ingredients costs of the alternatives as well as their effectiveness. The reason that we would choose the total ingredients costs is that, from a national perspective, we are usually concerned with the most efficient deployment of national resources rather than the cost to particular constituencies. Of course, even at the national level, we might have some concern about how the burden would be shared between the federal government and the states or between the public and private sectors.

As pointed out above, however, each constituency, or stakeholder, will typically be concerned with the costs to its members (and the benefits or results for its members) rather than the overall ingredients costs. A local school district, a state, or a parent group would normally wish to assess the costs and the benefits, or effectiveness, of each alternative for its constituents. Indeed, each constituency may rank the same alternatives differently if the distribution of costs and effects differs among them. Thus, a major dimension of cost analysis from the decision perspective is to consider who is making the decision or on whose behalf the decision is being made.

A second set of issues revolves around the nature of the decision. Let us take three types of decision questions:

1. In reviewing a number of alternatives, are all of them within the realm of cost-feasibility?

2. Are there "add-on," or incremental, programs that ought to be considered to improve an educational outcome?

3. Which program has the best average outcome per student relative to the per-student cost?

The first question refers to the area of cost-feasibility and the issue of whether the decision maker has adequate resources to consider the alternative. In this case, the potential educational outcomes are not taken into consideration. The only issue is whether the alternative is feasible from the cost perspective. The answer to that question is determined by comparing the total cost requirements and those for each constituency with the resource constraints of each constituency for every alternative. Alternatives that require greater cost outlays than available resources, in total or for the various constituencies, are probably not feasible. Thus, cost feasibility analysis simply determines which alternatives are within the boundaries of further consideration.

The second question arises when the decision maker wants to know if an ongoing program should be expanded or if some type of special program should be added to existing offerings. In this case, we are not concerned with developing and analyzing the costs of the existing program. We are interested only in doing a cost-effectiveness analysis of the additional increment, or add-on. This is known as marginal or incremental cost analysis, since the cost-effectiveness analysis will only be done on the additional ingredients required. This type of situation arises when a school is interested in considering ways of improving a learning outcome such as reading. One alternative might be to reduce class size, while a second might be to hire additional remedial specialists. A third alternative could be the use of computers or audiovisual aids. We are concerned then with comparing the costs of each of these add-on programs and the effects that they will have on raising reading scores. The analysis is limited to the additional costs and the additional results that are associated with each intervention rather than the overall costs of reading instruction in the school and the overall reading scores. Therefore, our analysis is called a marginal cost-effectiveness analysis, since we are concerned only with evaluations of the potential additional costs and effects of the alternatives.

The third question asks which alternative has the best educational result per student relative to its average cost per student. The actual comparison of alternatives with respect to their desirability is determined by dividing the cost by the number of students who will be served (average or per-student cost) and obtaining a measure of effectiveness on a per-student basis (e.g., average rise in test scores). We can view this as an analysis of average cost-effectiveness of each alternative, since the data are averaged on a per-student basis.

For example, we might compare the average costs and effects of private schools to the average costs and effects of public schools in order to determine which is the most cost-effective provider of outcomes. This type of comparison is quite prevalent and is usually satisfactory, with one major qualification. Average cost-effectiveness results are often sensitive to the scale of the application, such that the most cost-effective alternative for a small-scale implementation is not the most cost-effective one for a large-scale implementation.

The problem of scale arises because some interventions have a large component of "fixed costs," while others do not. Fixed costs refer to these ingredients that are relatively invariant, regardless of the number of students who are using them. Often, interventions with high fixed costs require a large investment even when the number of students served is very modest. For example, many technology-based interventions have large components of fixed costs. The installation of closed-circuit television in a school will require a large investment whether the technology is used widely for instruction or whether it is used only in a limited way. This means that when that fixed cost is apportioned over relatively few students and courses, its per-student cost will be very high. When apportioned over large numbers of students, however, the per-student cost may be very low (Jamison, Klees, & Wells, 1978).

In contrast, other interventions may have low components of fixed costs and be characterized by high components of variable costs. Variable costs refer to the costs of those ingredients that must be increased as enrollments increase. That is, they vary with enrollments. Teacher-based alternatives tend to have a large component of variable costs and low fixed costs.

At low enrollment levels, few teachers are needed, whereas at higher enrollment levels, more teachers are needed.

For this reason, a comparison of cost-effectiveness of alternatives on a per-student basis must take account of the scale of the application. Interventions with a high component of fixed costs tend to be very costly on a per-student basis for programs with low enrollments relative to those with low components of fixed costs and high components of variable costs. At very high levels of enrollments, however, the fixed costs are divided over more students and often become considerably less costly than programs characterized by large variable costs. As more students are enrolled, costs do not increase commensurately, since the same fixed investment can be used for more and more students.

The result is that cost-effectiveness findings for one level of enrollments may not be the same for higher or lower levels of enrollments. This means that a sensitivity analysis should be done over the range of enrollments that might be considered for the alternatives, and results of other studies that are being reviewed should be scrutinized for the enrollment levels on which they are based.

Summary

This chapter has addressed the analysis of cost information by showing how such data can be developed through the use of a worksheet and how the cost burdens can be analyzed among different constituencies, or stakeholders. It also discussed methods for adjusting costs when they occur over multiple years, and presented the technique of sensitivity analysis for cost estimation in the presence of uncertainty. Finally, the chapter discussed the use of different cost measures for different types of decisions. The next three chapters will discuss how to estimate the effects, benefits, and utility of educational programs, as well as how to combine that information with costs and interpret it.

RECOMMENDATIONS FOR FURTHER READING ◀

Although we have referred to our costing approach as the ingredients method, there are similar approaches in the education literature that go by other names, such as the resource cost method. The methods share a fundamental concern that cost analysis should attempt to identify and value all the ingredients or resources that constitute an educational intervention. On the resource cost method, the reader can refer to Chambers and Parrish (1994a, 1994b), contained in a larger edited volume of readings on educational cost analysis (Barnett, 1994). The applied work of Hartman (1981) on special education is also quite instructive.

Psacharopoulos and Woodhall (1985) and Coombs and Hallak (1987) provide discussions of costing methodology that are specifically focused on education in developing countries. In health, there are a wide variety of methodological readings that are inspired by the particular concerns of cost analysis in that field. In particular, the reader may wish to consult Dranove (1995), Drummond, O'Brien, Stoddart, and Torrance (1997), and Luce, Manning, Siegel, and Lipscomb (1996). Finally, Greenberg and Appenzeller (1998) provide a "hands-on" exposition of costing methodology, with a special focus on employment and training programs.

Exercises

1. Your school district is considering a dropout prevention program for high school youth. Two alternative programs have been suggested. Program A would expand the counseling program of the school to provide additional services to potential dropouts. On the basis of the characteristics of past dropouts, a profile of potential dropouts would be developed. These potential dropouts would be placed in counseling and guidance groups. Program B would place potential dropouts in part-time jobs. An employment registry would be established in the school, and employers in the community would be asked to provide part-time jobs. Using worksheets like the one in Table 5.1, develop a list of hypothetical ingredients for each alternative. How would you estimate the costs of each ingredient? That is, what procedures would you use? Provide some hypothetical costs that might be derived from these procedures.

2. For Program A, you are able to obtain a subsidy from the federal government of $10,000 under a program for disadvantaged children. For pro-

gram B, you are able to obtain volunteers to run the employment registry and to solicit jobs in the community. In addition, you are able to get a private foundation to contribute $5,000 for Program B. Show how you would use these data to distribute the cost burden among the various constituencies.

3. Assume that you do a cost-effectiveness analysis of different alternatives, in which you use the total ingredients cost (on a per-student basis) as well as a student-based outcome as a measure of effectiveness. Based upon this analysis, you are able to rank the alternatives according to their cost-effectiveness. Under what circumstances might a decision maker rationally choose an alternative different from the one that you have ranked as being the most cost-effective?

4. For what types of ingredients might costs be most uncertain? Can you give some specific illustrations? How would you do a sensitivity analysis for these ingredients, and how would you incorporate it into the overall comparison of alternatives?

5. It is possible to compare the costs of alternatives by estimating their overall costs over a multiyear period rather than following the more conventional approach of estimating their annual costs. Why is it not acceptable to simply obtain the sum of the annual costs to derive the multiyear costs?

6. What is the conceptual basis for using a present-value calculation to compare costs of multiyear alternative projects?

7. Assume that you are asked to review the costs of a 7-year project. After doing a careful identification and specification of ingredients and their costs, you obtain the following costs:

Year 1: $11,000

Year 2: $13,000

Year 3: $18,500

Year 4: $10,800

Year 5: $27,000

Year 6: $23,000

Year 7: $21,000

Use the expression in this chapter to derive the present value of this stream of costs for both a 5% and a 10% discount rate. Compare the present values obtained by these calculations with a simple summation of the costs for the 7 years. Why do they differ?

8. How would you use the cost information generated in Table 5.1 to determine if a set of alternatives is feasible from a cost perspective?

9. Under what circumstances should your cost analysis and effectiveness analysis be based on marginal costs and effects? Provide an example.

10. Assume that you derive cost-effectiveness results for a group of alternative interventions for a single school. The school district wants to know if the same cost-effectiveness findings are applicable for the entire school district. Discuss the issues involved in answering this question from the perspective of the cost analysis.

▶ **NOTE**

1. It is also common to use a similar index called the GDP (Gross Domestic Product) deflator.

CHAPTER 6

Cost-Effectiveness Analysis

OBJECTIVES

1. Address how to define measures of effectiveness.
2. Discuss three approaches to estimating the effectiveness of alternatives.
3. Emphasize the importance of assessing the distribution of effects among individuals.
4. Describe procedures for discounting effects in multiyear projects.
5. Discuss how to calculate cost-effectiveness ratios and use them to rank alternatives.
6. Describe the methods for conducting a sensitivity analysis of results.

Cost analysis in evaluation must consider both the results and costs of interventions. By comparing both costs and results among alternatives, one can choose the alternative that provides the best results for any given cost outlay or that minimizes the cost for any given result. In previous chapters, the assessment of costs and their measurement were presented. In this chapter, we discuss the assessment of effectiveness and how to combine that information with costs in order to evaluate the overall cost-effectiveness of interventions.

In a certain sense, this will appear to be a case of déjà vu for evaluators, for the heart of the evaluation exercise is often precisely that of ascertaining the effects of interventions on particular criteria. For example, evaluators often face situations in which they are asked to ascertain the impact of alternative curricula on reading scores or the effects of a teacher-retraining program on teacher performance. In this respect, the evaluation of outcomes is a familiar endeavor, and it is not the purpose of this book to provide an exhaustive description of evaluation designs. For this, the reader is advised to consult one of the excellent manuals on evaluation and research design that already exist (e.g., Cook & Campbell, 1979; Light, Singer, & Willett, 1990; Mohr, 1995; Rossi & Freeman, 1993; Smith & Glass, 1987; Weiss, 1998). We will limit ourselves to an overview of the main issues.

After discussing the important issue of defining the measures of effectiveness, we will review the main issues that arise when attempting to gauge the causal relationship between one or more alternatives and the chosen measure, or measures, of effectiveness. This is followed by discussions of the importance of analyzing the distribution of effects across different populations and the treatment of effects that occur across multiple years. We then describe how the information on costs and effectiveness can be combined and properly interpreted in a cost-effectiveness analysis. We conclude by reviewing the importance of conducting a proper sensitivity analysis to gauge how robust the conclusions are to different assumptions about the costs and effects of each alternative.

Defining Measures of Effectiveness

Linking Objectives and Effectiveness

Cost-effectiveness analysis is designed to compare the costs and effects of two or more alternatives with similar objectives. The measure of effectiveness chosen should reflect as closely as possible the main objective of the alternatives. For example, programs designed to increase mathematics achievement should elect an appropriate mathematics test as a measure of effectiveness. Drop-out prevention programs might be evaluated according to the numbers of potential dropouts that are averted. The effectiveness of various physical education programs could be evaluated in terms of the measured improvements that they bring about in the physical skills of participants.

As we discussed in Chapter 1, programs with different objectives will have entirely different indicators of effectiveness, so they cannot be readily compared within the CE framework. We cannot, for example, use a CE analysis to compare the cost-effectiveness of a drop-out prevention program and a physical education program because they necessarily use different measures of effectiveness. One way of comparing the relative attractiveness of each program would be to convert the outcomes of each program into pecuniary terms, in order to compare the programs within the framework of a cost-benefit analysis (see Chapter 7). For obvious reasons, this is a tall order and is rarely accomplished. The use of cost-utility analysis is also a possibility but has its own challenges (see Chapter 8).

The richness in potential of the CE approach is reflected in Table 6.1, which provides examples from the literature of how effectiveness has been assessed. Almost any particular program objective can be utilized as a basis for constructing an effectiveness measure. This table shows a number of examples of different educational program objectives—from increasing achievement to reducing drug consumption—each with a corresponding measure of effectiveness. Although many of these studies use measures of academic achievement, this by no means implies that a CE analysis must focus on such measures. If the program objectives warrant it, the evaluator could choose from a wide range of effectiveness measures. Some might be easier to collect than typical achievement data, because they are present in the administrative records of programs. Such measures might include the number of reported disciplinary problems, the number of graduates or trainees placed in jobs, or the number of students who attend college. Note that this task is embedded in any effectiveness study, with or without the cost dimension.

Nevertheless, we do not wish to understate the challenges involved in choosing a proper measure of effectiveness and the dangers involved in using a poor measure. It makes little sense to invest time and resources in accurate cost measurements and a rigorous evaluation design if the measure of effectiveness is not suitable. In choosing among measures of effectiveness, evaluators need to consider two general concepts: reliability and validity.

TABLE 6.1 Measures of Effectiveness Used in Selected
Cost-Effectiveness Studies

Objective	Study	Measure(s) of Effectiveness
To reduce lifetime drug consumption by individuals	(Caulkins, Rydell, Everingham, Chiesa, & Bushway, 1999)	Kilograms of cocaine consumption averted over a lifetime
To improve the functioning of disabled infants and toddlers	(Warfield, 1994)	Vineland Adaptive Behavior Scales; Nursing Child Assessment Scales (mother–child interaction)
To increase the number of secondary graduates in Malawi	(Murphy, 1993)	The number of students who pass the Junior Certificate examination
To improve achievement in Brazilian elementary schools	(Harbison & Hanushek, 1992)	Criterion-referenced tests of basic skills in Portuguese and mathematics
To improve reading skills of illiterate adults	(Lewis, Stockdill, & Turner, 1990)	Test of Adult Basic Education
To improve mathematics achievement in elementary schools	(Quinn, Van Mondfrans, & Worthen, 1984)	Iowa Test of Basic Skills; locally developed math test

A measure of effectiveness—such as a mathematics test—is said to be reliable if it yields the same results when applied on repeated occasions to the same individuals. Conversely, an unreliable test might produce vastly inconsistent results in several administrations of the test to the same population. Few measures of effectiveness will be perfectly reliable, but the evaluator's goal is to employ the most reliable measure available or the one that at least meets minimal standards. Common sense suggests that unreliable measures of effectiveness will be of little use in making broad statements about the overall effectiveness and cost-effectiveness of alternatives. A lack of reliability may stem from several sources, such as nonstandardized test administration (e.g., different groups of students have more or less time to complete a test) or the idiosyncrasies of a particular test and its component items. Since a complete discussion far exceeds the scope of this book, the reader is advised to consult textbooks on research methodology and psychometrics, such as Smith and Glass (1987, pp. 98-106) or Crocker and Algina (1986).

Even if a measure of effectiveness is reliable, it may not be valid. A valid measure is one that bears a close correspondence to the underlying concept that it is intended to reflect. For example, suppose that the overall objective of a program is to increase the job performance of beginning employees, and that effectiveness is gauged by a test of job-related competencies. If individuals score highly on the test but still perform poorly in their jobs, then the measure is said to have poor "construct" validity. Or, to provide another example, consider several programs that are intended to raise the self-esteem of students. If the measure is a single question that is self-reported by students, then there is a possibility that students will artificially overstate or otherwise misrepresent their feelings. Again, the measure is not a valid indicator of the underlying construct that it is intended to represent. The enormous literature on validity is well described by Smith and Glass (1987, pp. 106-113), Light et al. (1990, pp. 150-159), or Crocker and Algina (1986).

Intermediate Versus Final Outcomes

Most of the measures of effectiveness that we have discussed are directly related to some underlying program objective. These measures are usually associated with the attainment of a final outcome in children, such as academic achievement. For many reasons, often as simple as lack of data, evaluators can obtain measures of intermediate outcomes only. While these are hypothesized to have direct links with final outcomes, direct evidence is often lacking on their predictive validity.

Tatto, Nielson, and Cummings (1991) compared the cost-effectiveness of three Sri Lankan teacher-training programs in raising an intermediate outcome: teacher mastery of subject matter and pedagogy. As the authors observe, however, they are ultimately interested in ascertaining which program is the most cost-effective means of improving classroom teaching and student outcomes. To use the results, we must assume that increased teacher competencies will lead to higher student outcomes. Similarly, a CE analysis by Hartman and Fay (1996) compared two different methods of referring children to special education in Pennsylvania. The measure of effectiveness is the number of children who receive certain kinds of intervention services; the presumption is that this intermediate measure of effectiveness is related to final outcomes such as decreasing learning difficulties among children (on which little evidence was available).

Even many "final" outcomes in education may simply be intermediate ones. For example, academic achievement is probably not valued as an end in itself (though the rancor of educational debates might cause one to question this notion). Rather, it is valued for its supposed influence on other valuable outcomes such as higher wages or an increased capacity to participate in a democratic society.

In health, many CE analyses are obligated to employ intermediate outcomes as their principal measure of effectiveness (Drummond et al., 1997). Intermediate outcomes might include decreases in blood pressure or cholesterol, which are ultimately posited to lead to other desirable health outcomes, such as reduced mortality.

In most of these cases, intermediate outcomes are used because the authors are unable to obtain the proper measures of final outcomes. Tatto and her colleagues (1991) could only observe teachers during the period prior to and immediately following their training; they were unable to follow them into classrooms where student outcomes might be observed and measured. Similarly, to observe the lifelong outcomes of young students is not feasible given the time and resource constraints of many studies. In these cases, the best that can be done is to make a convincing argument that intermediate and final outcomes are strongly associated. Most often, this argument relies upon the intuition of the evaluator and audience.

It would be even more convincing to present empirical evidence from a secondary source that concretely establishes a link of certain magnitude. In a few cases, this evidence might be used—in concert with evidence on intermediate outcomes—to produce estimates of the final effectiveness of alternatives. One health study combined its evidence on the effectiveness of treatments in lowering cholesterol with secondary evidence on the lowered coronary heart disease risks associated with cholesterol reductions. In such a way, they were able to estimate indirectly how alternative treatments were eventually linked to disease risk (Oster & Epstein, 1987).[1] In their CE analysis of school-based drug prevention strategies, Caulkins, Rydell,

Everingham, Chiesa, and Bushway (1999) are ultimately interested in how such programs are related to a reduction in cocaine consumption. However, they have data only on how programs are related to reductions in marijuana use. By utilizing other statistical evidence on the relationship between marijuana and cocaine use, they are able to construct estimates of how prevention is eventually related to cocaine use.

These strategies make creative use of secondary data. However, by introducing additional assumptions into the CE analysis (such as the relation between cholesterol reduction and heart disease), they also reduce the reliability of the analysis. This should affect how we interpret and analyze the CE results. In particular, it underscores the importance of conducting a sensitivity analysis, to gauge whether the final conclusions are sensitive to assumptions made by the evaluator (see further discussion below).

Dealing With Multiple Outcomes

A cost-effectiveness analysis is intended to compare several alternatives according to their success in altering a single measure of effectiveness. This is reasonable if the alternatives have a single objective that is reflected by a single measure of effectiveness. Furthermore, there should be no compelling reason to believe that secondary effects will be produced in other areas, either intentionally or unintentionally. Of course, these assumptions are often unrealistic.

Most educational alternatives jointly produce a wide range of outcomes that require numerous measures of effectiveness. For example, we may wish to compare the cost-effectiveness of two school investments: lengthening the day in elementary schools and lowering the class size. The main objective of the alternatives may be to increase achievement in reading or mathematics, and effectiveness might be gauged by separate tests. In addition to these, the effects of the two alternatives may extend to other domains, such as student self-esteem, parental satisfaction, or disciplinary problems.

The issue of multiple outcomes is important even when the stated objectives of programs have a limited scope. One could imagine three separate programs, each focused on raising the English competencies of recent immigrants. To varying degrees, each program removes children from their standard classroom environments for part of the school day. The fact that children are deprived of some classroom instruction may yield effects (perhaps negative) in other areas, even if the programs succeed in improving English skills.

In each of these cases, it behooves the evaluator to measure the important intended and unintended outcomes of each alternative. With this information, there are several ways of proceeding. First, the evaluator could conduct a separate cost-effectiveness analysis for each measure of effectiveness. Such an analysis may reveal that a given alternative is to be preferred unambiguously by virtue of its consistently superior cost-effectiveness across many measures. That is, it may yield a given amount of mathematics achievement at a lower cost than other alternatives, and it may also yield a given amount of reading achievement at the lowest cost. In these cases, the evidence clearly supports the use of a particular alternative.

However, it is possible that one alternative is the most cost-effective means of raising mathematics achievement, whereas another is more cost-effective at improving reading. In such an instance, the evaluator could simply present the results of each CE analysis and clearly describe the relevant tradeoffs. In one CE analysis, Levin, Glass, and Meister (1987) compared the costs and effects of four interventions: cross-age tutoring, computer-assisted instruction, reducing class size, and increasing instructional time (see Example 6.3 for a description of this study). The analysis revealed that peer tutoring was the least costly method of obtaining gains in mathematics achievement, followed by class size reduction and then computer-assisted instruction. While peer tutoring was also the most cost-effective means of raising reading achievement, the analysis showed that computer-assisted instruction assumed the second place. Individual decision makers might use these data to make different investment decisions, depending on their priorities.

Alternatively, the evaluator may wish to conduct a cost-utility analysis. In the CU framework, multiple measures of effectiveness—weighted by their importance to parents, administrators, or another audience—are combined into a single summary measure of utility. The weights can be estimated subjectively, perhaps in informal consultations with the primary audience or decision maker. Using more rigorous methods, they could also be elicited from key stakeholders. Such an analysis might reveal, for example, that parents in a particular school district place somewhat higher weight on mathematics achievement than other outcomes. Chapter 8 describes cost-utility analysis in greater detail and discusses the few studies that have been conducted in education.

Methods of Establishing Effectiveness

Once measures of effectiveness are established, the next task is to determine whether a particular intervention is successful in altering these measures. In particular, we need to ascertain whether there is a cause-and-effect relationship between each alternative and the measure of effectiveness. Does reducing class size lead to increased mathematics and reading achievement? Does a drug prevention program reduce the likelihood that students will use drugs?

Typically, this involves comparing the measure of effectiveness for a group of individuals who have been "treated" by the alternative with that of a "control" or "comparison" group. There is a vast array of strategies—referred to as evaluation designs—for carrying out these comparisons. All designs are not created equal, however, and they inspire varying degrees of confidence in the cause-and-effect relationships that they purport to establish. An evaluation that establishes a causal relationship with great certainty is said to possess internal validity. In contrast, the causal claims of many evaluations are less certain because of a variety of "threats" to internal validity.

The next section delineates the most frequent threats to validity. This is followed by a discussion of three general approaches to evaluation: experimental, quasi-experimental, and correlational. Each approach has its strengths and weaknesses and is suited to dealing with the threats to validity in differing degrees. Thus, we also make some suggestions on which approach is best, even while recognizing that the particular circumstances of contexts will demand a flexible approach.

Impediments to Establishing Causality

We may find it fairly easy to establish a correlation between an alternative and a measure of effectiveness. That is, increasing amounts of the alternative might be positively (or negatively) associated with the measure. Unfortunately, this is not necessarily the same as saying that the alternative *caused* these changes. To make a strong causal statement, we must adequately rule out all the other explanations for this observed relationship. Campbell and Stanley (1966) coined the expression "threats to internal validity" to refer to these alternate explanations. The threats are of several varieties, including nonequivalence (also known as selection bias), attrition, history, maturation, testing, instrumentation, and regression to the mean. For a more detailed discussion, the reader may wish to consult Campbell and Stanley's original work or almost any textbook on evaluation and research methods.[2]

Nonequivalence (or Selection Bias)

Evaluation designs often obtain estimates of effectiveness by comparing the outcomes of two groups: one that participated in the alternative and one that did not. In order to causally attribute any difference in outcomes to the alternative, we must be assured that the two groups were equivalent from the beginning, their sole difference being a differential exposure to the alternative. If the two groups are not equivalent, then it becomes exceedingly difficult to disentangle the effects of the alternative from preexisting group differences.

Suppose, for example, that we wish to establish whether exposure to a new math curriculum causes mathematics scores to increase. It is decided that one classroom will use the old curriculum (the control group), while another uses the new curriculum (the treatment group). At the end of the year, the treatment classroom obtains higher scores on the math test. Nevertheless, it is later discovered that students in that classroom are from wealthier and more educated families. Moreover, it is revealed that some parents, prior to the school year, succeeded in having their children transferred from the "old" to the "new" classroom. The apparent nonequivalence of the two groups makes it difficult to determine whether the difference in math scores is due to the new curriculum or to better home environments provided by the wealthy and motivated parents of one classroom's children.

Attrition

Evaluations usually begin with a full complement of individuals in their treatment and control groups. However, a frequent occurrence is that members of either group drop out, a phenomenon referred to as attrition. Thus, even if the groups were equivalent at the beginning, the changing group composition induced by attrition may render them nonequivalent. For example, an after-school tutoring program may begin with 40 students, along with a control group of 40 students who do not participate. Suppose that a number of students do not attend regularly because they must care for younger siblings, and many are not present on testing days. These students, among the poorest, are also the lowest achievers, and their exclusion will tend to inflate the average scores of the treatment group. It no longer seems fair to compare the control and (diminished) treatment groups and attribute the entire difference in outcomes to the tutoring program.

History

A frequent evaluation design—even if used informally—is to examine a group's outcomes before and after the application of an educational alternative. We have all heard or read statements of the following sort: "The test scores of Lincoln Elementary School went up 5% between this year and last. It appears that the new principal (or new curriculum, new computers, etc.) is having the intended effects." It may well be that the actions of the school are causally related to increased test scores. However, it could also be the case that external events during the same time period—referred to as *history*—played a part in the increased scores. Perhaps changes in school district boundaries led to an influx of high socioeconomic status students from a neighboring community, who received higher scores. In order to make strong causal statements, an evaluation design should be able to convincingly rule out the external influence of history.[3]

Maturation

A related threat to validity stems from the natural growth experienced by research subjects. Let us return to the prior example. If the test scores of a group of students increase from one year to the next, it may be that growth is due to a natural process of maturation; perhaps test scores increase because the cognitive ability of students increased with the passage of time. Again, we are hard-pressed to attribute the entirety of the overall increase in test scores to maturation, history, or outside interventions.

Testing

A common feature of evaluations is the application of a pretest and a posttest. The intent of using two tests is to compare the growth in achievement (or another measure of effectiveness) that occurs in the interim period.

A limitation of this approach is that the pretest may provide opportunities to "practice." In cases where tests are applied several times—especially when the stakes are high—it may lead individuals to "teach the test." This could lead to higher scores on posttests, regardless of the effectiveness (or lack thereof) of the educational alternative that is being evaluated.

Instrumentation

If a before-and-after design uses slightly different measures of effectiveness, then it is subject to the threat of instrumentation. Perhaps the pretest, while similar in content to the posttest, is of a slightly higher difficulty. In this case, we may be left with the erroneous impression that the alternative led to a decline in test scores. Or it may be that the measure of effectiveness is based on the ratings of outside observers; however, the individuals conducting the observation changed between first and second rounds of observation. The turnover in personnel—and consequent change in rating methods—may be reflected, even if the educational alternative itself had little effect.

Regression to the Mean

In some cases, individuals are chosen to participate in a treatment because of their extreme scores—either high or low—on a particular assessment. However, in subsequent observations, it is likely that individuals will score closer to the mean; that is, high-scoring individuals will score lower and low-scoring individuals will score higher. The effects induced by regression to the mean are easily confused with those of the program that is being evaluated.

Experiments, Quasi-Experiments, and Correlational Evaluations

There are three general categories of evaluation designs: experimental, quasi-experimental, and correlational.[4] Each encompasses an enormous variety of methods which can involve a great deal of technical sophistication that is beyond the scope of this book. Rather than describe methods in exhaustive detail, we shall focus on explaining their key features and how these may assist us in ruling out some of the threats to internal validity. We will further illustrate some of these differences in Example 6.1 by discussing several evaluations of the common strategy of class size reduction (pp. 126-127). Above all, we wish to highlight the key points that should be of concern for a cost analyst who is contemplating an evaluation design or attempting to ascertain the quality of effectiveness results produced by others.

Experimental Designs

Like many evaluation designs, experiments use a control group and one or more treatment groups. Members of the control group do not participate in the educational alternative that is being evaluated; instead, they provide a baseline estimate of what the treatment group *would have* attained in the absence of the treatment. Ultimately, the estimates of effectiveness are based on the difference between the measured outcomes of the treatment and control groups subsequent to the application of the educational program or policy to the treatment group. The use of a control group is particularly helpful in eliminating the threats to validity of history and maturation, because the control group is subject to the same external events and natural growth as the treatment group.

For the difference between treatment and control groups to possess a strong causal interpretation, the groups must be equivalent at some initial point. As we discussed in the previous section, group nonequivalence (e.g., students with different levels of motivation or socioeconomic status) makes it exceedingly difficult to separate any program effects from effects that are simply due to preexisting group differences.

The best way of ensuring equivalence is to randomly assign subjects from the same population to either control or treatment groups. Indeed, random assignment is a prerequisite of experimental research. Randomization is akin to a series of coin tosses; those individuals obtaining heads are assigned to the treatment group, whereas others are assigned to the control group. In this case, each individual has a specified probability of participating in either group (0.5). The likelihood of participation is governed exclusively by chance and not by other attributes such as income, motivation, or ability. Because randomization provides assurances that the two groups are fundamentally equivalent prior to the application of the treatment, we can rule out the important threat to validity of group nonequivalence.[5]

A frequent component of randomized experiments is the use of a pretest and a posttest, although the former is not strictly necessary. A pretest— or another measure of effectiveness—is applied to treatment and control groups at some initial point. The program or policy is then applied to the treatment group and, subsequently, a posttest is applied to both groups. In order to extract an estimate of effectiveness, we subtract the control group's change in outcomes from the treatment group's. The basic logic of the randomized experiment using a pretest and posttest is diagrammed in Table 6.2. The pretest is a useful means of verifying whether the control and treatment groups are initially equivalent (although this can also be accomplished through comparisons of group composition on gender, race, parental education, and other characteristics).

For introductory discussions to the issues surrounding experimental designs, see Smith and Glass (1987, pp. 142-143) or any other textbook on educational evaluation. More recently, volumes by Boruch (1997) and Orr (1999) have provided comprehensive reviews of the issues related to the design and conduct of social experiments, as well as numerous citations to the applied literature. The degree to which experiments have been incorporated in cost-effectiveness analysis varies widely by field. There is widespread consensus in health care that experimental methods represent a "gold standard," and their use has grown substantially over the past 15 years (Detsky, 1995; Mandelblatt et al., 1996).

Cost-effectiveness evaluations in education have used randomized experiments to a lesser extent (in Chapter 7, we will review some experiments that have been used to conduct cost-benefit analyses). There are several recent examples of educational experiments, such as Tennessee's class size experiment and New York's voucher experiment (Krueger, 1999; Peterson, Myers, & Howell, 1998). However, these are not always accompanied by a comprehensive cost analysis. There is clearly a great deal of opportunity and need to incorporate educational experiments into cost analysis, and vice versa.

Quasi-Experimental Designs

In many instances, the random assignment of subjects to treatment and control groups is not feasible due to ethical or practical constraints on the evaluator. In these cases, evaluators sometimes use other methods to construct treatment and comparison groups. (When random assignment is not

TABLE 6.2 A Randomized, Controlled, Pretest/Posttest Experiment

Step 1: Subjects Are Randomly Assigned	Step 2: Pretest Is Applied	Step 3: Treatment Period	Step 4: Posttest Is Applied		Step 5: Effect Is Estimated
Treatment group	a	Treatment	b	$b-a=y$	If y is greater than z, the program has had a positive net outcome.
Control group	c	No treatment	d	$d-c=z$	

SOURCE: Adapted from Weiss (1998, Figure 8.1).

possible, a common convention is to refer to a "comparison" rather than a "control" group.[6]) For example, let us presume that a group of students volunteered to participate in a new after-school homework program. We wish to evaluate the effectiveness of the program but are unable to randomly assign a group of students to receive and not receive the treatment. One alternative is to match each participating student with a nonparticipating student, who is similar according to some batch of characteristics defined by the evaluator. In this case, one might attempt to match students according to their demonstrated ability on a pretest and their socioeconomic status. The goal is to construct a comparison group that is initially equivalent to the treatment group, so that later differences in outcomes can be attributed to the program. Such a matching procedure was employed in the cost-benefit analysis described in Example 1.4 (Stern, Dayton, Paik, & Weisberg, 1989). Participants in a high school drop-out prevention program were matched to a comparison group, based on a predefined set of characteristics. There are a variety of procedures and approaches to matching that are well described by Rossi and Freeman (1993).

Unfortunately, matching does not completely eliminate the threat of group nonequivalence. Despite initial similarities, even on a wide range of observed characteristics, it is still possible that groups are dissimilar in important ways. In the prior example, it may be that students who volunteered for the after-school homework program are substantially more motivated than other students—even those with the same pretest scores or socioeconomic status. This evaluation design might confuse the effects of student motivation and the homework program. Because of this, it is essential that the evaluator have a detailed knowledge of the program, which will allow the matching process to focus on the most relevant student characteristics.

Besides matching, quasi-experimental evaluations can assume a number of alternative forms, such as the interrupted time series and the regression-discontinuity design. For methodological details on these, see Smith and Glass (1987) or Rossi and Freeman (1993). As in the matching design, the prefix "quasi" is intended to suggest that these designs may parallel experiments in important ways. For example, most use treatment and comparison groups of some form, and in most of these designs, the evaluator has some degree of control over which individuals belong to each group and when the intervention is applied. Nevertheless, this control does not extend to completely randomized assignment.

Correlational Designs

In some cases, the evaluator has very little control at all over who receives and does not receive a given treatment, and neither randomization nor quasi-experimental matching is possible. Indeed, the researcher may begin collecting and analyzing data only well after the treatment has been applied. Correlational studies—also referred to as nonexperimental—are exceedingly common in education, though causal conclusions about effectiveness are sometimes derived from their results in a less-than-cautious manner.

One of the most famous correlational studies in education is the "Coleman Report." James Coleman and his colleagues (1966) collected an enormous sample of data on the characteristics of students and their schools. With these data they sought to explore the causal links between school resources and student achievement. At no time, however, were they able to consciously manipulate the levels of school resources. Instead, they compared students with greater and lesser quantities of school resources, using a statistical technique called multiple regression analysis to control for, or "hold constant," other variables like the socioeconomic status of students.

Since the Coleman Report, hundreds of studies have used nonexperimental data and multiple regression analysis to infer the causal links between school resources and student outcomes (these often appear in the literature under the rubric of "input-output," "production function," or "school effectiveness" studies). Hanushek (1986, 1997) has written influential reviews of this literature, which are skeptical of the possible links between school resources and student outcomes. Nevertheless, his conclusions have been disputed by other authors using different techniques of research synthesis such as meta-analysis (Greenwald, Hedges, & Laine, 1996). Our position is that firm conclusions are difficult to extract from this literature, because the nonexperimental features of the data limit our ability to rule out important threats to validity such as group nonequivalency.

When comparing students who receive and do not receive a given "treatment" (e.g., more text books or a new curriculum), we make statistical controls for measured characteristics of students (such as a pretest score or socioeconomic status). If the controls are complete and accurate, then the threat of group nonequivalency is adequately ruled out. Unfortunately, it is a fairly tall order to make complete and accurate controls. There are countless unobserved student characteristics that also affect outcomes, such as motivation, family wealth, or ability. If students who received a given treatment tend to possess more or less of these characteristics, then it is quite difficult to separate treatment effects from the preexisting student differences.

To provide one example, many studies compare the achievement of students who attend private schools (the treatment) to students who attend public schools (the comparison group).[7] It is often the case that families who choose to send their children to private schools are of a higher socioeconomic status. Thus, statistical comparisons of public and private achievement make controls for such background variables. Even with such controls, however, it is feasible that students in private schools are different in some important, but unobserved, ways. Perhaps their families choose private schools because they are deeply devoted to their children's success, which also leads them to provide greater assistance with homework. Group nonequivalence (also referred to as selection bias) causes the effects of in-household homework to be confused with those of private schools. Thus, the internal validity of the studies is thrown into question.

All is not lost, however. There are many sophisticated statistical procedures to address the threat of group nonequivalence (and, indeed, these methods have been applied to comparisons of public and private school outcomes). Many of these are summarized by Moffitt (1991) or in textbooks on econometrics and statistics.[8] These methods rely upon explicit attempts by the researcher to statistically model the process of selection into the treatment and comparison groups. These results, in turn, are used to produce a correction term that is included in a regression analysis comparing outcomes across the treatment and comparison groups. Suffice it to say that these methods require a detailed knowledge of the selection process and many technical assumptions that should be well understood prior to the implementation of any correction. Furthermore, although additional statistical methods can increase our confidence in the internal validity of estimates of effectiveness, they rarely provide the same degree of confidence as a well-designed randomized experiment.

Which Approach Is Best?

Randomized experiments provide an extremely useful guard against threats to internal validity such as group nonequivalence. In this sense, they are the preferred method for estimating the causal relationship between a specific educational alternative and measures of effectiveness. That said, we should endeavor to be critical but not dismissive of nonexperimental evidence. It is clear that a correlational evaluation that makes strong causal claims, with little acknowledgment of potential threats to validity, should be taken with a grain of salt. Regrettably, these studies are all too common in the field of education. On the other hand, a correlational study that provides a thorough discussion of potential biases, while credibly exploring the data for evidence of their existence, should be given greater attention.

In some respects, experiments may not be the most attractive or feasible option. By their nature, experimental treatments are conducted in strictly controlled settings, often on a small scale. In contrast, other evaluation designs (especially large-scale correlational studies) occur in more natural settings. Because of this, the results of experiments have been criticized for not being strictly generalizable to other settings (see the discussion in Weiss, 1998, pp. 229-233). We shall return to the problem of generalizability of study results—also referred to as external validity—in Chapter 9.

Furthermore, experiments are not always feasible in a practical sense. In some cases, the evaluator is simply given minimal control over which individuals (or classrooms or schools) are assigned to participate or not participate in a treatment, or groups are assigned far in advance of the evaluator's initial participation. In other circumstances, experiments that randomly deny service to individuals may be unethical or politically unacceptable.

For an illuminating debate on the relative merits of experiments versus other evaluation designs, the reader is advised to consult articles by Burtless (1995), who argues in favor of experiments, and Heckman and Smith (1995), who are more skeptical.

How Useful Is Meta-Analysis?

In recent decades, researchers in the social sciences have increasingly used techniques of meta-analysis to arrive at estimates of effectiveness. Often, there are numerous—perhaps hundreds—of individual studies that explore the causal relationship between a particular educational alternative and an outcome such as achievement. Results from individual studies may vary considerably. It is difficult to extract meaningful conclusions from the overall body of findings without resorting to additional analytical techniques.

EXAMPLE 6.1. Evaluation Designs for Estimating the Effects of Class Size Reduction

A contentious issue in educational research is the potential effect of class size reduction on student outcomes. Fortunately, a broad research base has developed that employs variations on all three evaluation designs: experimental, quasi-experimental, and correlational (or nonexperimental). For a student of evaluation, it is quite instructive to compare the methods and results of this diverse literature. Much of it is summarized and discussed in the summer 1999 issue of the journal *Educational Evaluation and Policy Analysis*.

The best-known and most influential experimental study, already described in Example 1.1, is Project STAR in Tennessee (Krueger, 1999; Mosteller, 1995). Its hallmark is the use of randomization to assign students to small and large classes. Seventy-nine elementary schools volunteered to participate in the experiment. At the beginning of the experiment, the newly entering kindergartners within each school were randomly assigned to three types of classes: (1) regular classes (22-25 students) without teacher aides; (2) regular classes with teacher aides; and (3) small classes (13-17 students).

Krueger's (1999) independent evaluation suggests that performance on standardized tests increases by about 4 percentile points during the first year in which students are assigned to smaller classes, with larger effects among minority and lower-income students. In contrast, teacher aides were found to have little effect on student achievement. In some ways, however, the experiment fell short of the ideal. Some students who began the experiment left for another school; likewise, new students continued to enter the experiment and were randomly assigned to treatment and control groups. Around 8% to 11% of participating children did not take exams for a variety of reasons. Hanushek (1999) believes that this casts some uncertainty on the results, perhaps exposing the estimates to the threats of attrition and group nonequivalence. Grissmer (1999) is more confident that the results are internally valid. For example, his review of the evidence suggests that there are no significant differences between characteristics of leaving and entering students across small and large classes, implying that group nonequivalence is less of a threat.

More recently, a quasi-experimental evaluation of class size reduction has been conducted in Wisconsin (Molnar et al., 1999). The SAGE program had several components, although a key element was substantial class size reductions—to between 12 and 15 students—in the early elementary grades. Schools were required to apply in order to participate, and applications were restricted to high-poverty schools. The evaluators were unable to randomly assign schools or students within schools to receive (or not receive) the treatment. Instead, they opted for a quasi-experimental approach. After the group of 30 participating schools was established, the evaluators chose a comparison group of 17 schools that were located in the same districts and that reflected similar family incomes, achievement levels, and racial compositions. The authors' statistical

EXAMPLE 6.1. continued

analysis compared outcomes of students in each school type, controlling for individual characteristics such as race and income. Their results were fairly consistent with those of the Tennessee experiment. Positive effects were found for all children, which were slightly higher in the case of African American children. While care was taken to ensure that group nonequivalence would not threaten the internal validity of results, the lack of random assignment might cause one to interpret the results with slightly more caution.

Since the famous Coleman Report, there have been literally hundreds of correlational studies that have explored the effectiveness of class size reduction. In these, the evaluators had no control over which students actually attended large and small classes. Instead, they compared achievement of students who were observed to attend large or small classes—or schools with high or low pupil-teacher ratios[9]—while making statistical controls for the socioeconomic background of students. Hanushek (1997, 1999) summarizes these studies and concludes that they show no consistent link of class size to student outcomes.

Before drawing such a conclusion, we might consider the causal interpretation of nonexperimental estimates of school effects. Consider the familiar issue of group nonequivalence. The prior estimates have a causal interpretation if adequate controls have been made for intervening variables such as family and student background. If controls are incomplete, then we have little guarantee that class size effects—or lack thereof—do not erroneously reflect unobserved family attributes. Research by Boozer and Rouse (1995) shows that the allocation of students to large and small classes is clearly nonrandom. In the United States, lower-ability students are often assigned to smaller classes. But if student ability is imperfectly controlled for in correlational studies, then smaller class sizes might appear to be associated with lower student achievement.

These shortcomings go far toward explaining why a single experiment in Tennessee has proven to be more compelling to policy makers than a vast array of correlational studies. Krueger concludes that "one well-designed experiment should trump a phalanx of poorly controlled, imprecise observational studies based on uncertain statistical specifications" (1999, p. 528).

From the perspective of the cost analyst, two points are important to emphasize. First, a cost-effectiveness analysis is only as good as its various components, including its estimates of effectiveness. One should be cognizant of the strengths and weaknesses of the evaluation design that was employed and suspicious of studies that obfuscate their methods or interpret their results too optimistically. Second, even clear-cut evidence on effectiveness provides just a portion of the information needed to make informed decisions. Without a rigorous cost analysis of class size reduction and comparison with other alternatives, we are hard-pressed to choose the alternative that provides the greatest amount of outcomes at lowest cost (Brewer, Krop, Gill, & Reichardt, 1999, p. 180; Grissmer, 1999, pp. 241–242).

Thus, many researchers use meta-analysis to estimate the "average" effect size of an alternative, which is typically used to support broad conclusions about its effectiveness (or lack thereof).[10] Meta-analyses have been conducted in many areas, ranging from the effects of within-class ability grouping (Lou et al., 1996) to class size reduction (Glass, Cohen, Smith, & Filby, 1982). They are an increasingly prominent feature of journals such as the *Review of Educational Research*. In health, their use has also been on the increase (Saint, Veenstra, & Sullivan, 1999).

Meta-analysis is not without controversy, however. It has been criticized on a number of grounds. Among these concerns are the issues of inclusion of studies that are based upon poor design and procedures; the "averaging" of results among different studies, coding, and classification; and inappropriate statistical analysis and interpretation of results (Hedges & Olkin, 1985; Slavin, 1984, 1986). From our perspective, the pertinent issue is whether meta-analytic summaries can be combined with cost-analyses in order to provide a cost-effectiveness comparison of different educational alternatives. Instead of using a single estimate of effectiveness, is it not preferable for a CE analysis to use an estimate derived from a comprehensive meta-analysis?

For many reasons, the incorporation of meta-analytic results into CE analysis warrants a fair amount of caution (Levin, 1988, 1991). Meta-analysis provides an estimate of the average results from many different versions of a single class of interventions (e.g., computer-assisted instruction, ability grouping, or tutoring). However, CE analysis is fundamentally oriented toward providing concrete information to decision makers on whether specific programs or policies are desirable to implement. Instead of specifics, a meta-analysis can only provide a general judgment of whether a general variety of policy is effective "on average."

The problem becomes more severe when we attempt to incorporate costs. In prior chapters, we discussed the importance of clearly defining an alternative, providing a detailed account of the ingredients, and carefully estimating the cost of each ingredient. But the effect size from meta-analysis is based on a mixture of many different programs, precluding any conceptual or practical way to identify costs. The effect size does not refer to an implementable program alternative with a set of specific ingredients. Consider a hypothetical meta-analysis of adult tutoring programs in elementary schools. In practice, each of these programs might obtain its tutoring services in different ways. Some might pay on-duty teachers to spend time after school, whereas others might pay local adults the minimum wage to participate. Still others could receive voluntary tutoring services from parents. Faced by such heterogeneity of resource use, there is no obvious way to define the ingredients and costs of a single program.

Under stringent conditions, it may be more acceptable to use meta-analytic results. If the specific studies all refer to different evaluations of precisely the same intervention, then it is more acceptable to ascribe a meaningful policy interpretation to the "average effect."[11]

Similarly, when the intervention is precisely the same, it is more likely that the particular cost ingredients will be similar across studies. For example, a specific intervention—such as a "packaged" reading program—may use a prescribed amount of materials, physical space, time, and human resources, even if it is implemented and evaluated in many different contexts (the messy reality of program implementation, however, provides good reason to be skeptical that this proposition will always hold). Overall, meta-analytic results should not be incorporated in CE analyses unless the underlying situations are derived from replication trials of a single intervention.

Discounting Effects

Many educational interventions are designed to last a single year, and the evaluations of costs and effects are necessarily confined to that period. The evaluator estimates the annual cost of the program via the ingredients method (making careful use of the annualization techniques developed in Chapter 4 to adjust downward the costs of facilities or materials that last for more than a year). The evaluator also uses an appropriate evaluation design to estimate the effectiveness during the year (e.g., achievement gained). Without further ado, one could calculate cost-effectiveness ratios and rank the alternatives, as described in the next section.

However, if the intervention lasts for more than a year, then both costs and effects need to be adjusted for the time pattern over which they arise. In Chapter 5, we discussed the importance of discounting the costs of multi-year programs. The same logic can be applied to the discounting of effects in multiyear programs, which is best illustrated with an example. Imagine that we are conducting a cost-effectiveness analysis of three approaches to drop-out prevention in high schools that are implemented over a period of

5 years. The measure of effectiveness is the number of dropouts averted in a given year by each program.

Table 6.3 presents the data on effectiveness for each year. Alternative A leads to a total of 100 dropouts averted in the first year, but none in subsequent years. Alternative B also reduces dropouts by 100, but the number is evenly spaced throughout 5 years. Finally, the effects of Alternative C are entirely deferred to the 5th year. If effects are not discounted, then the alternatives are judged to be equally effective, because they each reduce dropouts by 100. On the basis of effectiveness alone, we should be indifferent to which of the three alternatives is chosen. However, this reasoning is fallacious. Alternative A provides its effects much sooner than the others, and this makes it more attractive—even if only slightly—than the other alternatives. Just how attractive can be established with the same discounting formula that we used in Chapter 5:

$$PV = \sum_{t=1}^{n} \frac{E_t}{(1+r)^{t-1}} = 91$$

For example, if applied to Alternative B in Table 6.3, using a discount rate of 5%, the present value of the effect is the following:

$$PV = \frac{20}{(1+0.05)^0} + \frac{20}{(1+0.05)^1} + \frac{20}{(1+0.05)^2} + \frac{20}{(1+0.05)^3} + \frac{20}{(1+0.05)^4} = 91$$

If the same discounting formula is applied to Alternatives A and C, it shows that A has the highest effectiveness, because it manages to reduce dropouts by the same number but much sooner (see Table 6.3).

Educational CE analyses that discount their effects are rare (for an exception, see Caulkins et al., 1999). In general, this is because effects and costs occur during a single year and discounting is simply unnecessary, although other studies fail to discount effects (and even costs) over multiyear projects. The discounting of effects is much more common in the cost-effectiveness literature on health. Perhaps as a result of its greater use in health, as well as the special nature of health outcomes, discounting has also been the subject of some methodological controversy (for thorough discussions, see Drummond et al., 1997, pp. 107-109; Lipscomb, Weinstein, & Torrance, 1996; and Viscusi, 1995).

TABLE 6.3 Dropouts Prevented by Three Hypothetical Programs

Year	Alternative A	Alternative B	Alternative C
1	100	20	0
2	0	20	0
3	0	20	0
4	0	20	0
5	0	20	100
Total (undiscounted)	100	100	100
Present value (discount rate of 5%)	100	91	82

Much of the debate has centered on whether the rate used to discount effects should be less than the rate used to discount costs (or perhaps even set to zero, thus treating effects in the future as equivalent to current effects).[12] Some empirical evidence indicates that individuals discount health effects at a lower rate than costs (it remains to be seen whether the same could be true for educational outcomes). Moreover, the discounting of future effects naturally places greater weight on outcomes of this generation and less on future generations. Some feel that this unduly discriminates against future generations.

Notwithstanding these critiques, the evidence in favor of discounting is quite compelling. A failure to discount effects—even when costs are discounted—can lead to inconsistent or misleading results.[13] In Table 6.3, we found three programs to be equally effective in the absence of discounting, when in fact one should be favored because it provides the same effects much sooner. The question remains as to which discount rate should be employed, an issue discussed in Chapter 5. Regardless of the decision made, the analysis should ascertain how sensitive the CE results are to varying assumptions about the discount rate (for further details, see the discussion of sensitivity analysis on pp. 141-144, this volume).

Analyzing the Distribution of Effects

As with the distribution of costs, it is important to consider which constituencies receive the greatest (or least) effects of each alternative. For example, one might be concerned with the types of students that educational interventions assist the most. A specific alternative may increase total test scores by having profound effects on those with the highest initial score and little or no effect on those with the lowest initial scores. Alternatively, an intervention might have stronger effects for those with low scores initially or might have equal effects for all groups. Likewise, there can be different distributional consequences among races and income groups or between genders. For example, two recent evaluations of the effectiveness of class size reduction found that effectiveness was somewhat higher for lower-income and minority students than for other students (Angrist & Lavy, 1999; Krueger, 1999).

Not only is this an important issue to review in evaluations generally, but it also ought to be taken into account when incorporating costs into the analysis. If effectiveness differs across groups of students, but costs are roughly the same for each group, then cost-effectiveness ratios will also differ. A given alternative may prove to be a more cost-effective option for some groups and less so for others. In the class size studies just cited, it seems reasonable to presume that class size reductions will be relatively more cost-effective for low-income groups (although it remains to be seen whether reductions targeted at low-income students are the *most* cost-effective alternative of the many that could be considered). Another concrete example of such a case is provided in Example 6.2. In their study of two math programs, Quinn, Van Mondfrans, and Worthen (1984) find that one program is the most cost-effective option for low socioeconomic status (SES) students, but not for high-SES students.

When effects are unevenly distributed across groups of students, there are three ways of proceeding in the cost-effectiveness analysis. First, we can simply ignore the uneven distribution of effects and utilize a single estimate of effectiveness. In fact, this is what the majority of general evaluation and cost-effectiveness studies choose to do. By following this procedure, the single estimate of effectiveness is an "average" that may conceal larger effects for some groups and smaller (or even negative) effects for others. No one person's effect is treated as more important than another's.

Second, we can calculate separate estimates of effectiveness—and cost-effectiveness ratios—for each group under consideration (e.g., gender, income groups, or races). This is the procedure followed by Quinn et al. (1984). Decision makers might use these disaggregated results to choose an alternative that disproportionately benefits a particular social group.

Third, we can average the effectiveness measures for a number of groups into a single summary measure, weighting each group's estimate by the social importance that is attached to it. The summary measure of effectiveness is then used to calculate the cost-effectiveness ratio. Essentially, this is a variant of the multiple-outcome problem discussed above. Any overall measure of effectiveness can be decomposed among the populations that are affected to see how each shares in the outcome. Then, utility values can be used to weight the results according to social priorities. For example, effects on the educational performance of disadvantaged youngsters might be weighed more heavily than effects on the more advantaged.[14] Methods for deriving these weights are discussed in greater detail in Chapter 8 on cost-utility analysis.

Combining Costs and Effectiveness

Once estimates of costs and effectiveness are obtained, they should be combined in a ratio for each alternative. The ratios can then be ordered to identify the alternatives that provide a given level of effectiveness for the least cost, or the highest effectiveness for a given cost. Though perhaps obvious, some studies neglect to pursue this final step, making it difficult to properly interpret the results.

Cost-Effectiveness Ratios

To compute a cost-effectiveness ratio (*CER*), the cost of a given alternative (*C*) is divided by its effectiveness (*E*):[15]

$$CER = \frac{C}{E}$$

EXAMPLE 6.2. A Cost-Effectiveness Analysis of Two Math Curricula

The importance of analyzing the distribution of effects among students was demonstrated in the following cost-effectiveness study. The authors set out to compare the effectiveness and costs of two instructional approaches to fifth-grade mathematics instruction in a Utah school district. The approaches are a locally developed program called the Goal-Based Educational Management System Proficiency Mathematics (GEMS Math) and a more traditional, text-based approach (Text Math). The GEMS Math curriculum was designed to provide highly individualized instruction, using special instructional methods for teaching math concepts. In contrast, the Text Math approach relies upon one of six publishers' textbooks and a more traditional teaching approach.

It was found that students in the GEMS Math classes had higher mathematics achievement scores than those in the traditional classes, after controlling for SES. Moreover, it was found that the effect of GEMS Math relative to Text Math was even higher for students of lower SES. Put another way, the effectiveness of GEMS was moderated by SES. The cost analysis revealed that GEMS Math required more resources than Text Math. The annual cost per pupil of the former was $288, compared with $194 for the latter.

Initially, the authors calculated a single cost-effectiveness ratio for each program, dividing costs by program effects. These revealed that the GEMS Math cost $11.48 per raw score point on the Iowa Test of Basic Skills, while Text Math cost $13.45 per point. Their initial conclusion was that GEMS Math was the more cost-effective approach. Subsequently, they calculated several estimates of effectiveness for different socioeconomic groups. In concert with costs, these were used to calculate cost-effectiveness ratios for each level of socioeconomic status (see Table 6.4).

Based on these results, the study concluded that for low and medium SES students, the GEMS Math curriculum was considerably more cost-effective (i.e., the cost per score point for GEMS Math is uniformly lower). On the other hand, the GEMS curriculum was slightly *less* cost-effective for high-SES students (i.e., its cost per point is higher). The results provide useful information to decision makers. If a single math program is to be applied to a district with a heterogeneous group of students, it appears GEMS Math is the best option. If implemented in a rather high-SES district, the evidence provides some support for Text Math as the most cost-effective option.

SOURCE: Quinn et al. (1984).

TABLE 6.4 Cost-Effectiveness Ratios Among SES Groups

Socioeconomic Status Rating	Cost-Effectiveness Ratio (cost per raw score point on the Iowa Test of Basic Skills)	
	Text Math Program	GEMS Math Program
High	$8.29	$10.28
Medium high	$10.26	$10.87
Medium	$13.47	$11.52
Medium low	$19.60	$12.26
Low	$35.92	$13.09

SOURCE: Adapted from Quinn et al. (1984, Table 7).

The previous ratio is interpreted as the cost required to obtain a single unit of effectiveness (however the units of effectiveness are defined by the evaluator). Our decision rule is to choose the alternative that exhibits the lowest costs per unit of effectiveness. Thus, we should rank order the alternatives, ranging from those with the smallest cost-effectiveness ratios to those with the largest. Example 6.3 provides an additional example of a cost-effectiveness analysis that compared four alternative methods of raising mathematics and reading achievement.

There is an important caveat to the interpretation of cost-effectiveness ratios (in fact, this also applies to cost-benefit and benefit-cost ratios that are discussed in Chapter 7). Whenever comparing the cost-effectiveness ratios of several alternatives, the analyst should pay attention to the scale of alternatives. Hopefully, they will be of roughly similar scales, although in some cases, they may be of vastly different scales. For example, let's say that a program in a citywide school district will cost $10,000 and reduce high school dropouts by 20 (a cost-effectiveness ratio of $500). A different—and much larger—program will cost $100,000 and reduce dropouts by 160 (a cost-effectiveness ratio of $625). Based on our decision rule, the first program appears to be more cost-effective because it requires fewer resources for each dropout prevented.

Nevertheless, it is also of a much smaller scale. We might choose to implement a larger version of the first program, although this raises troubling issues of whether the costs and effects will be duplicated in the scaled-up version of the program. For example, the effects might be diluted because of implementation problems, or costs may be reduced because of economies of scale. In cases such as these, the analyst should think carefully about how modifications to the scale of a particular alternative might alter its effectiveness and costs (and, potentially, the cost-effectiveness ranking of alternatives).

On occasion, evaluators may be able to place monetary values on some outcomes but not on all of them (later on, in Chapter 7, we will review some of the methods for valuing outcomes). In this case, the evaluator may be in a position to apply a hybrid of cost-effectiveness and cost-benefit analysis, in which the cost estimate is adjusted for any monetary benefits that might be produced. The numerator is composed of costs minus benefits, and the denominator is the same as above:

$$CER = \frac{C - B}{E}$$

To provide an illustration, let's imagine that we conducted a cost-effectiveness analysis of two after-school tutoring programs that were designed to increase mathematics achievement. Thus, each alternative was evaluated according to its costs (C) and effectiveness (E) in raising math achievement. Along the way, it was discovered that the programs had the inadvertent outcome of reducing the incidence of vandalism and petty theft in the neighborhood, mainly because a large number of children were kept after school. This is an important finding, but how should it be incorporated in the analysis? One possible alternative would be to conduct a separate cost-effectiveness analysis, using a second measure of effectiveness (e.g., reduction in the number of crimes reported). However, it might be possible to place a monetary value on the benefits of crime reduction. Incidents of vandalism are costly to local businesses. By averting these costs, we have produced quantifiable benefits to the local community. These benefits can be subtracted from program costs (C–B). The resulting costs—net of selected monetary benefits—are divided by program effectiveness in raising math achievement.

Effectiveness-Cost Ratios

Some authors opt for a different approach to combining the same evidence on costs and effectiveness. In this case, an effectiveness-cost ratio is obtained by dividing the effectiveness of each alternative by its cost:

$$ECR = \frac{E}{C}$$

As Boardman, Greenberg, Vining, and Weimer (1996) note, this is often confusingly referred to as a cost-effectiveness ratio. It is interpreted as the units of effectiveness that are obtained by incurring a single unit of cost (generally a dollar or a multiple of a dollar). We should choose the alternatives that provide the greatest effectiveness per unit of cost. To do so, we need to rank order the alternatives, ranging from those with the largest effectiveness-cost ratios to those with the smallest. If properly interpreted, there is no difference in the conclusions produced by calculating cost-effectiveness or effectiveness-cost ratios.

CE studies in health are quite consistent in presenting cost-effectiveness ratios, a practice which is endorsed by a set of national guidelines (Gold, Seigel, Russell, & Weinstein, 1996; Weinstein, Siegel, Gold, Kamlet, & Russell, 1996). In contrast, education studies have tended to use both of these approaches, so one should exercise care in properly interpreting the results of these studies (as an example, Example 6.3 reports cost-effectiveness ratios; the original study to which it refers reported effectiveness-cost ratios). To standardize practices and avoid confusion, it is best to report cost-effectiveness ratios.

Accounting for Uncertainty

As one might imagine from prior discussions, our estimates of costs and effects necessarily involve some degree of uncertainty. Uncertainty might stem from at least three sources (Drummond et al., 1997). First, it is sometimes the case that imperfect data—or none at all—are available for a key component of the analysis, and an outright assumption has to be made. Second, a good estimate of a cost or effect might have been calculated,

EXAMPLE 6.3. A Cost-Effectiveness Analysis of Four Educational Interventions

There is never a shortage of suggestions in United States for ways to improve education. Unfortunately, all are costly, and only a few have been convincingly demonstrated to be effective at reaching a particular objective such as raising student achievement. In a wide-ranging CE analysis from the 1980s, the authors set out to compare the relative costs and effects for the elementary grades of four commonly suggested alternatives: a longer school day, computer-assisted instruction (CAI), cross-age tutoring, and reduced class size. In some cases, the results of this particular study are no longer applicable as a policy guide. For instance, the effectiveness and costs of computer-assisted instruction have probably changed substantially since the 1980s. Nevertheless, the study is still one of the few examples of a comprehensive educational cost-effectiveness analysis.

The extension of the daily school session is a recommendation of many national reports on educational reform. In this case, the alternative considered was to lengthen the school day by 1 hour, half devoted to reading and half to mathematics. Data on effectiveness were taken from the Beginning Teacher Evaluation Study (BTES) as reevaluated by Glass (1984).

The specific approach to CAI that was chosen was the drill and practice program of Computer Curriculum Corporation (CCC) as described in Ragosta, Holland, and Jamison (1982). In the 1980s, the CCC method was one of the most widely used in the United States, providing students with 10 minutes of daily practice through the use of student terminals connected to a mini-computer. Effectiveness results were taken from the 4-year experiment of the CCC system that was undertaken by the Educational Testing Service (Ragosta et al., 1982) and reevaluated by Glass (1984).

Cross-age tutoring utilizes older students to tutor younger ones, under the supervision of adults. The specific tutoring program that was used for measuring effectiveness was one that had received national recognition from the Joint Dissemination Review Panel of the U.S. Department of Education (Independent School District of Boise City, 1983). Fifth and sixth grade students tutored students in the lower elementary grades. For students in the fifth and sixth grades, adult tutors were provided. Thus, the study provided estimates of effectiveness for both peer and adult tutors (Glass, 1984).

EXAMPLE 6.3. continued

Then and now, a smaller class size is viewed as a principal means of improving achievement. Evidence for the CE analysis was drawn from a meta-analysis of 14 experimental evaluations of class size reduction (Glass, 1984). Specific estimates were made of effects on mathematics and reading achievement for reductions in class size from 35 to 30 students, 30 to 25, 25 to 20, and 35 to 20.

In each case, the annual per-student cost of each alternative was estimated via the ingredients method described in Chapters 3 through 5. The least costly interventions were reductions in class size of 5 pupils and increasing the length of the school day. The most costly were the adult and peer tutoring programs. The effectiveness of each intervention is reported in units of standard deviations (effect sizes) on mathematics and reading tests. Peer tutoring showed the largest effects by far, followed by adult tutoring. Small class size reduction and a longer school day showed the smallest effects.

Table 6.5 shows the results of dividing the costs by effects in order to arrive at cost-effectiveness ratios. These indicate the annual cost required to obtain one unit of student achievement. For example, to obtain an additional unit of mathematics achievement per year, it would cost about $2,033 a year with a longer school day, but only $219 with peer tutoring. In fact, a longer school day is less than half as cost-effective in raising mathematics achievement as CAI or reducing class size. The most cost-effective approach, peer tutoring, requires only one-ninth of the resources to obtain the same effect on mathematics achievement.

To obtain an additional unit of reading achievement would cost about twice as much for increasing the school day as using peer tutoring, with CAI almost as efficient as the latter. Reducing class size appears to be particularly inefficient with respect to raising reading achievement. For both mathematics and reading achievement, adult tutoring is not very cost-effective. Although its effectiveness is high, its cost is also high.

―――――――――――
Source: Levin et al. (1987); Levin (1988).

TABLE 6.5 Costs, Effects, and Cost-Effectiveness Ratios of Four Interventions

Alternative	Mathematics			Reading		
	Cost	Effect	CE ratio	Cost	Effect	CE ratio
Longer school day	$ 61	0.03	$2,053	$ 61	0.07	$ 871
Computer-assisted instruction	$119	0.12	$ 992	$119	0.23	$ 517
Cross-age tutoring						
Peer component	$212	0.97	$ 219	$212	0.48	$ 442
Adult component	$827	0.67	$1,234	$827	0.38	$2,176
Reducing class size						
From 35 to 30	$ 45	0.06	$ 750	$ 45	0.03	$1,500
From 30 to 25	$ 63	0.07	$ 900	$ 63	0.04	$1,575
From 25 to 20	$ 94	0.09	$1,044	$ 94	0.05	$1,880
From 35 to 20	$201	0.22	$ 914	$201	0.11	$1,827

SOURCE: Adapted from Levin et al. (1987, Tables 1 and 2).

which is nonetheless subject to a natural degree of uncertainty. This is almost always the case with estimates that are derived from a sample of individuals or schools rather than an entire population. The vagaries of statistical sampling imply that different samples drawn from the same population will yield different estimates of effectiveness. Although we would expect these to cluster around the true population effect, we almost always possess some degree of uncertainty as to the exact value. Third, there may be specific parameters such as the discount rate (see Chapter 5) that are simply chosen at the discretion of the evaluator but are nonetheless controversial or arbitrary.

Sensitivity Analysis

A simple and powerful technique for dealing with uncertainty is known as sensitivity analysis (we already provided a brief discussion of the technique in Chapter 5). The simplest version, called "one-way" sensitivity analysis, is characterized by a rather intuitive process. First, one identifies the parameters that reflect the greatest uncertainty. These could include almost any aspect of the analysis, including the discount rate, the cost of one or more ingredients, or the estimate of effectiveness. Second, one identifies a reasonable range over which each parameter might vary. The "middle" value is usually the baseline estimate that was calculated in the original analysis. The "high" and "low" values can be derived by a number of methods. In many cases, the evaluator might use his or her professional judgment, in concert with the raw material of the cost analysis, to estimate high and low values of the parameter in question. Often, parameters that are derived from the statistical analysis of a sample—including most estimates of effectiveness—are accompanied by a confidence interval. The upper and lower bounds of the interval could be used as high and low estimates. Finally, the evaluator should reestimate cost-effectiveness ratios over the entire range (or several points on the range) of a given parameter. This procedure should be repeated for each parameter with an uncertain estimate.

The main concern is to see if the CE ranking of alternatives changes when parameter assumptions change. For example, it may be that a ranking of projects according to their cost-effectiveness is invariant with regard to different assumptions about the discount rate or the cost of a particular ingredient. In this case, the sensitivity analysis will suggest that the results are highly robust with respect to different assumptions in estimating costs. If, however, the ranking of projects changes with different assumptions, it will be necessary to decide among alternatives by deciding which assumptions seem most reasonable. Or it may spur the evaluator to postpone a conclusion and seek new sources of data that provide additional certainty about the parameters of interest (Manning, Fryback, & Weinstein, 1996).

The basic idea of a one-way sensitivity analysis is illustrated in Figure 6.1. The costs and effectiveness of four alternatives (A, B, C, and D) are being compared. In the figure, a single parameter—the estimate of effectiveness for Alternative A—is varied while holding all others constant. Increasing the estimate of effectiveness from "low" to "high" estimates tends to reduce the cost-effectiveness ratio of Alternative A. We have also graphed the cost-effectiveness ratios for the other three alternative (B, C, and D). The figure shows that the three estimates of the cost-effectiveness ratio of Alternative A bracket the ratios of the other alternatives. In this simple example, uncertainty about the effectiveness of Alternative A prevents us from extracting firm conclusions about the cost-effectiveness rankings of the alternatives. By obtaining better data on effectiveness, we may be able to reduce the degree of uncertainty.

In addition to one-way sensitivity analysis, there are other procedures that can be applied. As a further step, the evaluator can conduct a multiway analysis, in which two or more parameters are varied at once (Drummond et al., 1997; Manning et al., 1996). Multiway analysis better reflects the actual nature of uncertainty because parameters rarely vary one at a time. However, it can quickly become unwieldy given the possible number of parameter combinations. Example 6.4 provides an example in which multiway sensitivity analysis was applied.

Sensitivity analysis is an essential feature of any CE analysis. Unfortunately, it is less common than its importance dictates. A review of numerous CE and CB studies in health shows that two thirds did not conduct a sensitivity analysis (Udvarhelyi, Colditz, Rai, & Epstein, 1992). Another review by Briggs and Sculpher (1995; cited by Drummond et al., 1997) found that only 14% of health studies provided a good analysis of uncertainty. When cost studies completely ignore the issue of uncertainty, the reader should interpret the results with a dose of caution.

General discussions of sensitivity analysis are given in almost every methodological discussion of cost-benefit and cost-effectiveness analysis.

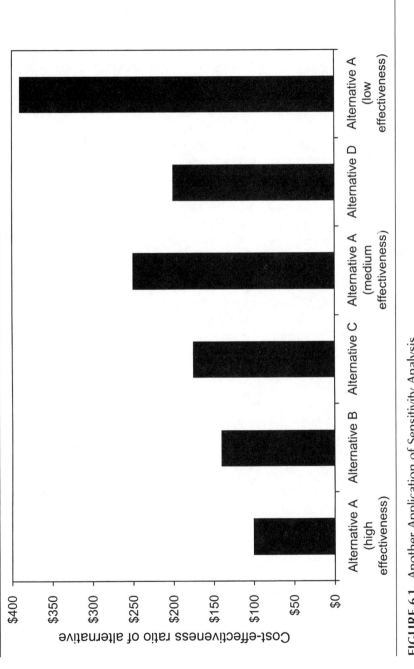

FIGURE 6.1. Another Application of Sensitivity Analysis

EXAMPLE 6.4. An Application of Multiway Sensitivity Analysis

The problem of illicit drug use can be addressed by any number of measures, including school-based drug prevention programs, mandatory minimum sentences for drug dealers, increased federal enforcement, and additional treatment of heavy drug users. However, given that government budgets are limited, which alternatives should be funded in order to produce the greatest possible decrease in consumption of illicit drugs for a set expenditure?

The study authors set out to explore the relative cost-effectiveness of several alternatives in reducing lifetime cocaine consumption, focusing attention on the alternative of school-based drug prevention programs. Unfortunately, there was no evaluation of effectiveness that provided a simple answer to their question: How much is lifetime cocaine consumption reduced by a prevention program? Instead, the authors used information from a variety of sources to construct estimates of effectiveness. Even using quite plausible assumptions, the authors recognized that this injected uncertainty into their results. Thus, they assessed how sensitive their conclusions were to key assumptions.

For a school-based prevention program, the authors established "low," "middle," and "high" estimates for both program costs and effectiveness. Nine effectiveness-cost ratios were calculated by dividing each estimate of effectiveness by each cost estimate (see Table 6.6). The ratios are interpreted as the kilograms of cocaine consumption averted for every million dollars spent. For

In particular, see Boardman et al. (1996, Chapter 6) who apply the concept to cost-benefit analysis, and Manning et al. (1996) and Drummond et al. (1997) who discuss sensitivity analysis in the context of health care evaluations. One-way and multiway sensitivity analyses are essential ingredients of any cost-effectiveness analysis. In addition to these basic methods, there are many other approaches of escalating complexity. A detailed examination would take us too far afield. However, we will briefly describe a few of these and provide some additional references to the literature.

Decision Trees and Expected Value Analysis

In some cases, we may have a fairly well-defined notion of just how certain or uncertain a particular outcome may be—that is, whether it has a example, dividing the low estimate of effectiveness by the high cost estimate suggests that consumption is reduced by only 7 kilograms for a cost of a million dollars. By using a higher estimate of effectiveness, the effectiveness-cost ratio increases to 26. Table 6.6 suggests that enormous uncertainty exists as to the cost-effectiveness of school-based drug prevention.

Table 6.7 compares school-based prevention programs to other alternatives for reducing drug consumption. In this case, the high cost estimate is used, in concert with the low, middle, and high estimates of effectiveness. Among four alternatives for the reduction of drug use, effectiveness-cost ratios vary widely depending on the assumptions about program effectiveness. For example, the effectiveness-cost ratios of increased federal enforcement range from 35 to 158, depending on the assumptions about effectiveness. The results make it difficult to provide sound advice about the most cost-effective strategies for reducing drug consumption. Given these disheartening results—and the urgent need to formulate cost-effective drug prevention policies—the authors note that "there may be substantial returns (in terms of reducing uncertainty about prevention's effectiveness) to allocating dollars to funding [additional] studies" (p. 56).

SOURCE: Caulkins et al. (1999), pp. 51-56.

high probability of occurring or a low probability. For example, let's say that we must choose between two alternatives, A and B. Alternative B will yield a monetary gain of $500, with absolute certainty. In contrast, the outcomes of Alternative A are subject to uncertainty. There is an 80% chance (or a probability of 0.80) that we will gain $1,000. Yet, there is a 20% chance that we will incur a loss of $1,000. How can we use our knowledge of uncertainty to choose between Alternatives A and B?

A quite powerful tool for doing so is called the decision tree. In Figure 6.2, we use a decision tree to illustrate the simple example from the preceding paragraph. On the left side of the figure, there is a square box, referred to as a "decision node." At decision nodes, the decision maker must choose among the available options—in this case, Alternatives A and B. If Alternative B is chosen, the lower branch leads directly to a payoff of $500. If Alternative A is chosen, there is some uncertainty as to the payoff. The

TABLE 6.6 Effectiveness–Cost Ratios of School-Based Drug Prevention Programs

| | Kilograms of Cocaine Assumption Averted Per Million Dollars Spent on School-Based Prevention | | |
	Low Estimate of Effectiveness	Middle Estimate of Effectiveness	High Estimate of Effectiveness
High estimate of costs	7	26	60
Middle estimate of costs	15	56	131
Low estimate of costs	521	1945	4550

SOURCE: Caulkins et al. (1999, Table 3.3).

TABLE 6.7 Effectiveness–Cost Ratios of Four Alternatives for Reducing Drug Consumption

| Alternative for Prevention of Drug Use | Kilograms of Cocaine Assumption Averted Per Million Dollars Spent on Four Alternatives | | |
	Low Estimate of Effectiveness	Middle Estimate of Effectiveness	High Estimate of Effectiveness
School-based prevention	7	26	60
Mandatory minimum sentences	17	36	75
Increased federal enforcement	35	63	158
Treating heavy users	90	104	147

SOURCE: Caulkins et al. (1999, Table 3.4).

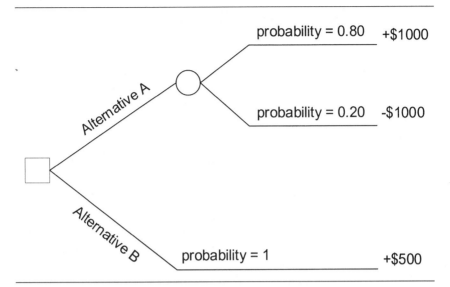

FIGURE 6.2. A Simple Decision Tree

small circle—a "chance node"—indicates that there are two possible outcomes of choosing Alternative A. A $1,000 gain will occur with a probability of 0.80 and a $1,000 loss with a probability of 0.20.

We must next calculate the expected value of Alternative A. To do so, each uncertain payoff is weighted by its respective probability, and the results are summed. Thus, the expected value of Alternative A is given by:

$$0.80 \times (+1,000) + 0.20 \times (-1,000)$$
$$= 800 - 200$$
$$= 600$$

Using this criterion, it appears that Alternative A is somewhat more attractive than the option of receiving $500 with certainty (if one is "risk neutral").

Decision trees can be enormously helpful in simplifying the decision-making process. First, they are useful frameworks for clarifying the fundamental decisions that confront individuals. Second, they can assist in choosing among alternatives that incorporate an often bewildering array of uncertainties. For a more detailed exposition of decision trees and their

EXAMPLE 6.5. Using Decision Trees in Cost-Effectiveness Analysis

You are the superintendent of a large urban school district in which the rates of high school dropouts are particularly severe.[16] Within the next year, the district has decided to implement a program to improve the situation, although a specific strategy has yet to be established. There are two main options. During the preceding year, Program A was implemented in a neighboring district with a fair degree of success. An experimental evaluation showed that it prevented 95 students from dropping out of high school, and cost about $100,000. Through a cooperative agreement with that district, many of your district's teachers were familiarized with the program and view it in a positive light. You are reasonably confident that these results can be duplicated in your district because of the similar demographics and favorable attitudes of key stakeholders.

A local university is currently promoting an innovative strategy to prevent dropouts (Program B). A cost analysis revealed that the program would cost the same as Program A ($100,000). There is, however, great uncertainty as to the effects that it might produce. A careful evaluation that was conducted in another state suggests that it may reduce dropouts by as many as 170, although that district was rural and poor, whereas the present one is urban and middle-class. After consultations with numerous experts and district personnel, you feel that Program B might produce one of three outcomes: (1) the program will be completely successful, reducing dropouts by 170; (2) the program will be partially successful, reducing dropouts by 75; and (3) the program will be marginally successful, reducing dropouts by 5. Furthermore, you have estimated the probabilities of each of these outcomes occurring at approximately 0.15, 0.60, and 0.25, respectively. These subjective probabilities were derived from discussions with the program designers, teachers, guidance counselors, and other school personnel. How can we use this information to choose between Programs A and B?

potential applications, see Boardman et al. (1996), Clemen (1996), or Stokey and Zeckhauser (1978). As one might imagine, decision trees are commonly used in health care evaluations to account for the uncertain outcomes that are inherent features of medical treatments (Drummond et al., 1997; Keeler, 1995).

Of course, the outcomes of educational programs are probably subject to no less uncertainty; nevertheless, it is rare to find decision trees used in educational program evaluations or cost analyses. Example 6.5 provides a

EXAMPLE 6.5. continued

The first step would be to summarize the available information in a decision tree, following the procedure described in the text (see Figure 6.3). In this case, we must choose between Programs A and B, each incurring the same cost of $100,000. If we were to choose Program A, it would lead to a reduction in dropouts of 95 with a high degree of certainty and a cost-effectiveness ratio of $1,053 (100,000 ÷ 95). Of course, we are never completely "certain" of educational outcomes in an educational program. We might decide that there is a small risk that Program A will fail to have its intended effects. By quantifying this smaller outcome and its probability of occurring, we could expand the lower branch of the decision tree in Figure 6.3, although we have chosen not to do so in this simple example.

In the case of Program B, we need to calculate the expected value by calculating the sum of the three outcomes, after weighting them by their probabilities of occurring:

$$0.15 \times 170 + 0.60 \times 75 + 0.25 \times 5 = 71.8$$

Given the expected value of 71.8, the cost-effectiveness ratio for Program B is $1,394 (100,000 ÷ 71.8). Program A's cost-effectiveness ratio is smaller than Program B's by more than $300, suggesting that it will require fewer resources per dropout averted. Of course, there is a possibility that Program B will yield spectacular outcomes (and a greater level of cost-effectiveness), but this is balanced by an important chance of failure. We may wish to probe how sensitive these conclusions are to the probabilities and outcomes that we have chosen (e.g., a worse outcome for Program A or a lower probability that Program B will produce the lowest outcome).

hypothetical example of how a decision tree might be incorporated into an educational cost-effectiveness analysis.

Other Methods

Scholars have developed a number of additional approaches to dealing with uncertainty. One of these is referred to as Monte Carlo sensitivity

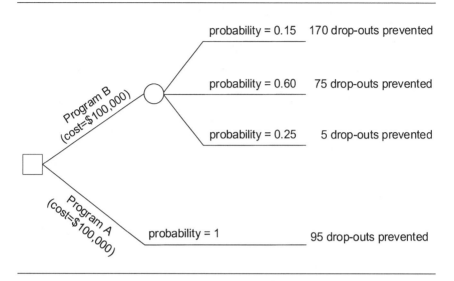

FIGURE 6.3. A Hypothetical Decision Tree for Drop-Out Prevention Programs

analysis. In a standard sensitivity analysis, we generally specify low, middle, and high estimates for an uncertain parameter. However, this may not accurately reflect the nature of the uncertainty. For example, perhaps the parameter is distributed according to a bell-shaped curve. In this scenario, the middle estimate is most likely to occur, while the low and high values are much less likely to occur.

In a Monte Carlo analysis, the evaluator specifies a statistical distribution for each parameter that is judged to be uncertain. Then, he or she takes a random draw from each parameter distribution. The resulting values can be used to construct a cost-effectiveness ratio, after which the same procedure is repeated. This yields many different estimates of the cost-effectiveness ratio. If the distribution of these ratios is tightly clustered around a single value, then it would appear that uncertainty does not greatly alter the conclusions about the true value of the cost-effectiveness ratio. If the distribution is spread rather widely, then it suggests that conclusions are less robust to uncertainty. With the advent of computer spreadsheets, it has become much easier for evaluators to conduct their own Monte Carlo sensitivity analyses. For details on this, as well as a more thorough description of the general method, see Boardman et al. (1996) or Chapter 11 in Clemen (1996).

A statistical approach to dealing with uncertainty has been developed and applied mainly by health care economists. The general aim of the method is to construct a statistical confidence interval around each cost-effectiveness ratio, with the interval denoting a likely range for the true value of the ratio. Then, through hypothesis testing, one can assess whether observed differences among various cost-effectiveness ratios are statistically significant. In general, the data requirements for these methods are quite exacting, because one must possess cost data that are stochastic rather than deterministic. That is, both cost and effectiveness data must be derived from a sample of individuals or sites rather than from a single estimate of the evaluator. For further details on these methods, see Chaudhary and Stearns (1996); Laska, Meisner, and Siegel (1997); Drummond et al. (1997, pp. 251-255); or Manning et al. (1996).

Summary

This chapter reviewed the main issues associated with defining measures of effectiveness, assessing the relative effectiveness of alternatives, and combining that information with costs. Each of these areas has its own literature—to which we provided some citations that should be pursued for further details. We placed particular emphasis on several issues that are often overlooked in CE analyses. First, it is important that the evaluation examine whether effects are unevenly distributed across groups of individuals, which can have important implications for the cost-effectiveness rankings. Second, effects should be discounted along with costs if the project lasts for more than a single year. Third, the final cost-effectiveness ratios should be subjected to a thorough sensitivity analysis before firm conclusions are drawn about investment priorities.

RECOMMENDATIONS FOR FURTHER READING ◀

The literature on educational evaluation and research design is vast, but most authors concentrate on the estimation of effectiveness. General references in this area include Light et al. (1990), Rossi and Freeman (1993), Smith and Glass (1987), Weiss (1998), and the classic works by Campbell and Stanley (1966) and Cook and Campbell (1979). Two recent volumes focus exclusively on evaluating effectiveness through the design and conduct of randomized experiments, citing many examples of social program evaluation (Boruch, 1997; Orr, 1999). In general, the prior references contain only a chapter or passing reference to cost analysis.

For specific advice on cost-effectiveness analysis, the reader may wish to explore the extensive literature in health. The textbook by Drummond et al. (1997) is easily accessible to a wide audience. They provide many references to the applied health literature. More advanced sources include the textbook by Johannesson (1996) and the edited volumes by Gold et al. (1996) and Sloan (1995).

Exercises

1. Select an evaluation of effectiveness with which you are familiar. Describe the problem that was addressed and the alternatives that were considered. What measures of effectiveness were used and why? Describe the evaluation design that was employed. Do you feel that the results have a high degree of internal validity? How would you do a study of costs to convert the evaluation into a cost-effectiveness analysis?

2. In the evaluation that you reviewed in the previous exercise, can you think of other dimensions of effectiveness that might have been considered? How would you add these dimensions to the overall design?

3. A school district is concerned about its shortages of mathematics and science teachers. An advisory group suggests the following alternative solutions to the problem.

a. Pay salary differentials to attract more mathematics and science teachers.

b. Ask local industry to contribute teaching time from among their scientists and mathematicians.

c. Use computer-assisted instruction and videocassettes, in conjunction with college mathematics and science students, to offer instruction.

You are asked to design a cost analysis that can evaluate these alternatives and select the one that will be most preferable for the district.

4. A school superintendent comes across an article on meta-analysis of school interventions where effect sizes are given for a wide range of interventions (e.g., Walberg, 1984). She asks that you calculate the costs of each of the interventions and do a cost-effectiveness analysis of them. In clear terms, what would you tell her about the usefulness of this approach?

5. You are faced with two alternatives for reducing first-year dropouts in a university. The first alternative is based upon the establishment of a learning community in which students work in cohorts and take similar courses. Instructors also work together to integrate learning among the courses. Students are provided with social and support activities as well as group counseling to make them feel a part of a larger community that cares about them. This program has already been tried on a pilot basis in the university and has yielded good results. However, there is a significant group of faculty that has suggested matching upper-level students with freshman so that each has a "buddy" to provide assistance and friendship. Results at another institution show even better results in terms of reducing freshman dropouts. How would you do a cost-effectiveness study? Which course of action would you recommend to the university if the second program were calculated to be 10% more cost-effective than the first program?

NOTES ◀

1. See Drummond, O'Brien, Stoddart, and Torrance (1997), who also cite this example, and the discussion therein.

2. We have relied on the extremely clear discussion by Smith and Glass (1987).

3. Of course, there are more sophisticated approaches than simply comparing outcomes at two discrete moments in time. For example, one might collect data at numerous points before and after a particular intervention. In this way, one can get a sense of trends in outcomes due to "history" that are independent of the intervention.

4. Correlational studies are referred to by many other terms, including nonexperimental, statistical, ex post facto, and causal comparative.

5. Obviously the groups will not be exactly equivalent. They may exhibit some differences in income, ability, or other characteristics due to statistical sampling. That is, chance may lead to some slight differences in individuals in the treatment or control groups. Nevertheless, the tools of statistics allow us to gauge the likelihood that such differences are due to chance or the concrete effects of the treatment.

6. See Weiss (1998).

7. Coleman, Hoffer, and Kilgore (1982) carried out the first study. Much of the later analysis and reanalysis is summarized in reviews by Witte (1992, 1996). For a methodological review, see Murnane, Newstead, and Olsen (1985).

8. The classic reference on selection bias is Heckman (1979). For other discussions, see Maddala (1983), Greene (1997), and Wooldridge (2000). For a discussion specifically aimed at the evaluation of medical treatments and procedures, see Mullahy and Manning (1995).

9. One critique of Hanushek's analysis is that the studies he reviewed did not have direct measures of class size but only of the pupil-teacher ratio. This ratio can differ significantly from class size. For example, the pupil-teacher ratio may include full-time substitute teachers, teachers of very small special education classes, teachers on pregnancy or sick leave, teachers assigned to other duties, and so on. These situations vary considerably from school to school, making the pupil-teacher ratio a poor indicator of class size.

10. For a good review of the methodological literature on meta-analysis, see Cooper and Lindsay (1998).

11. Focusing on the health field, Saint, Veenstra, and Sullivan (1999) also argues that studies to be included in meta-analyses (and later used in CE analyses) should be as homogeneous as possible.

12. See Drummond et al. (1997, pp. 107-108), Lipscomb, Weinstein, and Torrance (1996, pp. 222-230), and the citations therein.

13. Weinstein and Stason (1977) further demonstrate this with a variety of numerical examples. Also see Keeler and Cretin (1983) and the discussions in Drummond et al. (1997) and Lipscomb et al. (1996).

14. See Ribich (1968) and Weisbrod (1965). A comprehensive discussion of distributional weighting in cost-benefit analysis is provided in Chapter 14 of Boardman, Greenberg, Vining, and Weimer (1996).

15. See Boardman et al. (1996, pp. 397-398) for a similar discussion.

16. We are grateful to Daniel Sheinberg for suggesting this example.

CHAPTER 7

Cost-Benefit Analysis

OBJECTIVES

1. Address the conceptual underpinnings of cost-benefit analysis.
2. Discuss three general methods of estimating the monetary benefits of alternatives.
3. Emphasize the importance of analyzing the distribution of benefits among individuals.
4. Present three measures used to assess project worth by combining costs and benefits.

The outcomes of education can sometimes be expressed in money terms. Does a particular kind of vocational training tend to raise the wages of participating workers? Does early childhood education reduce the likelihood that individuals will eventually commit crimes as adults (thereby reducing the costs of crime)? In these and other cases, cost-benefit analysis can be used to compare monetary estimates of benefits and costs.

The technique allows us to determine whether the benefits of a given alternative outweigh the costs and thus whether the alternative is worthwhile in an absolute sense. It also allows us to compare several alternatives and choose that which provides the greatest amount of benefits relative to its costs. As long as the outcomes can be expressed in monetary terms, the alternatives do not necessarily have to share the same objective. For example, we could compare the net benefits (that is, benefits minus costs) of a primary education project, a public health campaign, and a rural electrification project. In this respect, cost-benefit analysis is distinct from a cost-effectiveness analysis, which compares two or more alternatives that necessarily share the same objectives and measures of effectiveness.

This chapter proceeds in several steps. It first describes the concept of willingness to pay, a key economic concept that organizes our thinking about the meaning of benefits and how we should go about measuring them. Given this foundation, we describe three general methods that have been utilized to place monetary values on benefits: traditional experiments, quasi-experiments, and correlational studies; contingent valuation; and methods that rely upon the observed behavior of individuals. The discussion is illustrated with several examples from education. Finally, we present three methods of combining costs and benefits to make decisions; these include the benefit-cost ratio, net present value, and the internal rate of return.

The Concept of Benefits

Some benefits of education lend themselves to being expressed in units of currency, such as higher earnings. Other benefits are harder to place in money terms, such as the increased self-esteem or happiness produced by higher achievement. At least conceptually, however, economists would use a similar approach in placing monetary values on these outcomes. They would attempt to determine the maximum amount that each individual affected by a program would be willing to pay to receive desirable outcomes. The sum of every individual's maximum willingness to pay provides an estimate of the total benefits. (Despite our casual use of the term "willingness," it does not necessarily imply that individuals have paid that amount or will be required to pay it.[1])

The notion of willingness to pay is best explained with an example. Suppose that the government funded a literacy program that succeeded in improving the reading ability of a small group of adults. The participants reap a broad range of "benefits" from participating in the program that are probably greater than $1 and less than $1 billion. To narrow the range, we require a means of structuring our thinking about the nature of benefits.

Let us assume that each individual derives increasing amounts of utility (or satisfaction) from two things: income (*y*) and literacy (*l*).[2] Each participant in the hypothetical program began with a certain amount of each at time 0, which produced an initial level of utility:[3]

$$u = u\ (y_0\ ,\ l_0)$$

Upon program completion, the new (and higher) level of literacy is l_1, which leads to an even higher level of utility. To place a monetary value on the literacy gains, we could ask each individual to conduct a simple thought experiment. In the wake of the program—and the literacy gains that it brings about—how much income must individuals sacrifice in order to return to the *initial* level of utility? This allows each individual to attach a specific money valuation to the literacy outcomes that they received. The amount is referred to as that individual's willingness to pay (*WTP*) for literacy (more technical discussions in welfare economics refer to it as the "compensating variation").[4] The same idea is expressed by the following equality:

$$u(y_0,\ l_0) = u(y_1 - WTP,\ l_1)$$

The left-hand side indicates the amount of utility produced by initial levels of literacy and income. Utility on the right-hand side is the same—despite a higher level of literacy—because income is reduced by the amount *WTP*. Again, the amount represents an individual's willingness to pay for added literacy, based on a personal valuation of literacy benefits. By summing the maximum *WTP* of each individual affected by the program, we arrive at the total program benefits.

Figure 7.1 gives a visual depiction of one individual's willingness to pay for increasing amounts of literacy. It is a demand curve for literacy that traces how the quantity demanded increases as the price declines. Economists refer to it as a utility-compensated demand curve, because the initial level of utility is held constant at all points on the curve.[5] As the quantity of literacy increases—leading to increased utility—a downward adjustment to money income is made "behind the scenes" in order to preserve the initial level of utility.

In our hypothetical example, the true price of literacy is fixed at zero because program participants do not pay a fee. Nevertheless, the curve still

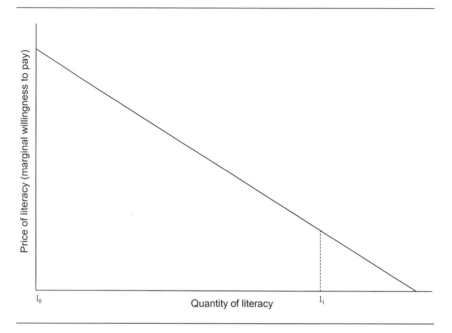

FIGURE 7.1. An Individual's Willingness to Pay for Literacy

provides an estimate of the individual's willingness to pay for different quantities of literacy and, hence, the benefits received. In this case, the program increases the individual's literacy from l_0 to l_1, and the willingness to pay for this outcome is given by the area underneath the demand curve, between l_0 and l_1. The area is equivalent to *WTP* in the previous equation. As before, the willingness-to-pay estimates for each person affected by the program are summed to arrive at a measure of total program benefits.

The concept of willingness to pay is a powerful one for at least two reasons. First, it does not place undue restrictions on the categories of benefits that we might consider. As we shall see, many cost-benefit analyses focus narrowly on earnings as the only measure of educational benefits. The previous discussion should make it clear, however, that better earnings are just one reason (albeit an important one) that individuals might evince a willingness to pay. By neglecting other outcomes, the benefits could be severely understated. Thus, the conceptual framework serves as a constant reminder that we should cast the widest possible net when delineating and measuring program benefits.

Second, the conceptual framework encompasses the benefits received by every individual who is directly or indirectly affected by the program or alternative under consideration, and not just those who are its immediate targets.[6] The goal is to obtain a broad estimate of the benefits that accrue to program participants as well as to other members of society (the benefits to those outside the program are often referred to as "externalities" by economists). In this respect, it parallels our discussion of costs in Chapters 3 through 5, where we emphasized the importance of measuring the costs to all groups of stakeholders in society, ranging from program participants to the government.

As one might imagine, the conceptual framework is almost never fully implemented. In an ideal world, we could costlessly obtain accurate information on each individual's maximum willingness to pay for valuable outcomes. In practice, demand curves such as those in Figure 7.1 are not readily available, because of data limitations or simply because many goods and services never pass through markets that would allow prices to be attached to them. Therefore, evaluators rely upon several practical alternatives to obtain estimates of program benefits. The next section describes several of these. When considering these methods and their applications in education, it is always helpful to keep the prior conceptual framework in mind. As one observer notes, "all . . . methods of valuing benefits in monetary terms are to be judged in terms of the closeness with which they approximate [willingness to pay]" (Pauly, 1995, p. 103).

Methods of Valuing Benefits

This section describes three approaches to placing monetary values on program outcomes.[7] The first relies on the evaluation designs that were introduced in Chapter 6. The additional benefits of an alternative—such as increased earnings—are estimated via experimental, quasi-experimental, or correlational evaluation designs. It is, by far, the most frequently used approach in educational cost-benefit analyses. Nevertheless, two other approaches hold great promise. The second, referred to as the contingent valuation approach, employs direct surveys of individuals to elicit their willingness to pay for outcomes. The third, referred to as the observed behavior approach, ascertains the willingness to pay of individuals based upon the economic decisions they are observed to make in the marketplace, rather than their stated opinions.

Experiments, Quasi-Experiments, and Correlational Evaluations

The vast majority of cost-benefit studies in education utilize one of the evaluation designs discussed in Chapter 6. To briefly reiterate, each design relies upon a comparison of outcomes between treatment and comparison groups. A key difference is the degree of control exercised by the evaluator over which individuals are assigned to each group. Experiments call for individuals to be randomly assigned to each group and, in doing so, provide assurance that subsequent differences in outcomes are not attributable to preexisting group differences. Quasi-experimental designs provide the evaluator with some control over group assignment that, nonetheless, does not extend to randomized assignment. In correlational designs, the evaluator exercises no control over group assignment and relies on statistical methods to control for group differences.

Cost-benefit evaluations usually focus on outcome measures that are easily expressed in units of currency, such as individual earnings. For example, did participation in a vocational training program increase the earnings of workers? Did students who attended schools with lower class sizes tend to receive higher earnings once they entered the labor market? Did children who received a preschool education eventually obtain higher earnings?

However, earnings are by no means the only (or even the most important) component of benefits. There are a wide range of additional benefits that education may confer upon individuals or society, although this will vary according to the educational alternative that is being considered. Individuals could derive an increased ability to enjoy literature and the arts, an improved sense of self-worth, or any number of intangible and hard-to-measure benefits (note that a perfect measure of willingness to pay should encompass all these benefits). Even individuals who are not direct targets of educational programs—often referred to as "society" or the "taxpayers"—could be indirect recipients of program benefits. For example, an educational program may reduce the likelihood that its participants commit crimes or receive welfare services. Both of these yield benefits, or reduced costs, for other members of society. As mentioned above, these benefits are referred to as externalities (Wolfe, 1995).

Experiments and Quasi-Experiments

Randomized experiments are an increasingly common feature of cost-benefit studies. They have been particularly helpful in evaluating programs that are specifically aimed at increasing earnings, such as employment and training programs. One of the largest examples to date is the experimental evaluation of the Job Training Partnership Act (JTPA) between 1987 and 1992. Over 20,000 potential job-training participants were randomly assigned to either receive training or serve as a control group. The earnings of each group were charted over a period of 30 months following the training. A comparison of earnings across treatment and control groups showed that adults received increased earnings from training, but that youth did not (Orr et al., 1996). For a summary of evaluations of JTPA and other employment and training programs, see Orr (1999) or Chapter 9 in Boardman, Greenberg, Vining, and Weimer (1996).

Cost-benefit analyses of JTPA and other training programs are usually based on a version of the framework in Table 7.1, taken from Orr (1999). The main benefit of training is the possible earnings gains to participants. Other benefits are produced because individuals may require fewer government-provided services (e.g., public assistance and criminal justice involvement) as a result of their job training. These benefits (or averted costs) are received by taxpayers and other members of society.

In some cases, training may reduce the reliance of individuals on state-provided welfare programs. Savings on welfare payments represent a benefit for society that is, nonetheless, offset by the cost to program participants of lost welfare payments. Similarly, a training program may provide subsidized wages to participants, which are funded by tax payments of other members of society. Both welfare and wage subsidies represent instances of transfer payments. A benefit to one group in society is balanced by a cost to another group. By ignoring the benefits or costs that are due to one group of stakeholders, we may derive misleading estimates of net benefits. Finally, program costs include the direct costs of operating the training program. As the ingredients method dictates, costs should also include the value of previous leisure and home time that is now devoted to work.

TABLE 7.1 Conceptual Framework for Cost–Benefit Analysis of Employment and Training Programs

	Benefits (+) and Costs (–) From the Perspective of:		
	Program Participants	*Other Members of Society*	*Total*
Benefits			
Earnings gains	+	0	+
Reduced costs of nonexperimental services	0	+	+
Transfers			
Reduced welfare benefits	–	+	0
Wage subsidies	+	–	0
Costs			
Operational program costs	0	–	–
Foregone leisure and home production	–	0	–
Net benefits	+/–	+/–	+/–

SOURCE: Orr (1999, p. 224).

Experiments are not limited to employment and training programs. One of the most well-known educational experiments is the Perry Preschool Project, in which a group of low-income children were randomly assigned to participate in a compensatory preschool program or in a control group that received no treatment. The children were followed into their early adulthood, allowing for a long-term assessment of program effects on many outcomes. A series of cost-benefit analyses by Steven Barnett expressed many of these outcomes in monetary terms.[8] Though wages are one category of benefits, several others were considered, such as the possible cost savings resulting from the reduced propensity of treated children to commit crimes as young adults. The principal methods and findings of this experiment are presented in Example 7.1.

Most educational experiments face time and resource constraints that limit the number of follow-ups that can be conducted with the individuals in treatment and control groups. In the JTPA evaluations, earnings were measured for 30 months after the training. In the Perry Preschool Program, follow-ups are ongoing even almost 30 years later. However, we often do not have the luxury of following individuals for a long period, even if many of the benefits of a program occur many years after it is completed. If these benefits are ignored, then we risk understating the overall benefits.

The usual solution is to use early measures of benefits to obtain projections of benefits over the entire lives of participants. For further details, see Orr (1999) and Barnett (1996). Even so, there is no perfect solution to this dilemma and the results will rest to some degree upon assumptions of the evaluator regarding the lifetime rate of growth or decline of earnings and other outcomes. In these cases, it is important to conduct sensitivity analysis in order to determine whether the key findings are robust to the use of alternative assumptions. For example, Barnett (1996) separately presents benefits that were calculated from measured observations of participants and nonparticipants and those that were projected (see Example 7.1).

Correlational Studies

Beginning with the Coleman Report in the 1960s, hundreds of studies have used nonexperimental data to search for causal links between school resources and student outcomes such as achievement. We reviewed some of the limitations of these studies in Chapter 6. Increasingly, researchers are using a similar approach to explore the links between school resources and longer-term outcomes such as success in the labor market. For example, do students who attend elementary and secondary schools with higher per-pupil expenditures eventually receive higher earnings in the labor market? Although not all authors have explicitly done so, the results of these studies can be incorporated in a cost-benefit analysis that weighs the costs of increased expenditures against the benefits of increased earnings.[9]

In a widely cited study, Card and Krueger (1992) purport to find a positive association between school resources such as class size and teacher sal-

EXAMPLE 7.1. A Cost-Benefit Analysis of the Perry Preschool Program

The Perry Preschool Program was designed to provide high-quality preschool services to children in at-risk situations. It included several components, including 2-hour classes on weekday mornings—with student-teacher ratios of around 6 to 1—and weekly 90-minute home visits by teachers. Over the course of the project, the curriculum varied between a traditional nursery school environment to a Piagetian approach.

The initial study included 128 African American students (born between 1958 and 1962) and their parents, all with relatively low incomes. Over the course of the study, attrition from the sample was quite low. The students were randomly assigned to either receive the preschool treatment or to serve in a control group. Following the treatment, follow-up surveys were conducted with individuals at several points, the latest at the age of 27. These data consistently showed significant advantages for the treatment group on a wide range of outcome measures, including test scores, earnings, arrest rates, and welfare participation. Because of the experimental design and low rates of attrition, estimates of effectiveness possess a high degree of internal validity.

A comprehensive cost analysis was completed, results of which were summarized in previous chapters (see Examples 3.2 and 4.2). Benefits were estimated by converting measured project effects into monetary terms. These benefits fall into seven categories, which are received by both program participants and other members of society (see Table 7.2). First, the project provided child care benefits to participating families, who otherwise would have had to pay for these services on the open market. Second, the project improved the later performance of children in K-12 education. This led to fewer children requiring special educational services or other costly interventions, which produced benefits (or averted costs) for taxpayers who did not have to fund these services. Third, the project participants had lower rates of participation in adult education

aries and later student earnings. In a later review article, the same authors conclude that "a 10% increase in school spending is associated with a 1% to 2% increase in annual earnings for students later in their lives" (Card & Krueger, 1996, p. 133). Nevertheless, the empirical studies and reviews of other authors have cast some doubt on these conclusions (Betts, 1996; Heckman, Layne-Farrar, & Todd, 1996). Much of the disagreement stems from the uncertainty that is inherent in causal estimates derived from the

EXAMPLE 7.1. continued

services such as high school equivalency (GED) examination preparation courses, which produced a small amount of benefits for taxpayers.

Fourth, the project increased rates of college attendance, which produced slight increases in costs to taxpayers (but, as we will observe, this was offset by higher earnings and other benefits). Fifth, the project led to increased earnings and fringe benefits for participants; these benefits were extended to other members of society in the form of higher tax payments. Sixth, the project yielded lower rates of crime and delinquency among participants. When possible, the monetary savings to society of reduced crime were estimated, and they turned out to be substantial. Seventh, the project lowered the rates of welfare assistance among participants. This represented a cost to participants in the form of lost payments but a gain to taxpayers. It is a good example of a transfer payment that simply shifts resources from one group to another. On the whole, however, slight cost savings were produced in the form of reduced administrative costs for the welfare system.

The most recent analysis provides data until the age of 27 for each child, and benefits were initially estimated just for this period (Barnett, 1996). Nevertheless, further benefits may exist over the entire lifetime of participants in the form of additional earnings, fewer crimes committed, and reduced welfare participation. These benefits were estimated separately using several projections that introduce additional uncertainty into the analysis. Even when projected benefits are excluded, however, the net benefits of the project—discounted benefits minus discounted costs—are positive. This suggests that the project was a desirable investment, both from the perspective of its participants and the rest of society.

SOURCE: Barnett (1985b, 1993, 1996).

correlational design. A natural way of resolving this uncertainty would be to randomly assign one group of individuals to receive higher-quality schooling and another to receive lower-quality schooling. After waiting a number of years, a comparison of their earnings would provide a clear measure of benefits. For obvious moral and practical reasons, experiments of this sort do not occur.

TABLE 7.2 Costs, Benefits, and Net Benefits of the Perry Preschool Program

	Estimated Benefits and Costs Per Program Participant (present value of 1992 dollars, 3% discount rate)		
	For Participant Only	*For General Public (taxpayers/crime victims)*	*Total (for society as a whole)*
Preschool cost	0	-12,356	-12,356
Measured preschool benefits			
Child care	738	0	738
K-12 education	0	6,872	6,872
Adult education	0	283	283
College	0	-868	-868
Earnings	10,270	4,228	14,498
Crime	0	49,044	49,044
Welfare	-2,193	2,412	219
Total measured benefits	8,815	61,972	70,786
Projected preschool benefits			
Earnings	11,215	4,618	15,833
Crime	0	21,337	21,337
Welfare	-460	506	46
Total projected benefits	10,755	26,461	37,216
Net benefits (measured and projected benefits minus costs)	19,570	76,077	95,646

SOURCE: Barnett (1996, Table 28).

Contingent Valuation

To obtain estimates of difficult-to-measure benefits, researchers are increasingly using a method called contingent valuation. Based on the conceptual framework outlined at the beginning of the chapter, it calls upon individuals to honestly assess their maximum willingness to pay for outcomes. For example, how much is it worth to preserve the scenic view of a forest or prevent a species of animal from going extinct? How much is it worth to provide quality educational services to the severely disabled? These are important benefits which should not be ignored when attempting to define investment priorities for society, even though they are difficult to monetize.[10]

In practice, we are unable to peer into each individual's mind and accurately determine their willingness to pay for a benefit such as increased literacy or better water quality. Contingent valuation relies upon direct surveys to elicit willingness-to-pay estimates from individuals. The method has mainly been applied in valuing environmental benefits such as pollution reduction and habitat conservation. To our knowledge, the method has been applied only once in education (Escobar, Barnett, & Keith, 1988). A brief overview of that study is provided in Example 7.2.

There are many approaches to contingent valuation, which, nonetheless, share several characteristics (Boardman et al., 1996).[11] First, the researcher defines an appropriate sample of individuals to survey about their willingness to pay and applies a questionnaire or survey instrument of some kind. Second, this information is used to calculate willingness-to-pay estimates for each individual. Third, the individual responses are used to estimate the benefits for the entire population of individuals that is affected by the policy or program.

Boardman et al. (1996) provide an excellent overview of several methods used to survey individuals. First, the open-ended method simply asks individuals to state their maximum willingness to pay for whatever good is being valued. Second, the closed-ended iterative-bidding method asks individuals whether they would be willing to pay a specified amount for a particular good. If they answer affirmatively, the amounts are gradually increased and the question repeated. This continues until the answer is negative. Third, a series of "payment cards" of different amounts are presented to individuals, and they are asked to select the card with the maxi-

EXAMPLE 7.2. Using Contingent Valuation to Measure the Benefits of Preschool for Disabled Children

The benefits of educational programs for disabled children may be substantial, but they are often difficult to measure. Many of the benefits are simply intangible, and others are difficult to assess with existing test instruments. Contingent valuation provides an alternative method of assessing the monetary benefits of such programs. By administering direct surveys to parents of disabled children, one can ascertain the willingness to pay of parents for preschool services.

The authors conducted 80 interviews with parents whose children experienced a wide range of disabilities, from mild to quite severe. Parents were reminded that no tuition would be charged and that educational services were guaranteed for their child. They were then asked the maximum amount that they would be willing to pay to have their child attend the preschool program. Respondents were asked to indicate one value in a range of indicated values, from $0 to $10,000; higher answers were also permitted.

The mean values of their estimates are presented in Table 7.3. In general, parents whose children have more severe disabilities evinced a higher willingness to pay for preschool services. The authors note that these estimates may not measure the full benefits of preschool services. For example, early childhood education could reduce elementary or secondary school expenditures on special education for the same children. This represents a benefit (or cost savings) for other members of society that is not fully captured by individual estimates of willingness to pay.

_____

SOURCE: Escobar et al. (1988).

mum value that they would be willing to pay for a good. Several other methods of escalating complexity are also available.

A vast literature has explored the possible biases in the estimates of benefits produced by these methods. We describe five of the biases outlined by Boardman et al. (1996, pp. 352-366). The following list is by no means exhaustive. First, it is challenging in surveys to properly convey the exact nature of the good or service that individuals are being asked to evaluate. When individuals are asked to place hypothetical values on goods that they do not fully understand, the results may not be valid. Second, it is possible

TABLE 7.3 Willingness to Pay for Preschool Services

Child's Disability	Mean Annual Willingness to Pay for Preschool Services	Number of Children
Sensory impaired	$1,396	12
Severe/profound	$ 770	5
Mentally retarded	$ 554	37
Mild	$ 181	26
All conditions	$ 573	80

SOURCE: Escobar et al. (1988).

that the description of the good or service in the survey instrument is not a neutral one, and it conveys a positive or negative attitude to the respondent. Thus, individuals may be swayed to place higher or lower values on it, regardless of their own preferences. Third, it is possible that individuals will exhibit a greater willingness to pay for goods when the economic decisions are not "real." Decisions that are made in the marketplace, rather than the laboratory, might be a more faithful reflection of the resources that individuals are really willing to sacrifice. Fourth, there may be a "starting point" bias in the iterative-bidding method. That is, the final willingness to pay could be influenced by the initial value that is posed by the researcher. Fifth, individuals may act "strategically" in providing answers and misreport their true willingness to pay. For example, they may fear that they will be required to pay for the service, and thus understate their willingness to pay. Or they may overstate their willingness if they feel that such an answer will influence the provision of the good, without affecting what they must pay.

These critiques are not intended to suggest that the method should be discarded. Rather, they emphasize that great care that should be taken in the design of survey instruments and application of the method. The potential for contingent valuation to contribute to educational evaluation is great, especially when used in concert with other methods. As Escobar et al. (1988) observe, the use of multiple methods to estimate benefits will ideally allow researchers to triangulate on a single estimate of benefits with greater confidence. Despite this potential, the method of contingent valuation is almost never applied in education (in health evaluations, however, it is being used with increasing frequency).[12]

Observed Behavior

One drawback of contingent valuation is that we are never completely sure that individuals have given an accurate portrayal of their maximum willingness to pay. Rather than relying on stated opinions, however, we might be able to infer willingness to pay by observing the real economic decisions that individuals make.

Of course, many goods and services are not bought and sold in markets, so we have little hope of directly observing the willingness to pay for these. For example, what are the benefits of a pristine mountain view, uncontaminated by air pollution? Mountain views are not directly purchased and sold in stores. Nevertheless, people *do* pay for things like a view, albeit indirectly. Most individuals are not indifferent between purchasing two homes, otherwise identical, if one has a mountain view and the other abuts a strip mine. If individuals receive benefits from the view, it should be reflected in the higher price they are willing to pay for that home. Presuming that the view is the sole difference between the two homes, the difference in price can be interpreted as the view's implicit price. It also represents an indirect estimate of the monetary benefits derived from the view. There is a large literature that attempts to derive the implicit prices of many goods and services from the observed market behavior of individuals.

An important assumption of this approach to valuing benefits is that individuals are rational and well-informed about the goods and services that they are purchasing. In the previous example, we assume that individuals are well briefed on each home and their respective views. If they are not, the difference in purchase price can hardly be said to faithfully reflect a true willingness to pay.

To further illustrate these ideas, we consider two additional questions that can be addressed in a similar fashion. First, what are the benefits of being able to send one's child to a high-quality public school? Second, is it possible to estimate the value of human life?

The Value of Better Schools

Most CE and CB studies estimate the effects or benefits of schooling with traditional evaluation designs. For example, do schools with higher expenditures tend to raise student test scores or educate students capable of earning higher wages? However, parents may value schools for a wide range of reasons, and an accurate measurement of benefits should reflect that.

Although we do not directly observe willingness to pay for public schools, we may be able to observe it indirectly in home purchase decisions. It is common in the United States for public school attendance to be defined by a zone of residence, or catchment area. It is also common that home purchasers will consider the characteristics of local public schools when deciding to move to an area (indeed, real estate agents frequently boast of school quality in home advertisements). To extend the discussion of the previous section, it is unlikely that a family with children will be indifferent between two identical homes, if one has access to much better public schools. The difference in purchase price between the homes can be interpreted as the implicit price of school quality, and it indicates the family's willingness to pay.

The predominant method of estimating the implicit price is the "hedonic price function."[13] Researchers obtain data on home prices and other variables and estimate a multiple regression of the following form:

$$\text{Home price} = f \text{ (home characteristics, neighborhood characteristics,} \\ \text{public school characteristics)}$$

The intent of the analysis is to hold constant all the relevant determinants of home prices, so that we may observe how home prices are directly affected by additional quantities of one or more school characteristics (e.g., test scores, per-pupil expenditures, and class size) In practice, the results can be misleading if only limited data are available to researchers. For example, the procedure assumes that we are perfectly controlling for *all* relevant determinants of home prices. But perhaps we fail to control for yard size, and it happens that homes in better school districts also have larger yards. We will probably confuse the separate effects of the two variables in raising home prices.

Several researchers have addressed this problem by seeking better data. Instead of comparing prices of homes scattered across a wide geographical area, they directly compare homes on opposite sides of a school attendance boundary. By comparing similar homes in a limited geographic area, we are more confident that differences in home prices are directly influenced by access to different public schools rather than unobserved factors. Two of these studies are briefly described in Example 7.3. For general reviews of this literature, see Black (1998) and Crone (1998).

As with contingent valuation, there is potential to incorporate estimates of monetary benefits from these studies in educational cost-benefit analyses, although progress in this area is limited. For example, Black's (1999) study estimated the implicit price of better schools in the Boston suburbs (see Example 7.3). Although it has not been done, she suggests that her results might be incorporated in a cost-benefit analysis of Boston's Metco program, which provides inner-city children with opportunities to attend outlying suburban schools.

The Value of a Human Life

In economic evaluations of medical treatments, cost-effectiveness analysis is frequently the method of choice. Two treatments might be evaluated according to their effectiveness in saving lives (or reducing the probability of death). The most cost-effective treatment is the one that provides a given reduction in mortality at the least cost. Nevertheless, this does not assist in determining whether a particular treatment is worth implementing in an absolute sense. In other words, do its money benefits outweigh the costs? To proceed would require some method of placing money value on a human life. Although some find this to be a distasteful enterprise, it is an active topic of research (for numerous references to work in this area, see Jones-Lee, 1989; Viscusi, 1992).

Researchers infer the value of a "statistical" life by exploring the revealed preferences of workers for on-the-job risk. If given the choice between two jobs that paid the same wage and were similar in every respect except job safety, most workers would choose the less risky job. In a freely functioning labor market, we might expect a wage premium to be paid to workers in the more dangerous job. The amount of this premium reflects the implicit price of job risk, or the willingness to pay for an increased risk of death. To estimate the implicit price, researchers use a hedonic price function:[14]

EXAMPLE 7.3. How Much Is It Worth to Attend a Good Public School?

A recent study attempted to derive the implicit price of better schools by analyzing over 20,000 home prices in several suburbs of Boston (Black, 1999). Home prices vary for many reasons, including lot size, the size and age of the home, the distance to Boston, and other features of the home and neighborhood. They could also vary because residents are constrained to attend public schools of different qualities. In this study, school quality is measured with average test scores in elementary schools, although the author acknowledges that test scores might serve as a proxy for many features of schools that parents would find desirable.

To gauge the willingness to pay for school quality, a standard approach would simply compare housing prices within the framework of a hedonic price function (see above text). The author improves upon this approach by directly comparing the prices of homes that are on opposite sides of school attendance boundaries. By doing so, the approach holds constant many features of local neighborhoods that could also affect home prices and perhaps interfere with our ability to isolate the implicit price of school quality. For example, homes that are relatively close to one another have similar crime rates and access to amenities such as parks. They are also located in the same city and school district, so tax rates on property and income are the same. Therefore, after controlling for characteristics of specific houses, we are relatively assured that any remaining difference in prices is exclusively due to differences in the quality of public schools.

In fact, the author finds that a 5% increase in average test scores (equivalent to about 1 standard deviation) leads to an increase of $3,948 in the average home price. The results indicate a substantial willingness to pay for higher school quality on the part of residents in suburban Boston.

Another study used a similar approach to assess willingness to pay for public schools in Ohio (Bogart & Cromwell, 1997). The analysis was limited to three geographic areas of greater Cleveland. Each area is composed of two neighborhoods that are both part of the same municipality (such as the city of Cleveland). Due to historical accident, however, the children of each neighborhood are constrained to attend public schools in higher- and lower-quality districts. In each case, the analysis controls for a wide variety of variables that may influence home prices, such as the size and quality of the housing. Even after making these controls, there is still a substantial difference in housing prices across neighborhoods that cannot be explained. The authors attribute this residual to differences in school quality. Nevertheless, they were unable to directly measure school quality, and the unexplained difference in home prices might still be attributed to other neighborhood characteristics that are unobserved.

Wage = f (education and experience, other individual characteristics, risk of fatal injury)

After controlling for other characteristics of workers that might affect wages, such as education, the implicit price of risk is given by the amount that wages increase in response to greater risk of death. Holding all else equal, let us assume that the probability of fatal injury increases slightly, by 1 in 20,000, and that the results of the hedonic wage function imply wages rise by approximately $200 per year. The implied value of a statistical life for these workers is $4 million.[15]

Discounting Benefits

When benefits occur over several years, it is important to properly discount future benefits (at the same rate as costs). One hundred dollars that are received now should be considered relatively more valuable than the same amount received 10 years hence, because they can be invested in the meantime or used to consume other goods and services. The rationale and procedure for discounting are exactly the same as in prior chapters on costs (Chapter 5) and effects (Chapter 6). Thus, we shall not repeat the discussion here, although a numerical example in an upcoming section will reinforce the general idea.

Analyzing the Distribution of Benefits

Also similar to cost-effectiveness analysis is the importance of assessing the distribution of benefits across different groups in society. Groups can be defined quite broadly. Among program participants, for example, we may wish to separately calculate benefits by income level, gender, or race, in order to assess whether one group obtains a larger share of benefits. (In some cases, this is precluded by an already limited sample of individuals in an evaluation. In the Perry Preschool Program, for example, the sample was relatively small and already limited to low-income, minority children.) We can also calculate benefits separately for program participants and for other members of society (the "taxpayers"). As with costs, it is common that benefits received by one group are not the same as benefits received by another group. Example 7.1 provided a concrete illustration of this.

Once benefits are separately estimated for each group, there are three ways to proceed. The first and least attractive option is to simply ignore the distribution of benefits across groups and present the sum of total benefits, even though this limits our understanding of the program. Second, we can separately calculate and present the benefits (and costs) that are received by each group. Individuals who read the evaluation can use this information to form their own opinions about whether the distribution of benefits should figure in judgments about the program desirability. Third, we can multiply each group's benefits by a set of distributional weights before they are summed in an overall measure of benefits, thereby placing greater (or lesser) emphasis on the benefits received or costs borne by certain groups.[16] (Even when doing so, however, it is important to also present the unweighted, baseline estimates.)

Imagine that we are assessing a program for both lower- and middle-income children. The discounted sum of benefits was separately estimated for each group. The benefits for each group are $10,000 and $15,000, respectively. The unweighted sum of benefits is $25,000, which does not treat one group's benefits as more important than the other's. We may decide that benefits accruing to low-income children are one and a half times as important as those received by middle-income children. In this case, total benefits are given by:

$$1.5 \times 10{,}000 + 1 \times 15{,}000 = 30{,}000$$

Our choice of weights in this example was quite arbitrary, although in Chapter 8, we will explore some additional methods for determining these weights.

Combining Costs and Benefits

To make investment decisions, we need to compare the benefits of each alternative with the costs. In Chapter 6, we described how to calculate and interpret cost-effectiveness ratios. Because outcomes are monetized in cost-benefit analysis, we have a larger array of measures from which to choose. We shall discuss three of these: the benefit-cost ratio, net benefits, and the internal rate of return.[17] Each measure relies upon the sum of discounted benefits and the sum of discounted costs, which are expressed by the following formulas:

$$B = \sum_{t=1}^{n} \frac{B_t}{(1+i)^{t-1}}$$

where B is the benefit, t is the year in a series ranging from 1 to n, and i is the discount rate, and

$$C = \sum_{t=1}^{n} \frac{C_t}{(1+i)^{t-1}}$$

where C is the cost and the other symbols are the same. These may be easier to interpret if we are able to replace the symbols with numbers. So, let us assume that a particular project was evaluated and produced the stream of undiscounted benefits and costs that is presented in Table 7.4.

Assuming a discount rate of 5%, the discounted sum of benefits is given by the following:

$$B = \frac{150}{(1+0.05)^1} + \frac{150}{(1+0.05)^2} + \frac{150}{(1+0.05)^3} + \frac{150}{(1+0.05)^4}$$

$$= 142.86 + 136.05 + 129.58 + 123.41$$

$$= \$531.89$$

The discounted sum of costs is given by:

$$C = \frac{300}{(1+0.05)^0} = \$300$$

In this example, costs only occur at the beginning, during Year 1. Because they are incurred immediately rather than in the future, they are not discounted. However, we could easily construct a different example with costs spread out over several years.

TABLE 7.4 Undiscounted Benefits and Costs From a Hypothetical
              Project

	Benefits	Costs
Year 1	0	300
Year 2	150	0
Year 3	150	0
Year 4	150	0
Year 5	150	0

Benefit-Cost Ratio

The benefit-cost ratio should be a familiar counterpart to the cost-effectiveness ratio. It is given by:

$$BCR = \frac{B}{C}$$

Using the numbers from our example, the benefit-cost ratio is:

$$BCR = \frac{\$531.89}{\$300.00} = 1.77$$

It can be interpreted as the number of monetary units of benefit for each unit of costs. If the ratio is greater than one, it implies that benefits outweigh costs and that the project is desirable. Note that we could also construct a cost-benefit ratio (C/B), which would have the opposite interpretation. That is, if it is greater than one, it implies that costs are greater than benefits. By convention of the cost-benefit literature, however, this is rarely done.

Net Benefits

The net benefits of a project are calculated by subtracting the discounted sum of costs from the discounted sum of benefits:

$$NB = B - C$$

In our example, the net benefits are:

$$NB = \$531.89 - \$300.00 = \$231.89$$

Because the net benefits are positive, it implies that the project is a desirable one.

Both the benefit-cost ratio and net benefits require us to choose a discount rate. In our numerical example, we used a discount rate of 5%, but had we used 10%, future benefits would have been more heavily discounted and the discounted sum of benefits would have been somewhat smaller (\$475.48).[18] This would have altered the cost-benefit ratio and the estimate of net benefits, and the project would have appeared somewhat less desirable. In Chapter 5, we briefly discussed some issues on choosing a discount rate. Regardless of the rate that is chosen, it is important to conduct a sensitivity analysis, to assess whether conclusions about project desirability are significantly altered when a higher or lower discount rate is employed.

Internal Rate of Return

A third measure of project attractiveness, the internal rate of return (*IRR*), has a key advantage in that it does not require us to choose a discount rate beforehand. The *IRR* is defined as the discount rate (*i*) that causes the net benefits to equal zero:

$$NB = \sum_{t=1}^{n} \frac{B_t}{(1+i)^{t-1}} - \sum_{t=1}^{n} \frac{C_t}{(1+i)^{t-1}} = B - C = 0$$

or, equivalently,

$$NB = \sum_{t=1}^{n} \frac{B_t - C_t}{(1+i)^{t-1}} = B - C = 0$$

The *IRR* in the numerical example turns out to be approximately 0.349 (or 34.9%). We can convince ourselves of that by calculating the discounted sum of benefits when i = 0.349:

$$B = \frac{150}{(1+0.349)^1} + \frac{150}{(1+0.349)^2} + \frac{150}{(1+0.349)^3} + \frac{150}{(1+0.349)^4}$$

$$= 111.19 + 82.43 + 61.10 + 42.59 = \$300$$

The discounted sum of costs is unchanged:

$$C = \frac{300}{(1+0.349)^0} = \$300$$

Thus, by definition, using the IRR of 0.349 as the discount rate equates the stream of discounted benefits and costs. This is illustrated in Figure 7.2, which graphs the net benefits against the discount rate. Note that the net benefits are equal to zero when the discount rate is equal to 0.349. At lower values of the discount rate, the net benefits are positive; at higher values, the net benefits are negative. To use the IRR to assess the desirability of a project, we should compare it to the prevailing discount rate. If the IRR is larger than the prevailing discount rate (probably between 0%-10%), then the project is a desirable one. In this example, that is clearly the case.

In many examples of educational cost-benefit analysis, the *IRR* is simply not calculated, and analysts rely on the *BC* ratio and the net benefits. In one genre of study, however, the *IRR* is used almost exclusively. Described in Example 7.4, these studies compare the benefits and costs of obtaining additional years of schooling.

Which Measure Is Preferable?

In practice, it is helpful to compute and present all three measures of project desirability. Nevertheless, as a guide to decision making, each measure has its strengths and limitations. The benefit-cost ratio provides a sim-

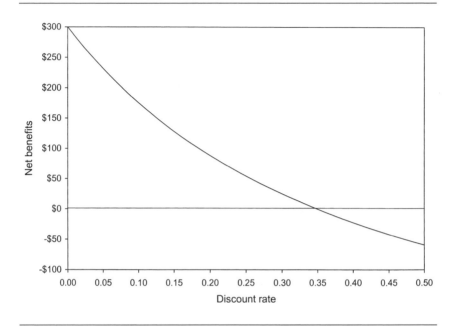

FIGURE 7.2. Net Benefits as a Function of the Discount Rate

ple indicator of whether benefits outweigh costs, but it does not provide any clues to the overall scale of the project. We could imagine a project with benefits of 100 and costs of 50 that yields a *BC* ratio of 2 and net benefits of 50. A second project has benefits of 1,000 and costs of 500, also yielding a ratio of 2. However, its net benefits are 500, much larger than the first project. Thus, the *BC* ratio can provide a misleading guide when the scales of two or more alternatives are vastly different. It is most useful when comparing projects of roughly similar scale (perhaps each costs about the same, but we are interested in which provides greater benefits).

Net benefits provide the best overall indicator of project desirability. However, as we just mentioned, a single measure of net benefits must assume a value for the discount rate. Because net benefits can be sensitive to the discount rate, it is always good practice to calculate net benefits under a range of assumptions. The corollary is that one should be cautious in interpreting evaluations that present only a single estimate of *NB*. It is important to ask what discount rate was employed and whether estimates of net benefits might be sensitive to this assumption.

The *IRR* has an important strength in that it does not require us to explicitly assume a discount rate, although it has two important weaknesses (Boardman et al., 1996). First, it does not provide any indication of the project scale. Thus, we could estimate identical *IRRs* for two separate projects, indicating that they are equally desirable, even when the *NB* of one project is larger (this dilemma of interpretation is similar to that of the *BC* ratio). Second, it is sometimes difficult to calculate a unique value for the *IRR*. This does not occur in instances like our numerical example in which all the costs occur at the beginning of the project and benefits come later (in fact, this closely parallels most projects). If, however, costs and benefits are dispersed unevenly throughout the project cycle, it is sometimes possible to calculate more than one *IRR*.

Accounting for Uncertainty

All the methods for incorporating uncertainty that were discussed in the previous chapter are also applicable to the case of cost-benefit analysis. In particular, it is essential that sensitivity analysis be used to test whether conclusions are fundamentally altered by varying key assumptions. These assumptions include the discount rate, prices, and any other parameter in the analysis that is subject to uncertainty.

Summary

This chapter has provided a summary of several issues that are pertinent to cost-benefit analysis, including its conceptual foundations, three methodological approaches to valuing benefits, and three methods of combining cost and benefit measures. In several cases, we made only passing reference to issues that are crucial elements of a good cost-benefit analysis but that were previously discussed in the chapter on cost-effectiveness analysis. These include the need to discount benefits that occur over time, the importance of evaluating the distribution of benefits across social groups, and the need to conduct a sensitivity analysis of results.

EXAMPLE 7.4. The Rate of Return to Additional Years of Schooling

In many poor countries, a large portion of the young population does not attend school, even at the primary level. Governments are forced to make difficult decisions about which levels of education—primary, secondary, or higher—should be the recipients of scarce investment funds. To allocate these resources across levels of education, one could attempt to compare the costs and the benefits of each of the three alternatives. The investment that yields the highest net benefits—or benefit-cost ratio or internal rate of return—would produce relatively greater benefits for a given cost. In fact, there are hundreds of studies that do exactly that, albeit with somewhat restricted definitions of what constitutes benefits and costs. For extensive reviews of this literature, see Psacharopoulos (1994) and Psacharopoulos and Ng (1994).

Figure 7.3 illustrates a basic schematic that is followed in estimating the benefits and costs of education (for further details on the method, see Carnoy, 1995; Psacharopoulos & Woodhall, 1985). The researcher first obtains data on individual earnings, usually from a census or household survey. Using these data, the researcher constructs an "age-earnings profile" for each level of education, which traces out the average lifetime earnings of individuals who have attained a given level of education. The figure depicts hypothetical age-earnings profiles for two levels of education: secondary and higher. The secondary profile begins at age 18, following graduation from secondary school; the higher education profile begins at 22, after graduation from university. Both end at the retirement age of 65, when individuals cease working.

The benefits of higher education are calculated as the difference at each age between what individuals earn as higher-education graduates and what they might have earned as secondary graduates. This is represented by the area B. The costs of higher education are divided into two components. The first is the cost of income forgone while receiving a university degree—an opportu-

▶ RECOMMENDATIONS FOR FURTHER READING

There are numerous general textbooks on the concepts and methods of cost-benefit analysis. Among these, the classic work of Mishan (1988) provides a thorough treatment that is well-grounded in economic theory. Nas (1996) covers much of the same material in a concise and up-to-date fashion. For readers without a minimal grounding in economic theory, both of these may be somewhat advanced. The presentation in Boardman et al.

EXAMPLE 7.4. continued

nity cost of studying instead of working (represented by the area C1). The second includes all the direct costs of studying, like books, tuition, and so forth (represented by the area C2).

In this simple framework, the internal rate of return for university education is calculated by finding the discount rate that equalizes the discounted sum of benefits and the discounted sum of costs. In summarizing the results of studies from many countries, Psacharopoulos (1994) finds that the average internal rate of return to university education is somewhat lower than that of primary education (11% vs. 18%).[19] In a simplistic way, this suggests that primary education is a better candidate for scarce investment funds than higher education.

Despite the relative ease of conducting these studies, there are also many critiques of the method (for an excellent summary and an alternative method, see Glewwe, 1999). First, the method assumes that the sole benefit of education is higher earnings, despite suggestive evidence of many other benefits. Second, it focuses exclusively on the rate of return to a greater *quantity* of education, when decision makers may be more interested in the return to the *quality* of education. Third, many authors assume that the only cost of education is forgone income (C1), when it is well-known that the direct costs of education may be substantial (C2). This may bias estimates of the return (McEwan, 1999).

Fourth, the age-earnings profiles are usually constructed with data from a single cross section, rather than longitudinal data that track a group of workers over their careers. Implicitly, this assumes that the earnings of a 65-year-old today are a good approximation of what a 25-year-old will earn in 40 years, although this assumption may not be entirely accurate. Fifth, it assumes that the earnings of a current secondary graduate are a good approximation of what current university graduates *would have* earned without a degree. In fact, we have few assurances that this does not overstate or understate the benefit, because of unobserved differences between the two sets of individuals.[20]

(1996) is thorough but also more accessible to the applied policy analyst and well illustrated with examples. The useful surveys of cost-benefit analysis in Drummond, O'Brien, Stoddart, and Torrance (1997) and Johannesson (1996) are focused exclusively on health care.

There are few textbooks devoted exclusively to educational cost-benefit analysis. Psacharopoulos and Woodhall (1985) discuss educational cost-benefit analysis in the context of developing countries (although their discussion is largely focused on rate-of-return studies like those in Exam-

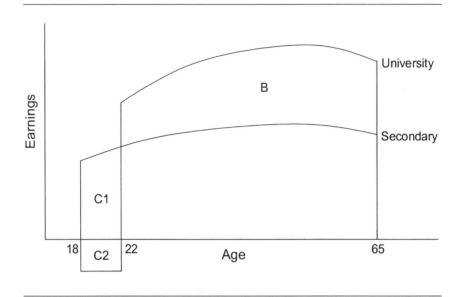

FIGURE 7.3. A Schematic for Calculating Rates of Return

ple 7.4). Although not strictly methodological, the applied work of Steven Barnett on the Perry Preschool Project is notable for its clarity and thoroughness (Barnett, 1996). A careful reading of his monograph would provide a useful methodological guide to readers.

Exercises

1. What types of educational interventions lend themselves best to CB analyses? Why?

2. Three years ago, a community college district considered the establishment of a number of new vocational curricula. A special committee was appointed by the college trustees. The committee was composed of local businessmen and taxpayers as well as students, faculty, and administrators. The committee reviewed various employment surveys and interviewed area employers. On the basis of these activities, it recommended 12 new programs

for the college district. The college followed this advice, only to find that some of the programs were experiencing low enrollments and relatively poor placements. After three years, the district has asked you to do a cost-benefit analysis of the programs to see which should be continued and which should be phased out. Design a study that would meet those objectives. What are the benefits, and what are the costs? How would you measure them? How should your results be used to make a decision?

3. Some studies of educational investments for at-risk students attempt to do cost-benefit analyses. Basically, they take the improvements in achievement scores and convert these to grade-level equivalents so that they can measure achievement gain in terms of additional months or years of schooling associated with the test scores. Thus, one alternative might provide an additional 3 months of achievement, whereas another provides an additional 2 months of achievement. These gains in achievement are converted to gains in earnings by assuming that if a person's test score is higher in terms of months or years of schooling equivalents, the earnings will also be higher as if the students had spent that additional time in school. Thus, an intervention with one-half year of achievement gain in 10th grade would be evaluated as if the students had had a half year of additional schooling. Of course, the benefits as measured in this way would be properly discounted to get present values and to compare with the present values of costs. Is this a legitimate way of converting a study on educational achievement into a cost-benefit analysis? Why or why not?

4. The state of New Jersey wants you to do a cost-benefit analysis of investing in dropout prevention. How would you go about this study? How would you measure costs? How would you measure benefits?

5. The state of Idaho is considering a large investment in making welfare recipients economically independent. Three programs have been recommended to the state. One group has argued that job development with living wages must be the centerpiece. A second has pushed for high school equivalency completion and job training. A third has claimed that counseling and child care are the keys. The state wants to know the costs and benefits of each of these separately and in various combinations. How would you formulate and carry out the study?

▶ NOTES

1. Stokey and Zeckhauser (1978) make a similar point.

2. The following explanation is inspired by that of Johannesson (1996).

3. For those unfamiliar with this notation, the equation can be verbally interpreted in the following manner: "utility is a function of (or produced by) income and literacy."

4. Virtually every textbook on cost-benefit analysis or welfare economics provides a full discussion of compensating variation (and its close relation, equivalent variation). In particular, see Boardman et al. (1996), Johannesson (1996), and Layard and Walters (1978).

5. Utility-compensated demand curves are also commonly referred to as Hicksian demand curves. They are different from the Marshallian demand curves that are familiar to most beginning students of economics. In the latter, money income—rather than utility—is held constant.

6. Stokey and Zeckhauser (1978) also make this point.

7. Boardman et al. (1996) employ a similar taxonomy, and we have borrowed their organization. Their three approaches are covered in their Chapters 9, 10, and 11.

8. The most comprehensive cost-benefit analysis is presented in a recent monograph (Barnett, 1996). Other articles provide summaries of the principal findings (Barnett, 1985a, 1992, 1993).

9. For an important exception, see Betts (1996).

10. Many individuals find the mere thought of placing money values on some of these outcomes to be repugnant. Thus, a common alternative is to conduct a cost-effectiveness analysis in which valuable outcomes are expressed in other than financial terms. Several alternative programs might be compared according to their cost in attaining a specified level of outcomes (e.g., a thousand lives saved or students educated). The alternative that provides the effect at least cost is chosen. If it is possible to place monetary values on outcomes, however, there is still much to be gained. By doing so, we can make judgments about the overall desirability of implementing a single project and compare it to a wide range of programs with different objectives.

11. Chapter 11 in Boardman et al. provides a superb overview of the strengths and weaknesses of contingent valuation as well as numerous citations to the applied literature in cost-benefit analysis. Other methodological reviews—focusing on valuation of environmental benefit—include Cummings, Brookshire, and Schultze (1986) and Mitchell and Carson (1989).

12. See Johannesson (1996) and Drummond et al. (1997) for references to contingent valuation studies in health.

13. Hedonic price functions are generally described by Boardman et al. (1996).

14. See Boardman et al. (1996) for a similar discussion.

15. Fisher, Chestnut, and Violette (1989) and Drummond et al. (1997, p. 212) give similar examples.

16. See Chapter 14 in Boardman et al. (1996) for further details on distributional weighting schemes in cost-benefit analysis.

17. For additional details on these, see any textbook on cost-benefit analysis (e.g., Boardman et al., 1996; Nas, 1996).

18. The discounted sum of benefits with a discount rate of 10% is given by:

$$B = \frac{150}{\left(1+0.10\right)^1} + \frac{150}{\left(1+0.10\right)^2} + \frac{150}{\left(1+0.10\right)^3} + \frac{150}{\left(1+0.10\right)^4}$$
$$= 136.36 + 123.97 + 112.70 + 102.45 = \$475.48$$

19. See Psacharopoulos (1994, Table 1).

20. See Willis and Rosen (1979) or, for a recent review, Levin and Plug (1999).

CHAPTER

Cost-Utility Analysis

> ### OBJECTIVES
>
> 1. Present the "multiattribute utility function" and describe its use.
> 2. Discuss methods for estimating the utility produced by alternatives.
> 3. Discuss whose utility should be measured.
> 4. Discuss how to calculate cost-utility ratios and use them to rank alternatives.

In Chapter 6, we described how a cost-effectiveness analysis can be used to compare the costs and results of programs when they share a single objective (and measure of effectiveness). Only in rare cases, however, does a single measure of effectiveness fully describe a program's outcomes. For example, two elementary school programs—say, class size reduction and tutoring—may improve achievement in both mathematics and reading. Further analysis may reveal that class size reduction is the most cost-effective means of raising reading achievement but that tutoring is more cost-effective in raising mathematics achievement. Given these conflicting findings, how can we choose between the alternatives?

One solution is to estimate the relative utility of the alternatives, based on their success in raising mathematics and reading achievement. Utility is a shorthand way of describing the relative strength of preference or satisfaction that parents (or students or teachers) have for each outcome within a range of possibilities. Once the utility and costs of each alternative are obtained, we choose the program that provides a given amount of utility at the lowest cost. In the preceding example, parents may have a preference for both types of achievement. However, they may feel that reading is particularly important and should weigh most heavily in the overall estimate of each program's utility. Because higher reading scores contribute most to the final estimate of utility, the cost-utility analysis may reveal that class size reduction provides a given amount of utility at the least cost.

The tricky part, of course, is coming up with a good estimate of the utility provided by each alternative. Toward doing so, researchers have developed a vast array of techniques in "decision analysis," a vibrant academic field that draws upon the work of economists, psychologists, and other scholars. This chapter will review only some of the most basic approaches, which are also the most straightforward to apply. We shall illustrate the discussion with a few examples from the education literature—in fact, the few that actually exist—and one from health. First, we will provide a general overview of multiattribute utility theory, which serves as a convenient framework to organize the rest of the discussion. This is followed by a review of the methods for estimating utility and a discussion of whose preferences (or utility) should be measured.

Multiattribute Utility Theory

Multiattribute utility theory is a complicated name for a fairly intuitive idea. An educational program produces outcomes in a multitude of categories: student achievement, student and teacher attitudes, and so on. Within each category, we could imagine a variety of subcategories. For example, student achievement can be divided into mathematics, reading, science, and so on. In Chapter 6, we referred to each subcategory as a "measure of effectiveness," although the literature on utility theory refers to each measure as an "attribute." We shall adopt the latter terminology in the following discussion. Stakeholders may derive utility from—or have a preference for—each of these attributes. Multiattribute utility theory provides a set of techniques for accomplishing two tasks: (1) quantifying the utility derived from individual attributes and (2) combining the utility from each attribute to arrive at an overall measure of utility. The general tool for carrying out these tasks is called the multiattribute utility function.

The Multiattribute Utility Function

Imagine that we exhaustively catalogued the attributes of a particular educational program. We could use a simple notation to refer to each of these attributes: x_1, x_2, x_3, and so on, all the way to the final attribute, x_m. As it stands, these attributes are measured in their "natural" units. For example, gains on an achievement test might be expressed in percentage points, the number of test items, or months of learning gain (you can assume that we already carried out an evaluation that allowed us to estimate the program's success in improving each of these attributes). Let's say that we want to express each attribute on a new scale, a common "utility" scale. That is, we would like to describe the strength of preferences for a given increase in achievement, for an improvement in student attitudes, or for a change in any of the attributes.

We need to estimate a series of single-attribute utility functions: $U_1(x_1)$, $U_2(x_2)$, and $U_3(x_3)$, all the way to $U_m(x_m)$. The preceding notation is an efficient way of saying "the utility produced by the attribute x_1," "the utility produced by the attribute x_2," etc. For the time being, we will refrain from specifying exactly how each attribute is to be "converted" to a utility scale.

Once single-attribute utility functions are obtained, the next step is to combine them in an overall measure of utility. The tool for doing so is referred to as the multiattribute utility function. The overall utility from a given alternative (and its m attributes) is expressed as:

$$U(x_1, \ldots, x_m) = \sum_{i=1}^{m} w_i\, U_i(x_i)$$

It is nothing more than a weighted sum of the utilities produced by individual attributes. To make this more concrete, let's assume that the outcomes of a particular alternative are fully described by three attributes:

$$U(x_1, x_2, x_3) = w_1\, U_1(x_1) + w_2\, U_2(x_2) + w_3\, U_3(x_3)$$

Prior to summing the three single-attribute utility functions, each is multiplied by an "importance weight" (w_1, w_2, and w_3). These weights— also referred to as "tradeoff weights"—are intended to reflect the relative importance of each attribute to the stakeholders. In general, the importance weights for all the attributes should sum to 1 (so in the preceding case, $w_1 + w_2 + w_3 = 1$). For example, if $w_1 = 0.80$, this suggests that the overall utility of stakeholders is primarily—but not entirely—determined by attribute x_1. The importance weights for the other two attributes are both 0.10, indicating their lesser importance to the stakeholders. For now, we refrain from specifying exactly how importance weights should be elicited from stakeholders.

This type of multiattribute utility function is referred to as "additive," because it involves simply adding up the weighted utilities of individual attributes. It makes intuitive sense to most people, and it can be usefully applied in a wide variety of circumstances. Example 8.1 provides a simple illustration of its application. Nevertheless, the additive utility function places some restrictions on the analysis that may not reflect the true nature of individual preferences. Most important, it assumes that the preference for each attribute is independent of the preferences for the other attributes.

To provide an illustration of this restriction, let's define attribute x_1 as mathematics achievement and attribute x_2 as student satisfaction. Overall utility increases with increasing amounts of either attribute. The additive utility function implies that the amount of utility produced by greater student satisfaction is independent of the level of math achievement. That is, whether the level of math achievement is high or low, student satisfaction will still yield the same amount of utility. Conversely, the amount of utility produced by greater math achievement is independent of the level of student satisfaction. Are these reasonable assumptions? We could easily imagine that student satisfaction produces somewhat less utility in the presence of extremely low levels of math achievement. If so, it may lead the analyst to use other forms of the multiattribute utility function that escalate rapidly in their complexity. Standard references on different forms of utility functions include Keeney and Raiffa (1976, 1993). A quite accessible presentation is given by Clemen (1996).[1]

Further Steps in the Analysis

The multiattribute utility function provides a simple framework for determining the overall utility of an alternative. It builds upon the components of a good cost-effectiveness analysis. First, a set of alternatives is clearly delineated. Second, the attributes—or measures of effectiveness—are laid out; these are the basic yardsticks by which alternatives will be judged. Third, the effectiveness of each alternative in altering the attributes

EXAMPLE 8.1. A Simple Multiattribute Utility Function

A school district is faced with a difficult decision. It must choose among four instructional strategies that teach students how to type (see Table 8.1). After careful deliberation with teachers, parents, and other stakeholders, it is determined that the success of any of these strategies should be measured according to three attributes: typing speed, typing accuracy, and the ability to apply typing abilities in other areas. Each of these attributes is measured on a 0 to 100 scale. By relying on prior studies of instructional effectiveness, the evaluators are able to determine the scores of each alternative for each of the three attributes. It is assumed that the scores will represent a utility scale; that is, there is an exact, 1-to-1 correspondence between units of effectiveness on each attribute and units of utility.

The importance weights for each attribute were determined through further consultation with teachers and parents. They are designed to sum to 1. The weight of 0.48 that is associated with speed indicates that it is considered more than twice as important as applications (0.19). Typing speed will account for roughly half of the overall utility score for each strategy. To derive the overall measure of utility for each alternative, it is a simple matter of obtaining a weighted average of the attribute scores.

The overall utility of the first alternative is given by:

$$0.48 \times 24 + 0.33 \times 49 + 0.19 \times 21 = 31.7$$

The utility of the other three is obtained in the same way—by multiplying each attribute score by its importance weight and then summing the results. Ultimately, teacher-based tutorials obtain the highest utility score, despite the fact that they produce somewhat lower typing accuracy than computer-based tutorials. The ranking of alternatives might have changed if accuracy were given a larger importance weight, relative to the others. As an exercise, you might try recalculating the overall utilities with a different set of importance weights.

Of course, we are still missing an important part of the analysis. Now that a single utility score has been estimated for each alternative, it is important to combine this with estimates of costs. This allows a cost-utility ratio to be estimated for each alternative, thereby allowing us to choose the alternative that provides a given amount of utility for the lowest cost. Later, in Example 8.4, we provide an example in which this is done.

TABLE 8.1 The Utility of Strategies to Improve Typing Ability

| Alternative | Attribute | | | Overall Utility |
	Speed	Accuracy	Applications	
Large group television presentation	24	49	21	31.7
Large group lecture	39	65	34	46.6
Teacher-based tutorial	95	69	80	83.6
Computer-based tutorial	87	83	41	76.9
Importance weight	0.48	0.33	0.19	

SOURCE: Adapted from Lewis (1989).

is established. For most attributes, such as student achievement, it will be necessary to employ one of the evaluation designs described in Chapter 6.

Before overall utility scores can be obtained, however, there are two remaining steps. These were only touched upon in the previous section. First, we need to convert each attribute into a common utility scale that expresses the strength of preference for the attribute. That is, we need to define the functions—$U_1(x_1)$, $U_2(x_2)$, and so on—that describe exactly how additional units of the attributes are associated with utility. Second, we need to establish the weights—w_1, w_2, and so on—that reflect the relative importance of each attribute in overall utility. Toward accomplishing this, scholars in the field of decision analysis have devised a wide variety of techniques, and the following sections explore a few of these.

Methods of Assessing Single-Attribute Utility Functions

This section describes several approaches to assessing single-attribute utility functions: proportional scoring, the direct method, and the variable probability method. To better illustrate each approach, we shall employ

TABLE 8.2 Hypothetical Data From an Evaluation of Four Programs for Computer-Assisted Mathematics Instruction

	Mathematics Scores
Alternative A	4
Alternative B	20
Alternative C	12
Alternative D	16

some hypothetical data on effectiveness. Imagine that we have just evaluated four separate programs for computer-assisted instruction of mathematics. The four alternatives (A, B, C, and D) are each evaluated according to a single attribute: mathematics scores. The test is composed of 25 items, results of which are presented in Table 8.2. In the following sections, we will convert these attribute scores to a utility scale.

Proportional Scoring

The first method, proportional scoring, is simply a linear rescaling of each attribute to a common utility scale. The rescaling can be accomplished via graphical or mathematical means. In Figure 8.1, we provide a graphical representation of proportional scoring. Each mathematics score is plotted on the x axis, ranging from the value of the lowest-scoring alternative to that of the highest-scoring alternative. The utility scale, on the y axis, ranges from 0 to 100. The low and high values of the utility scale are quite arbitrary. In applying the method, we could just as easily set the endpoints at any values. The important point is that the same utility scale is shared by each of the attributes that we assess (and eventually combine in a single measure of utility).

By examining Figure 8.1, we can see that the lowest score on mathematics is assigned a utility of 0 and the highest a utility of 100. The straight lines connecting these points imply that increasing mathematics scores lead to constant increases in utility (in this case, a 4-point increase in mathemat-

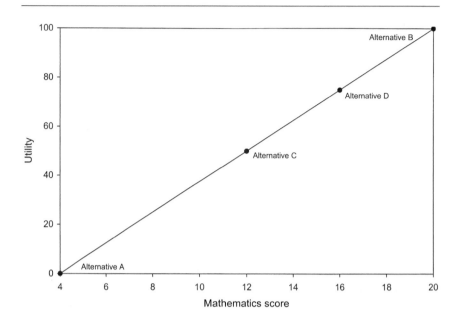

FIGURE 8.1. Assessing Utility Functions With Proportional Scoring

ics scores produces a 25-point increase in utility). Of course, this is an assumption that we are making. We have no direct evidence that people really evince this preference structure. It might be that when reading scores are low, a small increase leads to a substantial utility increase, but when they are higher, the same increase in scores leads to a somewhat smaller gain in utility. This would be represented by a curvilinear, rather than linear, utility function. Later on, we will allow for this possibility.

We could derive the same utility scores mathematically, without resorting to graphs. The formula is quite simple:

$$U(x) = \frac{x - \text{Lowest}}{\text{Highest} - \text{Lowest}} \times 100$$

Applying the formula for a reading score of 12 (Alternative C) yields a utility score of 50 (this can be verified by examining Figure 8.1):

$$U(12) = \frac{12 - 4}{20 - 4} \times 100 = 50$$

In a sense, proportional scoring isn't really a "method" because it does not rely on the expressed preferences of stakeholders. It simply assumes that increasing amounts of an attribute are linearly associated with utility.

The Direct Method

Instead of using proportional scoring, we could obtain direct input from individual stakeholders on the utility that they derive from varying amounts of an attribute. The simplest approach for doing so is the direct method. To apply the direct method, one identifies the low and high values on the relevant attribute scale. In this case, the low mathematics score is 4 and the high score is 20. As before, these are arbitrarily assigned low (0) and high (100) values, respectively, on the utility scale. The respondent is then asked to directly rate the preference for middle levels of the attribute, relative to these endpoints. In our example, the middle levels are the mathematics scores that were obtained by the middle alternatives. For comparison's sake, it would also be helpful to rate other possible scores. Let's say that such a process turned up the following results:

$U(4)$ = 0 (arbitrary assignment)

$U(8)$ = 40 (judgment, relative to arbitrary assignment)

$U(12)$ = 75 (judgment, relative to arbitrary assignment)

$U(16)$ = 95 (judgment, relative to arbitrary assignment)

$U(20)$ = 100 (arbitrary assignment)

The mathematics scores and corresponding utilities are plotted in Figure 8.2. A researcher could use visual means to draw a smooth curve through the points. Alternatively, many researchers use statistical methods to find the curve that provides the best "fit" to the data. In this case, the data suggest a curvilinear relationship between mathematics scores and utility. More specifically, increasing mathematics scores tend to increase utility, but at a decreasing rate. Despite this example, it should be emphasized that utility functions can assume many different shapes.

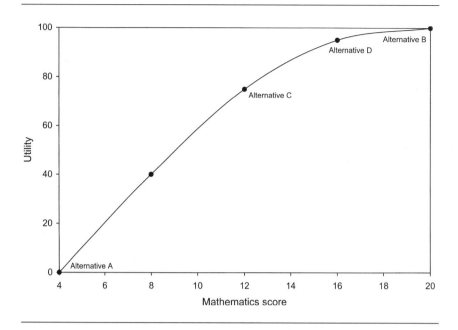

FIGURE 8.2. Assessing Utility Functions With the Direct Method

The structure of the prior example was borrowed from von Winterfeldt and Edwards (1986). These same authors describe many variations on the direct method, in addition to providing a variety of examples from the decision analysis literature. Drummond, O'Brien, Stoddart, and Torrance (1997, pp. 151-152) describe several variations on direct rating that have been employed in the health literature.

The Variable Probability Method

The variable probability method also calls upon stakeholders to assess their preferences for varying amounts of a given attribute. However, it requires a different sort of thought experiment than the direct method. In particular, it makes use of the decision tree that was briefly introduced at the end of Chapter 6. Imagine that you are able to choose between two different options. On the one hand, you could opt for a gamble in which the

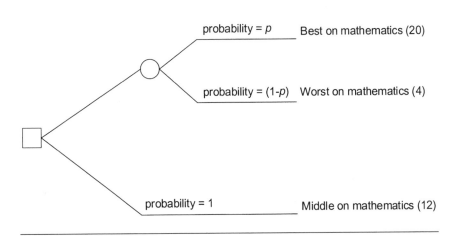

FIGURE 8.3. Assessing Utility Functions With the Variable Probability Method

"winning" hand leads to the highest attribute score (in this case, a mathematics score of 20) and the "losing" hand produces the lowest (a mathematics score of 4). The probabilities of attaining the highest and lowest scores are, respectively, p and $(1-p)$. Instead of this risky option, you could obtain a given mathematics score with certainty. For the time being, let's fix this middle score at 12. This particular gamble is represented by the decision tree in Figure 8.3.

To assess the utility of the middle score, individuals choose the probability (p) that makes them indifferent between the risky alternative (with a potentially high or low payoff) or the riskless alternative (with a middling payoff). Let's say, for example, that we suggested an initial probability of 0.99. That is, individuals would be faced with the option of receiving the best score with a probability of 0.99 (and, conversely, the worst score with a probability of 0.01) or receiving a middling score with certainty. It seems fair to presume that many individuals would find the risky option to be most attractive.

What if we suggested an initial probability of 0.01 instead of 0.99? In this case, chances are that most individuals would not favor a gamble that offered such a small probability of an attractive payoff. Instead, they might prefer the certainty of obtaining a middle score.

Between 0.99 and 0.01, there is a probability at which individuals would be indifferent between the two options. In the case of Figure 8.3, suppose that a probability of 0.60 leads to indifference for a particular individual. We can then interpret this probability as the utility of a mathematics score of 12 (with the endpoints of the utility scale set at 0 and 1). In order to employ the same utility scale as prior examples, we multiply 0.60 by 100, yielding a utility of 60. The same exercise is repeated for several different mathematics scores. Doing so produces a number of pairs of mathematics scores and their associated utilities. These can be graphed, just as we did in Figures 8.1 and 8.2.

A Brief Caveat

In the previous discussion, we used the word "utility" rather loosely. In fact, many scholars prefer to distinguish between "value" functions and "utility" functions. The two are distinguished according to whether the outcomes of interest are treated as certain (riskless) or uncertain (risky). In the direct method, for example, outcomes are treated as certain. When preferences are elicited by variants of this method, they are said to reflect the underlying value of outcomes, rather than utility. In the variable probability method, outcomes are treated as uncertain. Preferences that are elicited by this method are referred to as utilities.

There is an important reason that some scholars, particularly economists, prefer to make this distinction. First, the variable probability method is directly based on a seminal theory of utility that was developed by John von Neumann and Oscar Morgenstern in 1944. (A complete discussion of this theory would take us far afield. For an excellent discussion, see Clemen, 1996.) In contrast, most other methods bear little relation to an underlying theory of utility, and some fear that this may produce ad hoc measures of preferences.

Second, utilities estimated by the variable probability method incorporate the attitudes of individuals toward risk.[2] An individual is said to be "risk-neutral" if she is indifferent between receiving $100 with certainty or taking a 50/50 gamble of receiving $200 or nothing. If she prefers the gamble, she is said to be "risk loving," whereas if she prefers the certainty of $100, she is said to be "risk averse." In the real world, most outcomes are far from certain (even so, many educational evaluations refer to outcomes

---

TABLE 8.3 Further Data From an Evaluation of Four Programs for
Computer-Assisted Mathematics Instruction

	Mathematics Scores	*Student Satisfaction*	*Computer Literacy*
Alternative A	4	2	10
Alternative B	20	1	16
Alternative C	12	3	2
Alternative D	16	5	20

---

as if they were a "sure thing"). Thus, it seems appropriate to try to capture the notion of risk attitudes.

Methods of Assessing Importance Weights

After single-attribute utility functions are defined for each attribute, we require some method of obtaining the relative weight or "importance" of each attribute in overall utility. This section describes two general approaches to estimating importance weights: the direct method and the variable probability method.[3]

To illustrate the methods, we shall return to the previous example, in which four programs for computer-assisted mathematics instruction were evaluated. In addition to mathematics scores, let's assume that the programs were evaluated on two additional attributes: student satisfaction with each program and computer literacy. Student satisfaction is gauged on a scale from 1 (low) to 5 (high). Computer literacy is measured by a 25-item test. Table 8.3 presents hypothetical data on all of the attributes.

The Direct Method

There are many variants of the direct method. One of the simplest, which doesn't even make use of the data in Tables 8.2 and 8.3, asks individuals to "allocate" a total of 100 points among attributes, according to their relative importance. Let's say that mathematics scores are considered by individuals to account for about half of overall utility and, consequently, are assigned 50 out of 100 points. Computer literacy is the next most important attribute and is assigned 30 points. Lastly, student satisfaction receives 20 points. Each estimate is divided by 100 in order to obtain a set of three importance weights—0.50, 0.30, and 0.20—that sum to 1.[4]

Another variant of the direct method calls for individuals to rank the attributes in order of their importance. The most important attribute is assigned a value of 100. Each of the remaining attributes is assigned a value, relative to 100, that reflects its importance (thus, a value of 50 indicates that an attribute is half as important as the most important attribute). Using this method, let's assume that math achievement was fixed at 100, and computer literacy and student satisfaction were assigned values of 80 and 60, respectively. The final step is to normalize these weights, such that they sum to 1. To do so, each weight is divided by the sum of all weights. In this case, the weight of math achievement is 0.42 (100/240); of computer literacy, 0.33 (80/240); and of student satisfaction, 0.25 (60/240).

The Variable Probability Method

The variable probability method can also be used to derive importance weights. Individuals are asked to choose between two options, represented by the decision tree in Figure 8.4. First, they can opt for an uncertain gamble with two outcomes. Individuals might obtain the best scores on all three attributes, with probability p. Or individuals might obtain the worst possible scores on all attributes, with probability $(1-p)$. Instead of this gamble, individuals can choose to receive another set of scores with certainty. For now, let's define this outcome as the best possible score in mathematics (20) and the worst possible scores on computer literacy and student satisfaction (2 and 1, respectively).

What if the probability (p) is set at 0.99? In this case, many individuals would be inclined to choose the gamble. There is an excellent chance of obtaining the best scores on all attributes. If the probability is set at 0.01, the gamble is much less appealing. In this case, it seems more prudent to choose the certainty of obtaining the best score on at least one attribute. Between

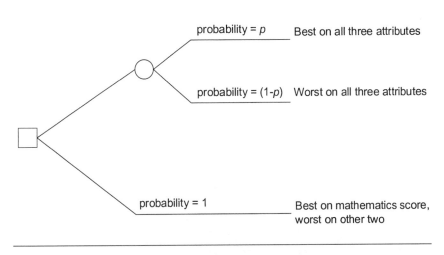

FIGURE 8.4. Assessing Importance Weights Using the Variable Probability Method

these two values of *p*, there lies a probability that would cause an individual to be indifferent between the two options.

In the case of Figure 8.4, let's say that this probability is estimated at 0.40. It can be interpreted as the importance weight of mathematics scores. To assess the utilities of computer literacy and student satisfaction, we would apply the same procedure. Therefore, for the next step, we would replace the lower branch of the decision tree with "best on computer literacy, worst on other two." The resulting indifference probability is interpreted as the importance weight of computer literacy.

Once importance weights are estimated for all three attributes, they should sum to 1, or at least be somewhat close. If they are close (but do not sum to 1) we can normalize them by dividing each individual weight by the sum of the weights. If the sum is not close to 1, this is a signal that the additive utility function does not adequately represent an individual's preferences (Clemen, 1996). The analyst might need to use more complex versions of the utility function that incorporate interactions among the attributes. These were briefly mentioned in a previous section. For further details, the reader is encouraged to consult Clemen (1996) or Keeney and Raiffa (1993).

EXAMPLE 8.2. Quality–Adjusted Life-Years in Health Research

Health interventions are frequently evaluated according to their effects on life expectancy. That is, by how many years does a particular medical treatment tend to lengthen one's life? While a useful means of evaluating some interventions, life expectancy still does not capture the quality of life or the satisfaction that individuals may derive from additional years of life. Two medical treatments may each add 2 years to an individual's life. Yet, if one of these leaves the individual significantly impaired or incapacitated, then it is clearly less desirable.

One tool for incorporating both the quality and quantity of life is referred to as the Quality–Adjusted Life-Year (QALY). The notion of the QALY is illustrated in Figure 8.5. Imagine that we have assessed a medical treatment and determined that it increases the length of life by 2 years. However, it is also determined that it improves the quality of life. The quality of life is measured on the y axis by weights that range between 0 (death) and 1 (perfect health). Without the medical treatment, the quality of life begins at a lower point and declines more rapidly. With the treatment, the quality of life is immediately improved and declines more slowly. The total gain in QALYs that is produced by the treatment is calculated as the area between the two descending curves.

To estimate the QALYs that are produced by a medical treatment, it is necessary to estimate quality-of-life weights that reflect the satisfaction derived from different health states. These weights can be obtained by most of the methods that have been described in this text, as well as by many variants that have been specifically developed by health researchers (for a review of these, see Drummond et al., 1997). A particularly common one is the variable probability method, also referred to as the "standard gamble." The method is illustrated in the Figure 8.6. Individuals are given a choice between two alternatives: (1) a risky gamble that could result in perfect health, with probability p, or in death, with probability $(1-p)$, and (2) the certainty of living with an impaired health state. The individual must choose the value of p (a number between 0 and 1) that makes him indifferent between the two alternatives. If, for example, this probability is determined to be 0.5, then the utility of the impaired health state is 0.5 (relative to the endpoints of 0 and 1). Each year of life that is lived in the impaired health state is weighted by 0.5.

Drummond et al. (1997) provide a more thorough review of the theory and methods of QALYs, as well as a number of practical examples.

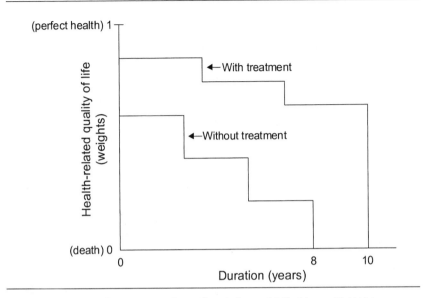

FIGURE 8.5. An Illustration of Quality-Adjusted Life-Years (QALYs)
SOURCE: Adapted from Drummond et al. (1997), p. 170.

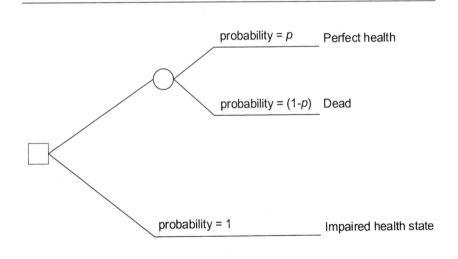

FIGURE 8.6. Applying the Variable Probability Method to Health

Which Method to Use?

As we mentioned, many economists prefer the variable probability method because of its explicit links to a theory of utility and because it incorporates risk attitudes (e.g., Drummond et al., 1997). Even so, it is not without its limitations. For example, many individuals find it difficult to think about probabilistic choices, and some evidence indicates that individuals will make seemingly contradictory decisions when faced with gambles.[5]

Other methods, including many variants on direct rating techniques, are attractive because they are easily understood by most individuals and are straightforward to apply (Gold, Patrick, et al., 1996). However, they are not explicitly linked to economic theories of utility, which unnerves some practitioners. And doubts have been expressed as to whether these methods can produce true interval data and thus whether they can be regarded as a true reflection of strength of preferences.[6]

In practice, many scholars—especially those involved in the "nuts and bolts" of conducting these analyses—are not inclined to make sweeping recommendations in favor of one method or another (for examples of these views, see Clemen, 1996; von Winterfeldt & Edwards, 1986). They recognize that all methods are potentially error-prone, and none is likely to provide a completely faithful reflection of preferences. However, all of the preceding methods are helpful ways of eliciting information about individual preferences. When possible, it is especially desirable to use multiple methods to check on the consistency of results and, ideally, triangulate on a small range of likely values. As Robert Clemen puts it, "human decision makers need help understanding objectives and tradeoffs, and all . . . assessment techniques . . . are useful in this regard" (p. 553).

Utility to Whom?

Thus far, we have addressed several techniques for assessing the utility of individuals, but we have not specified exactly *whose* preferences should be assessed. There are at least three groups that might be considered: (1) the entire population in a given community, (2) the population that is directly affected by an intervention (such as families with children enrolled in school), and (3) a smaller group of representatives such as teachers, administrators, or school board members. In choosing among these, evaluators will usually be forced to make tradeoffs between what is theoretically appropriate and what can be accomplished in a practical sense.

In previous chapters, we emphasized that cost analyses should usually be conducted from the societal perspective. In measuring costs (Chapters 3 through 5), we attempt to identify the resources that are sacrificed by the entire community. In measuring benefits (Chapter 7), we attempt to identify the benefits that accrue to every member of the community, whether or not they are direct targets of the intervention. (Of course, we also emphasized the importance of separately analyzing how the burden of costs and benefits may differ across different groups.)

In keeping with this approach, a cost-utility analysis should attempt to measure the preferences of an entire community, usually by surveying a representative sample of community members (Gold, Patrick, et al., 1996; Kaplan, 1995). Let's say that a large school district is choosing among three different curricula that will affect several outcomes (or attributes). In order to assess the importance weights of each attribute, we should obtain a representative sample of individuals within the district boundaries. For each individual, we can then apply one or more of the techniques that were discussed in the previous section. It might appear that we are unjustly ignoring the preferences of families with school-age children. However, these families will appear in our sample in proportion to their presence—often quite substantial—in the community.

In some cases, however, it will not be possible to obtain the views of a large sample of community members. Perhaps time is a binding constraint, or the monetary costs of a community survey are judged to be prohibitive. There are two alternatives that might be pursued. First, one can assess the preferences of a representative sample of parents or students who are directly affected by the intervention. Second, one can obtain the views of appropriate representatives of the community, such as school board members or elected officials of civic and community organizations. In other cases, it may be possible for administrators or teachers to determine the utility of the alternatives.

We should keep in mind that the preferences of the groups that we have mentioned may bear little resemblance to one another. Even within a particular community or school, the preferences for different educational outcomes may vary by income level, education, or another social grouping. It is hard to judge the degree of variability in preferences. In education, there

EXAMPLE 8.3. A Cost-Utility Analysis of Special Education Alternatives (Part 1)

The outcomes of special education programs are difficult, if not impossible, to express with a single measure of effectiveness (or attribute). In fact, there are multiple objectives that can be represented by a large number of attributes, and multiattribute utility theory seems especially appropriate in these cases.

Darrell Lewis and his colleagues set out to compare the utility and costs produced by three different administrative structures for special education. These alternatives include

> an independent school district (representing school districts of sufficient size to offer special education services to all students residing within their geographic boundaries), an intermediate school district (representing consortia of typically suburban districts in jointly offering services for students primarily with low-incidence handicapping conditions), and a joint powers special education cooperative (representing cooperative groups of small- to medium-sized independent school districts in the shared delivery of special education). (Lewis, Johnson, Erickson, & Bruininks, 1994, p. 83)

In collaboration with a group of stakeholders—including teachers, administrators, and parents—the evaluators defined the attributes by which the success of alternatives would be judged (see Table 8.4). These are grouped into four categories, including student participation in school life, satisfaction with the program, program accomplishments, and program processes.

The same group of stakeholders participated in the process of assigning importance weights to each attribute. The evaluators employed a variant of the direct method (discussed earlier in the text). Individuals ranked all the attributes in order of their importance, with the most important being assigned a value of 100.[7] The rest of the attributes were assigned lesser values, relative to 100.

is simply little evidence to guide us. To our knowledge, educational cost-utility analysis has only elicited the preferences of small groups of administrators or other stakeholders (e.g., Fletcher, Hawley, & Piele, 1990; Lewis et al., 1994). In health, there is a much larger body of research on utility assessment. In reviewing this research, at least one author feels that evidence does not support the notion that preferences vary strongly across individuals (Kaplan, 1995, p. 51).

EXAMPLE 8.3. continued

These values were normalized to sum to 1 (using methods described earlier in the text). The final importance weights are presented in the second column of Table 8.4.

The evaluators then visited school districts and conducted surveys in order to collect the performance data on each attribute. These attributes were measured on a variety of scales. However, it was necessary to convert each of these to a common utility scale, with the lowest possibility utility of each attribute specified as 0 and the highest utility as 100. In order to convert each attribute score, the evaluators used the method of proportional scoring (described earlier in the text). The third column in the table presents the unweighted attribute utilities for one of the three alternatives—independent districts.

The final step is to combine importance weights and unweighted utilities in order to arrive at an overall measure of each alternative's utility. To do so, the evaluators employed the additive multiattribute utility function. Each attribute's utility was multiplied by its respective importance weight (see the fourth column). The weighted utilities were then summed, thereby yielding the overall utility of the alternative. The table shows that the overall utility of the independent district alternative is 63.9. Other calculations, not shown in the table, implied a utility of 70.4 for the intermediate alternative, and 65.2 for the cooperative alternative.[8]

The results suggest that the intermediate alternative is the most attractive, since it provides the highest level of utility. However, it is important to combine these results with cost estimates in order to determine which alternative provides a given level of utility at least cost. Later on, in Example 8.4, we describe the final cost-utility analysis that was conducted by the authors.

———————————
SOURCE: Lewis et al. (1994).

Whatever the evidence, the cost-utility analyst should always consider the possibility that preferences will vary across subgroups, which has great potential to affect the conclusions. Let's say that parents attach a large importance weight to mathematics achievement, but that teachers place a much smaller weight on this attribute. Using either set of importance weights might produce a different cost-utility ranking of educational alternatives. When evaluators are aware that preferences vary—or might vary—

TABLE 8.4 Estimating the Utility of Special Education Alternatives

Attribute	Importance Weight	Independent District Alternative		Weighted Attribute Utility
		Unweighted Attribute Utility (0–100)		
Student participation in school life				
Students have access to educational/social experiences	0.09	×	32.5	=	2.9
Students participate in extracurricular/social activities	0.07	×	13.3	=	0.9
Students participate in mainstream programming	0.09	×	80.0	=	7.2
Satisfaction with program				
Parents express satisfaction	0.05	×	84.7	=	4.2
Students express satisfaction	0.05	×	48.0	=	2.4
Teachers and administrators express satisfaction	0.04	×	82.7	=	3.3
Public expresses satisfaction	0.05	×	90.0	=	4.5
Accomplishments of program				
School completers demonstrate appropriate social behaviors	0.06	×	77.5	=	4.7

School completers live in independent/semi-independent settings	0.06	×	54.0	=	3.2
School completers have social and recreational networks	0.06	×	89.9	=	5.4
School completers participate in meaningful vocational settings	0.06	×	88.5	=	5.3
Students complete all years of offered schooling	0.04	×	100.0	=	4.0
Process of program					
Program provides appropriate curriculum components	0.10	×	74.7	=	7.5
Program provides training and support for parents	0.08	×	59.3	=	4.7
Program provides appropriate staff support	0.09	×	40.0	=	3.6
Sum	1.00				63.9

SOURCE: Adapted from Lewis et al. (1994, Tables 3 and 6).

across groups of individuals, it behooves them to conduct a sensitivity analysis (see below).

Discounting Utility

In some cases, the utility of a project is confined to a single year. In other words, we may focus upon the gains in achievement (and utility) that occur over a single year. In many other cases, however, utility gains occur over a period of many years. In these cases, utility needs to be appropriately discounted (at the same rate as costs) to its present value. The rationale and methods for discounting were already reviewed in Chapters 5 and 6, and we shall not discuss them further.

Combining Costs and Utility

After estimates of utility are obtained for each alternative, it is important to combine these estimates with costs. The procedure for doing so is exactly the same as in Chapter 6. The cost (C) of each alternative is divided by its utility (U) to yield a cost-utility ratio:

$$CUR = \frac{C}{U}$$

The ratio is interpreted as the cost of obtaining a single unit of utility. The cost-utility ratios of each alternative are rank ordered from smallest to largest. The smallest ratios indicate the alternatives that provided a given amount of utility at the lowest cost. As with CE and CB ratios, it is important to consider the scale of alternatives when comparing CU ratios.

Accounting for Uncertainty

After cost-utility ratios are calculated, it is important to assess whether the ranking of alternatives is sensitive to key assumptions of the analysis. The

EXAMPLE 8.4. A Cost-Utility Analysis of Special Education Alternatives (Part 2)

In Example 8.3, we described an evaluation of three alternatives for the provision of special education alternatives. Using multiattribute utility theory, the evaluators were able to calculate the overall utility of each of the three alternatives. To complete the evaluation, it is important to estimate the costs of each alternative, so that cost-utility ratios can be calculated.

The evaluators estimated the costs of each alternative using an approach similar to that of Chapters 3 through 5. They created a complete list specifying all the activities and services carried out under each alternative. Then, consulting administrative records and school personnel, they identified, measured, and valued all the resources (or ingredients) used in all aspects of service delivery. The total cost estimates for each year were divided by enrollments in order to arrive at estimates of the average cost per student per year (see Table 8.5).

Costs were then divided by utility, yielding three cost-utility ratios. These are interpreted as the annual cost per student of obtaining a 1-unit increase in overall utility. Upon examining the results, it is immediately apparent that the independent district alternative is the least attractive of the three. Not only is it more costly than the other alternatives, it also results in lower overall utility; unsurprisingly, its cost-utility ratio is the highest. The other two alternatives have slightly different costs and utilities. However, their cost-utility ratios are quite similar. From an efficiency perspective, it appears that both alternatives are similarly attractive. As we will note in Chapter 9, when alternatives are equal or close in their estimated efficiency, other considerations should be used in making decisions, such as ease of implementation.

SOURCE: Lewis et al. (1994).

procedures for conducting such a sensitivity analysis are exactly the same as those described in Chapter 6. The principal difference lies in the parameters that will be varied. For example, a key parameter in most cost-utility analyses is the importance weight that is assigned to each attribute. Depending on the circumstances of each study, these weights may have been estimated with some uncertainty, or they may vary among different social groups. It is important to gauge whether the cost-utility rankings of alternatives are modified when alternative sets of weights are employed.

TABLE 8.5 Costs, Utility, and Cost–Utility Ratios of Special Education Alternatives

	Independent District Alternative	Intermediate Alternative	Cooperative Alternative
Average cost per student per year	$28,056	$14,496	$13,413
Overall utility	63.9	70.4	65.2
Cost-utility ratio	$ 439	$ 206	$ 206

SOURCE: Adapted from Lewis et al. (1994, Table 7).

Summary

This chapter has provided an overview of cost-utility analysis. It began by briefly reviewing the concept of utility and the challenges to measuring individual preferences. It then described the framework of multiattribute utility theory and the additive utility function, which are helpful tools for organizing a cost-utility analysis. To carry out an analysis, it is important to clearly define and measure the attributes of each alternative; then, each attribute can be converted to a utility scale by using one of the methods described in the text. These individual utilities are multiplied by "importance weights" that reflect the relative contribution of each attribute to overall utility (the importance weights can also be derived by one of several methods). The sum of weighted utilities provides a simple estimate of overall utility. Once this is obtained for each alternative, the analysis proceeds much like a standard cost-effectiveness analysis. Cost-utility ratios are calculated, and a sensitivity analysis is conducted to assess whether the ranking of alternatives is robust to alternative assumptions.

► RECOMMENDATIONS FOR FURTHER READING

Keeney and Raiffa (1976, 1993) is still the standard reference on multiattribute utility theory, but both editions of their book require some sophistication in economics. The discussion of von Winterfeldt and Edwards (1986) is exceedingly thorough and perhaps a bit more accessible to the noneconomist or nontechnical reader.

Fortunately, there are a number of excellent textbooks that provide comprehensive reviews. Clemen (1996) provides a very readable discussion of the major issues, including multiattribute utility theory and various methods of assessing individual utility. He also provides many helpful exercises and examples. The texts of Edwards and Newman (1982), Golub (1997), and Pitz and McKillip (1984) provide more concise reviews of the field.

Cost-utility analysis is now a common tool of research in health policy, much of it utilizing the concept of QALYs that was introduced in Example 8.2. For reviews of theory, methods, and evidence, see Drummond et al. (1997); Gold, Patrick, et al. (1996); and Kaplan (1995). In contrast, multiattribute utility theory and cost-utility analysis are rarely used in education. There are just a few examples of empirical studies, including Fletcher et al. (1990), Lewis et al. (1994), and Lewis and Kallsen (1995).

Exercises

1. What are some of the advantages and disadvantages of CU in comparison with CB and CE analyses?

2. A high school offers 2 years of each of the following languages: French, German, Russian, and Spanish. It wishes to offer 4 more years of language instruction by adding 1 or 2 more years of instruction for each of these languages and/or by offering up to 2 years of Latin. Design a CU analysis that will assist the high school administration in choosing the best combination of languages for which to offer additional instruction.

3. Different educational alternatives have different educational results among different student groups (e.g., disadvantaged versus advantaged, Latino versus white, males versus females). How can CU analysis be used to consider these distributional effects as well as the overall educational results of each alternative?

4. An evaluator has just completed a cost-effectiveness analysis that compared two new math curricula. In accordance with the program goals, two

measures of effectiveness were established: mathematics achievement and student attitudes towards mathematics. The cost-effectiveness analysis revealed that the first curriculum is the most cost-effective means of raising math achievement, whereas the second curriculum is the most cost-effective means of improving student attitudes toward math. Informal discussions with school personnel and parents reveal that they consider achievement to be somewhat more important than attitudes. Is there a systematic way that you can help them choose between the two alternatives, given the conflicting CE results?

► NOTES

1. For a presentation that focuses specifically on health, see Drummond et al. (1997).

2. For a deeper discussion of utility theory and risk attitudes, see Clemen (1996), Drummond et al. (1997), or Stokey and Zeckhauser (1978). The example that follows in the text is taken from Drummond et al.

3. Another method called swing-weighting is frequently advocated by researchers in decision analysis, though we have chosen not to introduce the topic in this limited space. For further details, see von Winterfeldt and Edwards (1986) or Clemen (1996).

4. Instead of asking individuals to allocate points, the same method could be applied graphically. For example, individuals can divide a pie chart into three parts. The size of each part is proportional to the relative importance of each of the three attributes.

5. See Kaplan (1995) and the citations therein.

6. See Drummond et al. (1997) and Kaplan (1995) for a thorough discussion of this literature.

7. In fact, the evaluators pursued a two-step procedure, which is helpful when there are a large number of attributes. With input from the stakeholders, they first assigned importance weights to each of the four general categories of attributes; these four weights were normalized to sum to 1. Then, within each category, importance weights were assigned to individual attributes; within each of these categories, weights were normalized to sum to 1. The final importance weight for each attribute was obtained by multiplying the initial category weight by the initial attribute weight.

8. The utilities for the alternatives are not vastly different. In these cases, it is usually advisable to conduct sensitivity analyses in order to determine whether the ranking of alternatives is sensitive to key analytical assumptions (e.g., the importance weights).

The Use of Cost Evaluations

OBJECTIVES

1. Describe the potential uses of cost evaluations.
2. Establish three factors to consider when applying the results of cost analyses.
3. Suggest a quality checklist for cost studies, and apply it to a particular study.
4. Review the issues to consider in using "league tables."
5. Present suggestions for implementing cost analysis in evaluation.

The previous chapters explained the importance of using cost analysis in evaluations as well as the different modes of analysis within the cost family. In addition, attention was devoted to identifying the problem, specifying alternatives, and choosing an appropriate cost-analysis approach. Following these introductory issues, chapters were devoted to the identification, measurement, and distribution of costs as well as to the measurement of effects, utility, and benefits. In this chapter, we focus on how cost analyses are used, or might be used, in the decision-making process. We also provide some advice for decision makers who wish to design and implement their own studies.

Diverse Applications of Cost Analysis

The general uses of cost evaluations might be divided into two broad categories.[1] First, they may be put to direct, or instrumental, use. This is most often the case when a cost study has been commissioned—perhaps by a school district or state office of education—usually with the expressed intent of providing input into a decision. The decision maker is usually the primary audience that was referred to in Chapter 2, though a secondary audience may also take advantage of a study to directly inform a decision.

Second, cost evaluations may be used in a conceptual manner. In conceptual use, a cost evaluation does not directly influence a decision to adopt or eliminate a program; rather, it influences the thinking of key stakeholders about educational issues. For example, a CB analysis of a specific program for early childhood education may have little effect on the immediate support received from local policymakers. However, the results could have far-reaching impact—if widely disseminated—on the general importance with which politicians and parents view early childhood education.

The health care field has witnessed several attempts—some more successful than others—to put CE analysis to a direct use in the decision-making process. Oregon attempted to construct a cost-utility "league table" in order to determine the medical benefits that would be available to recipients of Medicaid (Eddy, 1991; Sloan & Conover, 1995). (See below for further details on league tables.) A panel of experts and consumer representatives was convened in order to prioritize hundreds of medical interventions; high-priority items exhibited the lowest costs per unit of utility. The initial rankings were conducted via a cost-utility analysis, in which each intervention was assigned a cost-per-QALY (quality-adjusted life-year). Following the completion of the list, the rankings were subjected to much public debate and subsequent modification. The initial CU results "were ultimately abandoned in favor of a hybrid process in which cost was not a major factor in determining the final rankings" (Sloan & Conover, 1995, p. 219).

Similarly, the World Bank commissioned a large number of CE, CB, and CU studies on the costs and outcomes of various approaches to disease control in developing countries (see the volume edited by Jamison, Mosley, Measham, & Bobadilla, 1993). These studies were used to rank the desirability of many alternative investments, and they were eventually incorporated into a wide-ranging report of the World Bank's investment priorities in the health systems of developing countries (World Bank, 1993). This may have directly affected World Bank lending strategies.

CE analysis has also been applied to determine which drugs should be reimbursed by public agencies. Typically, these decisions are made on the basis of safety, effectiveness, or costs, but not cost-effectiveness. Since 1993, Australia's government has required manufacturers to submit a cost-effectiveness evaluation in order for their drug to be included in the Australian Pharmaceutical Benefits Scheme (Drummond, O'Brien, Stoddart, & Torrance, 1997; Sloan & Conover, 1995). The costs and effects of the new drug must be compared to those of a relevant alternative, such as another drug that is frequently used to treat the same condition. A similar system is under way in the Canadian province of Ontario (Drummond et al., 1997; Sloan & Conover, 1995).

There have been few investigations of how cost evaluations are used by educational decision makers. However, most evidence leaves reason to be skeptical. Educational cost analyses are carried out infrequently in education, both in absolute terms, and when compared with cost analysis in other fields (Levin, 1991; Monk & King, 1993). A survey of state departments of education in the 1980s revealed that almost no cost-effectiveness analyses were carried out. Moreover, such units usually lacked the capabilities to do such analysis and were not called upon to do so (Smith & Smith, 1985). The logical corollary is that cost analysis rarely features prominently in educational decision making, even if references to the term are common.

There are some quite important exceptions to this rule. The national evaluation of the Job Training Partnership Act (JTPA), briefly described in Chapter 7, probably had direct effects on the funding decisions of the Republican congress and Democratic administration (Orr, 1999; Orr et al., 1996). Many states have vocational rehabilitation (VR) agencies for people with disabilities. Lewis, Johnson, Chen, and Erickson (1992) note that "almost all state VR agencies employ some form of benefit-cost analysis and its related ratios for reporting to legislatures and policymakers on likely efficiency effects" (p. 267).

Perhaps more common than such direct uses are the conceptual uses of cost evaluations. During several decades, developing-country researchers devoted great energy to comparing the costs and benefits of various levels of education, including primary, secondary, and higher (see Example 7.4). Influential reviews of the accumulated literature by George Psacharopoulos (e.g., Psacharopoulos, 1994; Psacharopoulos & Woodhall, 1985) purported to show that rates of return were generally higher for primary education. This, in turn, influenced the lending priorities of the World Bank and other international agencies. Primary education supplanted higher education as the focus of much development aid.

In the United States, the economic analyses of the Perry Preschool Program appear to have been put to "conceptual" use (see Example 7.1, as well as Barnett, 1985b, 1993, 1996). While the evaluations dealt with a small-scale version of a single program, they nonetheless played a role in modifying overall perceptions of the benefits and costs of early childhood education. As a result, they may have affected investments in larger initiatives such as Head Start.

Levin, Glass, and Meister (1987) compared the cost-effectiveness of four educational alternatives: class size reduction, computer-assisted instruction (CAI), peer and adult tutoring, and increased instructional time (see Example 6.3). The CAI and tutoring interventions were specific programs; nonetheless, the research spurred a larger debate about the relative cost-effectiveness of all these interventions. One might also note, however, that despite the cautionary findings on the relative cost-effectiveness of class size reduction, the intervention has been embraced by state and federal policymakers in the 1990s, with little apparent regard for cost-effectiveness.

Guidelines for Using Cost Analyses

Three questions arise in considering the consequences of a given cost study for informing a decision. The first question is whether the study or report that is under consideration is of sufficient quality. The second is the degree to which the results of that study—even if high-quality—can be generalized to the particular setting of the decision maker. The third question is whether outside information should be used in concert with the cost analysis in order to enrich the decision-making process. Each of these will be considered in turn.

Quality of Analyses

The reason that it is often difficult to evaluate cost-effectiveness or cost-benefit studies is that the reader of such literature normally lacks the skills to understand what issues should be raised in such a literature evaluation. Indeed, one of the underlying motives behind this book has been to provide a reader with enough of an understanding of these issues to competently judge such studies. But the reader should bear in mind that CE and CB studies often have the status of the "emperor's new clothes." In other words, very poor analyses are implemented or published because few readers or referees have the competence to evaluate them. The quality of evaluation studies may be problematic in virtually all areas of educational and social evaluation, but these evaluations are even more susceptible to deficiencies when cost analyses are integrated.

There are several areas where CE, CB, and CU analyses can fall short. First, the overall decision framework of the study may be poorly specified, or key alternatives may have been omitted from consideration. Second, costs could be measured in a flawed or incomplete manner. This problem can assume a number of forms. Key ingredients are often excluded, such as the time commitments of stakeholders or the fringe benefits that accompany wages. Mistakes are sometimes made in valuing ingredients. A frequent problem is that costs occurring in the future are not properly discounted, or the costs of expensive and durable goods like buildings are not annualized. Third, effects may be measured incorrectly. Sometimes, this is because the wrong measures are chosen or because important secondary effects are not considered in the analysis. Even if the measures of effectiveness are correct, the researcher's ability to identify a causal link between an alternative and a measure is sometimes doubtful. Identifying links is mostly a feature of the evaluation design, whether experimental or quasi-experimental. Fourth, costs and effects (or benefits) may not be properly integrated by calculating CE ratios and ranking alternatives accordingly. Once ranked, the fragility of these conclusions might not be tested by conducting a sensitivity analysis that varies the key assumptions underlying the analysis.

The sheer quantity of cost studies in health has led several authors to review how well studies adhere to these dimensions of quality. Their conclusions are sobering for research consumers. Udvarhelyi, Colditz, Rai, and Epstein (1992) assessed 77 CE and CB studies in health. Only 18% explicitly stated the perspective of the study (e.g., society, hospitals, or patients) so it was difficult to assess which were the relevant costs to consider. In cases where costs and benefits occurred over a longer time horizon than 1 year, 48% of studies failed to properly discount these. Similarly, about half the articles failed to calculate and report summary measures such as CE or CB ratios, which are required to properly rank the alternatives.

Lastly, around two thirds of the studies failed to conduct sensitivity analyses in order to evaluate the overall robustness of findings.

Another review by Gerard (1992) focuses on 51 CU studies in health that used quality-adjusted life-years (QALYs) as their utility measure (see Chapter 8 for a discussion of QALYs). About 70% of studies were judged to have included a "comprehensive" set of ingredients in calculating their cost estimates; for others, it was rarely possible to evaluate this because studies omitted key information. Only 63% of studies provided a clear description of the procedures used to value ingredients, and only 61% clearly described the sources of their cost data. Where discounting should have been employed, 15% of studies failed to do so. Only 37% of studies conducted "extensive" sensitivity analysis. Overall, Gerard's opinion is that the execution of almost half of the studies should be deemed "limited."

Finally, a review of health-related cost studies conducted in Australia is similarly pessimistic (Salkeld, Davey, & Arnolda, 1995). Of 33 studies, the authors note that "only 55% gave an adequate description of how the costs were measured. . . . Certain costs such as capital and overheads were often omitted completely and inappropriately" (p. 117).

There are fewer CE and CB studies in education and, consequently, fewer methodological reviews. However, some evidence is suggestive that the existing studies should inspire a cautious approach on the part of research consumers. In an early review of cost studies in early childhood education, Barnett and Escobar (1987) found that 5 of 20 studies provided no details on their cost estimates. Others focused exclusively on program costs, ignoring the costs to parents and other clients. A number neglected to consider the costs of facilities. These omissions probably affected conclusions about the cost-effectiveness of alternatives, particularly if one alternative tended to make greater use of omitted cost ingredients.

To assist the reader in evaluating cost studies, a later section will describe a quality checklist and then utilize its criteria to evaluate the quality of a particular CE study.

Generalizability of Analyses

A second issue is the relevance of even an excellent study to a different setting. The question of generalizability from one sample or setting to another pervades the field of evaluation, and social science research in general. A study that can be adequately generalized to another population or

context is said to possess "external validity." Unfortunately, there is no rec-
ipe for determining external validity; judgments are best made on a case-
by-case basis, depending on both the cost study and the setting to which it
might be applied. There are three varieties of external validity to consider,
relating to the population, the environment, and the operations (see Smith
& Glass, 1987, or most evaluation textbooks for a complete discussion of
external validity).

There is population external validity when the results of a particular
cost study can be generalized to a larger group of individuals. Frequently,
the data on effectiveness or costs are estimated from a small sample of individuals. If the sample was drawn at random from a well-defined population
(e.g., elementary students in the state of Washington or secondary students
in Argentina), then study results can be generalized to that population. This
population is referred to as the "accessible" population.

Quite often, however, the researcher or decision maker would like to
apply results from such a cost study to a different population, referred to as
the "target" population. For example, a researcher may wish to apply results from a random sample of Argentine secondary students to others in a
neighboring country. Or a researcher may have data on a nonrandom sample of second graders in New York City, chosen because their parents volunteered them for a study. Nonetheless, the researcher would like to make
broader statements about second graders in Los Angeles. In these cases, we
should ensure that individuals in the sample resemble individuals in the target population as closely as possible—in gender, age, socioeconomic status,
ability, or other important characteristics. Short of conducting a new study,
however, there is no way of guaranteeing that results can be applied from
one group of individuals to another.

Environmental external validity exists when the environment of a
study is comparable to other settings in which the cost study might be applied. In many cases, the environments will be quite different. For example,
many studies of effectiveness are carried out in a well-managed laboratory
setting, which would not carry over to a large-scale implementation of the
intervention. We could imagine an experimental study in which second
graders are given a particular kind of instruction in a laboratory classroom
under pristine conditions. When placed in the less-controlled environment
of a public school, the same instructional method may not produce identical results.

In cost studies, it is particularly important to consider the economic
environment. The prices of key educational ingredients, such as teacher sal-

aries, textbooks, and even parent time could vary drastically from one set-ting to another (Rice, 1997). Thus, even if the alternatives under consider-ation are equally effective in two settings, a different set of costs could alter the cost-effectiveness rankings of alternatives. The best remedy is to care-fully examine the environment of the study and the environment to which the study might apply in order to ensure that they are roughly similar. In the case of cost data, it may be possible to collect new costs, which can be com-bined with the existing evidence on effectiveness.

Finally, there is the issue of operations external validity. To apply the results of a study, we must be sure that the educational "treatment" is faith-fully replicated in the new setting—an issue of program implementation. In some cases, this might be relatively straightforward, such as reducing a class size from 30 students to 25. In education, this is usually the exception rather than the rule. We often refer blithely to interventions such as "text-books" or "teacher training." However, the form and content of these in-terventions can change drastically from one setting to another. In many cases, these changes are probably necessary, in order to adapt interventions to a new context or language. But the process of change makes it difficult to assume that the effects or costs of a study alternative will be duplicated by the modified alternative. A related aspect of operations external validity is the measure of effectiveness used to gauge success or failure. For example, we often say that an alternative is effective in raising mathematics achieve-ment. But often, that mathematics test has been designed for its particular setting, perhaps because it is meant to reflect elements of a curriculum. The alternative could prove to be less effective if applied in a setting where ef-fectiveness is gauged by other means.

In sum, a cost study is generalizable to another setting when the study setting and the new one reflect similar populations, environments, and op-erations. However, one should be wary of factors that are not similar (and not observed) between the two situations and their consequences for gen-eralizability. There is no method of guaranteeing generalizability, beyond the good judgment and experience of individuals.

Incorporating Outside Information

We have argued that when cost-effectiveness analysis and other cost analyses are integrated into evaluations, the evaluation exercise is more likely to yield the types of information that are crucial to decisions than when costs are ignored. This does not mean that even the best CB, CE, or CU studies can be used mechanically to make decisions. Perhaps the most important principle is that of viewing such studies as sources of information rather than as sources of decisions. The fundamental problem is that as helpful as evaluation studies can be in providing information on alternatives, they must necessarily be incomplete.

All evaluations reduce complex organizational and social dynamics to a manageable set of relations for analysis. Although every effort should be made to consider the principal issues, there may be other factors that can be taken into account only as one reviews the results of cost evaluations. For example, there may exist institutional or organizational factors that make one alternative easier to implement than another. Implementation of a new intervention is hardly a mechanical task, and many alternatives that show promise at the drawing-board stage are relegated to failure at the implementation stage because of the simplistic assumptions underlying them (Berman & McLaughlin, 1975). Those alternatives that are presently being used or are similar to present approaches are more likely to provide the predicted results than those that represent a radical departure from existing practices. Clearly, this information must be taken into account in considering the implications of cost evaluations. For example, if one alternative seems slightly more cost-effective than another but will require massive changes in organizational structure, it may be appropriate to select the slightly less cost-effective approach that is more easily implementable.

The important point is that there are always considerations that cannot be fully incorporated into the evaluations. At the decision stage, however, these considerations should be explicated and brought into play in using the information generated by the cost evaluations. Example 9.1 provides an example of such an instance.

A Checklist for Evaluating Cost Studies

At this point, the reader may find it useful to have a checklist of criteria for evaluating the quality of cost-effectiveness analyses in education. These criteria are drawn from the methodological discussions of previous chapters, and can be applied to CE, CB, or CU analyses. Of course, no cost study will

EXAMPLE 9.1. Making Decisions With Cost-Effectiveness Findings

The constituents of a certain school district are deeply concerned about the problem of dropouts at the secondary level. After interviewing former students who dropped out, it is concluded that the main reasons contributing to dropping out are poor academic performance, boredom, and pregnancies among female students. Accordingly, three alternative programs are formulated to reduce dropouts. All three programs provide greater information on birth control and responsible sexual behavior in order to reduce pregnancies. In addition, Alternative A concentrates on upgrading the academic skills of dropouts by instituting a program of token rewards in which students obtain scrip for good behavior and performance. When enough scrip is obtained, it can be exchanged for merchandise. Alternative B focuses on additional academic assistance through peer tutoring as well as placement in part-time jobs for those students who desire them. Alternative C focuses on an intensive counseling program incorporating group and individual counseling methods to address both academic and nonacademic problems of students.

On the basis of evaluations of former dropouts, the school district concludes that the following students are dropout-prone: those with test scores in the bottom 30% of the population; those who have been characterized by disruptive behavior; and those with poor attendance records and, especially, unexcused absences. Any one of these characteristics or any combination of these seems to provide an early warning of dropout-proneness on the basis of past records. The school district randomly assigns 300 tenth-grade students who are characterized as dropout-prone into four groups of 75. The first group is a control group that will not receive any special treatment. Each of the other three groups will be the focus of one of the three program interventions to reduce dropouts. On the basis of a 1-year intervention, data are collected on dropouts for all four groups. The control group has the highest proportion of dropouts, as expected. The difference between the number of students who dropped out of each treatment group and the number who were expected to drop out, as reflected in the experience of the control group, is used to assess the effects of each program in reducing dropouts.

Table 9.1 shows the costs for reducing dropouts for the three alternative programs. Of the 75 students in the control group, 35 had dropped out by the end of the year. Among the other groups, there were fewer dropouts, suggesting that each had prevented some dropout-prone youngsters from leaving. Using the control group as a basis for estimating the number of dropouts in the absence of program interventions, it appears that 17 students were saved from dropping out by Program A; 15 students were saved by Program B; and 10 students were prevented from dropping out by Program C. Costs for each program were fairly similar, but the "cost per dropout prevented" showed

EXAMPLE 9.1. continued

that Program C was the most costly, while Programs A and B were rather close in costs per dropout prevented.

Because Programs A and B were so close in the cost per dropout prevented, other information was sought to inform the decision. One of the crucial factors determining the implementation of a program is that of teacher attitudes. Accordingly, a survey was made of teacher attitudes toward the three alternatives. First, teachers were given a description of each program and what would be required in terms of teacher participation. Second, they were asked to rank the programs according to their own preferences and to give the reasons for those preferences. Third, they were asked to provide any information that they thought ought to be considered by the administration in making a program decision. On the basis of this survey, it was concluded that teachers would be resistant to the adoption of Program A, enthusiastic about Program B, and neutral about Program C.

When this information was combined with the cost per prevented dropout, the decision makers concluded that Program B should be implemented. Although Program A was less costly for each success in its experimental setting, a higher risk was attached to its full implementation by the apparent resistance of teachers to the program of token rewards. Since the teachers were enthusiastic about Program B, it was assumed that they would cooperate to implement it. Accordingly, the additional information convinced the decision makers to adopt a program that appeared to be slightly more costly than another alternative, because the judgment was that with a full adoption it would be less problematic. The decision makers concluded that teacher enthusiasm more than compensated for the slight difference in cost, and that Program B was more likely to succeed than Program A, when fully implemented, in reducing the cost per prevented dropout.

TABLE 9.1 Costs, Effects, and Cost-Effectiveness of Drop-Out Prevention Programs

Alternative	Incremental Cost of Alternative	Dropouts Prevented	Cost Per Dropout Prevented	Teacher Attitudes
A	$12,750	17	$ 750	resistant
B	$12,375	15	$ 825	enthusiastic
C	$13,500	10	$1,350	neutral

EXAMPLE 9.2. A Checklist for Evaluating Cost Studies

1. **Establishing the decision framework**
   1.1. Does the study carefully define a problem?
   1.2. Does the study delineate the alternatives under consideration? Are the alternatives ostensibly related to the probable causes of the problem? Are these the only relevant alternatives, or are there others that ought to be considered?
   1.3. What is the analytical technique designated to choose among the alternatives (CE, CU, or CB)? Is it the appropriate one?

2. **Evaluating costs**
   2.1. Are the ingredients for each alternative set out carefully (e.g., personnel and facilities)? Are all the ingredients included in the costing exercise, or does it include only those that are paid for by the sponsor?
   2.2. Are the methods for costing these ingredients appropriate?
   2.3. If relevant, is there an analysis of the distribution of cost burdens among constituencies (e.g., sponsor, government, and clients)?
   2.4. Is the cost analysis differentiated for different levels of scale of the alternatives? Is the appropriate cost concept (e.g., total, average, or marginal cost) used in the comparison?
   2.5. If necessary, are costs that occur over a number of years annualized? If necessary, are costs discounted appropriately for their distribution over the time horizon?

be perfect. Sometimes, the methodological failings of a study are due to errors or omissions by the authors. More often, they are due to unavoidable constraints such as limited data or time available to authors. We are not encouraging readers to immediately discard a study if it fails to meet each of the following criteria. However, the careful reader should attempt to understand the limitations of each study and ask whether its results can still be utilized. In the best studies, the authors assist in identifying the strengths and weaknesses of their study's methodology, data, and conclusions. In doing so, they establish caveats to its interpretation. In the worst studies, there are outright errors or insufficient detail to completely understand what the authors did; in these cases, it is best to set aside the study.

EXAMPLE 9.2. continued

3. **Evaluating effects, utility, or benefits**

 3.1. Is the measure of effectiveness appropriate? Does it neglect important outcomes of the alternative that should be taken into consideration? If there are multiple outcomes, how are they taken into account? In a CB analysis, are all the important benefits included in
 the analysis?

 3.2. Is the experimental, quasi-experimental, or correlational evaluation
 design sufficient to ensure that estimates of effectiveness (or benefits) are internally valid?

 3.3. If benefits are not derived from an experiment, quasi-experiment, or
 correlational study, is the alternative methodology clearly described
 (e.g., contingent valuation)?

 3.4. In a cost–utility analysis, is the methodology (e.g., for assessing importance weights) clearly described? Whose preferences are employed (e.g., community members, school parents, or school personnel)?

 3.5. Is there an adequate analysis of distributional effects of the alternatives across different groups?

 3.6. If necessary, are the effects, utility, or benefits discounted for their
 distribution over the time horizon?

(continued)

Each of the items in this checklist refers to a systematic attempt to evaluate a report and to ascertain its strengths and weaknesses. The specific
questions are divided into five general categories. The first category refers
to the overall decision context in which the study is situated. The decision
framework and the alternatives under scrutiny should be described explicitly in order to understand the nature of the decision problem and the alternatives that were considered in addressing it (see Chapter 2). The second
category refers to the procedures for estimating and analyzing costs that
were extensively discussed in Chapters 3, 4, and 5. The third category addresses the conceptualization, measurement, and analysis of effects, benefits, or utility (these topics were discussed in Chapters 6 through 8). The

EXAMPLE 9.2. A Checklist for Evaluating Cost Studies *(continued)*

4. **Comparing costs and outcomes**

   4.1. Is the information on costs and effects used to calculate cost-effectiveness ratios? Are these results used correctly to rank alternatives? Does it appear that errors or omissions in the estimates of costs and outcomes might be sufficient to alter these rankings? In the case of a CB study, are costs and benefits used to calculate cost-benefit ratios, net present values, or internal rates of return? In the case of a CU study, are cost-utility ratios calculated and interpreted?

   4.2. Are the differences in estimates among alternatives large enough that you would have confidence in using them as a basis for decisions? Did the authors present results of a sensitivity analysis? How robust are the results with respect to different assumptions about the ingredient requirements, ingredient values, choice of discount rates, estimates of effectiveness, and the weighting of different dimensions of effectiveness?

5. **Applying the results**

   5.1. How generalizable are the results to the immediate decision context? Are they generalizable to other decision contexts? For example, could they be applied to alternatives for similar populations and environments in other settings? Is it possible to make cost-estimate adjustments that would enable such generalizability?

fourth category includes questions on the calculation of cost-effectiveness ratios, the ranking of alternatives, and sensitivity analysis (again, see the appropriate sections of Chapters 6 through 8). Once alternatives are ranked with some degree of confidence, the fifth category addresses the generalizability (or external validity) of results, a matter discussed in this chapter.

Applying the Checklist

To better explain the key elements of the preceding checklist, we shall apply it to a particular cost-effectiveness analysis. We focus on the book-length study of primary school achievement in northeast Brazil by Harbison and Hanushek (1992). The authors present both CE and CB analyses. The main elements of the CE analysis were already described in Example 1.3, so they should be somewhat familiar. After following this checklist, readers may wish to examine the original study more closely.

1. Establishing the decision framework

1.1. Does the study carefully define a problem?

The book presents compelling data that northeast Brazil is educationally disadvantaged relative to the rest of the nation and that rural areas are disadvantaged relative to urban areas. During the early 1980s, the Brazilian government set out to improve the situation of primary education by investing in a program called EDURURAL, which provided some schools with a basic package of inputs such as repairs to school facilities, training, and textbooks. Thus, a part of the analysis is devoted to evaluating a specific educational program (EDURURAL) and asking whether it accomplished its goals. However, the majority of the analysis is devoted to answering a broader question: "What works in education and what educational policies flow from this?" (p. 5).

1.2. Does the study delineate the alternatives under consideration? Are the alternatives ostensibly related to the probable causes of the problem? Are these the only relevant alternatives, or are there others that ought to be considered?

The study considers a number of educational alternatives, focusing on basic school inputs (see Table 6.1, Harbison & Hanushek, 1992). These include: water provision, school furniture, school facilities, writing materials, textbooks, in-service training courses for teachers, and additional formal education for teachers. Other alternatives such as class size reduction were initially considered but excluded from the final analysis because they were not shown to be consistently effective. They acknowledge the potential relevance of other alternatives such as increasing subject matter knowledge of teachers but exclude these from the analysis due to difficulties in attaching costs to these characteristics. Although other alternatives might have been considered, the preceding ones are consistent with their available data and with their focus on basic education policies in the primary grades.

1.3. What is the analytical technique designated to choose among the alternatives (CE, CU, or CB)? Is it the appropriate one?

The authors apply two main analyses. First, a CE analysis is used to compare the relative costs and effects of each alternative in raising student achievement (pp. 135-142). The analysis is intended to show which alternatives provide the greatest achievement gains per dollar invested in that alternative. Second, a CB analysis is used to compare the costs and a limited range of (monetary) benefits for each alternative (pp. 145-157). These benefits include the monetary savings that may be produced by reducing the repetition rate among students. It is intended to show which alternatives provide the largest ratios of benefits to costs. It is also intended to show which alternatives, if any, have benefits that outweigh costs in absolute terms (i.e., a benefit-cost ratio greater than one).

2. Evaluating costs

2.1. Are the ingredients for each alternative set out carefully (e.g., personnel and facilities)? Are all the ingredients included in the costing exercise, or does it include only those that are paid for by the sponsor?

The authors followed the ingredients approach that was described in Chapters 3 through 5 of this volume. Some details of their approach are provided (pp. 135-140), although most are confined to a separate document (Armitage, Gomes-Neto, Harbison, Holsinger, & Leite, 1986). They appear to have included a comprehensive range of ingredients. These include sponsor-provided resources such as texts and materials, but also frequently ignored ingredients such as donated resources and the time of other stakeholders (e.g., the cost of teacher time spent in training).

2.2. Are the methods for costing these ingredients appropriate?

There are few details on the source or methods used to value ingredients (as mentioned, these appear to have been confined to a separate document). Much information was apparently drawn from the records of the Secretariat of Education (Ceará) in one state. Because estimates of effectiveness are based on a wider sample of states, this is potential bias if costs from Ceará are not representative of other states. It is difficult to evaluate this with the existing data.

2.3. If relevant, is there an analysis of the distribution of cost burdens among constituencies (e.g., sponsor, government, and clients)?

Harbison and Hanushek state that some costs are borne by local government, such as donated spaces for teacher training, or by teachers, such as time spent in training (p. 137). However, it is difficult to ascertain how costs might be distributed across all the constituencies (local and national governments, teachers, parents, etc.). This might be helpful in assessing the likelihood that any one alternative will encounter acceptance or resistance from various stakeholders.

2.4. Is the cost analysis differentiated for different levels of scale of the alternatives? Is the appropriate cost concept (e.g., total, average, or marginal cost) used in the comparison?

The authors attempt to estimate marginal (or incremental) costs of replicating each alternative in a new school. To do so, they exclude the fixed costs associated with the initial development of alternatives (e.g., curriculum design of teacher training). To arrive at per-student costs, these marginal costs are divided by the number of students, relying on the average number of students currently attending the school.

2.5. If necessary, are costs annualized that occur over a number of years? If necessary, are costs discounted appropriately for their distribution over the time horizon?

The authors estimate the per-student cost of each alternative in a single year (in order to compare it to its effectiveness or benefits in the same year). Thus, there is no need to discount and include recurrent costs that occur many years hence. However, there is a need to carefully consider the issue of facilities and equipment costs. In calculating a single year's costs, the authors recognize that it would be misleading to include a large expenditure on a building, for example, because facilities last for many years. For these ingredients, they apply the annualization technique discussed in Chapter 4, assuming an interest rate of 10% (p. 137). For example, they annualize tangible inputs such as infrastructure, after estimating their useful lifetime by interviewing teachers and school personnel. They also annualize the costs of teacher training, recognizing that the skills it imparts to teachers last for more than a single year.

3. Evaluating effects, utility, or benefits

3.1. Is the measure of effectiveness appropriate? Does it neglect important outcomes of the alternative that should be taken into consideration? If there are multiple outcomes, how are they taken into account? In a CB analysis, are all the important benefits included in the analysis?

The CE analysis uses achievement tests in Portuguese and mathematics as measures of effectiveness. These appear to be well suited to the task of measuring basic skills. The tests were criterion referenced to minimally acceptable levels of performance in the second and fourth grades and were designed to reflect the prevailing curriculum. An extensive discussion of the tests is given in their Appendix A. The authors note that other measures of effectiveness or benefits might be useful: "the ability of educated people to compete in the labor market, to increase the productivity of their farms, to participate in democratic society, to care for and nurture children" (p. 82). However, these occur subsequent to primary schooling and could not be measured. Each measure of effectiveness (Portuguese and mathematics) is considered in a separate CE analysis (i.e., utility weights are not applied to arrive at a single measure of utility).

In their CB analysis, the authors clearly state that not all benefits have been monetized. Because some benefits are excluded—such as the subsequent wage gains of students—they refer to it as a "partial" CB analysis. They argue that even a "partial" analysis provides useful evidence if a portion of overall benefits is shown to outweigh total costs (the implication is that a more complete measurement of benefits would simply cause a desirable alternative to appear even more desirable).

3.2. Is the experimental, quasi-experimental, or correlational evaluation design sufficient to ensure that estimates of effectiveness (or benefits) are internally valid?

The authors calculate effectiveness with a correlational design, using an extensive database spanning 4 years in the 1980s. It contains information on approximately 6,000 second and fourth graders in roughly 600 schools. Although the data were obtained by methods of random sampling, they are nonetheless not part of a randomized experiment. In an experiment, different groups of students would have been randomly assigned to receive different quantities of each alternative (e.g., textbooks). In this case, the authors still compare the outcomes of students who are exposed to greater and lesser quantities of each alternative. However, they rely on statistical methods to "control for" or "hold constant" the many background characteristics of students and their families (in a true experiment, randomization obviates the need to make such controls).

As the authors themselves point out, their approach is not the ideal method of establishing effectiveness. If important student or family control variables are omitted, then estimates of effectiveness could be biased. Nevertheless, the authors include an excellent discussion of potential biases and make some additional attempts to address these (see pp. 84-94). In any case, there was simply no opportunity to conduct a true experiment.

3.3. If benefits are not derived from an experiment, quasi-experiment, or correlational study, is the alternative methodology clearly described (e.g., contingent valuation)?

In their CB analysis, benefits are measured as the monetary savings produced when a given alternative causes a student to be promoted more swiftly through the education system due to higher achievement. By increasing promotions, students spend less time in primary schools and incur fewer costs. The analysis is based on a detailed set of statistical models and assumptions, all of which are described in depth (pp. 147-148). The incorporation of additional assumptions, however reasonable, implies greater uncertainty about the final estimates of benefits. Thus, it is important to gauge the sensitivity of the estimates to key assumptions.

3.4. In a cost-utility analyses, is the methodology (e.g., for assessing importance weights) clearly described? Whose preferences are employed (e.g., community members, school parents, or school personnel)?

Not applicable to this study.

3.5. Is there an adequate analysis of distributional effects of the alternatives across different groups?

The estimates of effectiveness do not include an assessment of distributional effects. In the statistical models, additional units of each alternative are presumed to have a similar effect on each child. If the students in the underlying data are homogeneous, this may be a reasonable assumption. But although northeast Brazilian states are generally much poorer than Brazil as a whole, there is still a good degree of heterogeneity among states in the northeast (p. 30). It is possible that effectiveness (and cost-effectiveness) of alternatives varies across states or student populations.

In their CB analysis, the authors do explore distributional effects. They calculate different levels of benefits for different regions of Brazil, using methods described on pages 153 through 155. In general, results suggest that benefits are higher in the rural northeast than in the urban southeast (the latter is a more developed region of Brazil) and higher in low-income areas.

3.6. If necessary, are the effects, utility, or benefits discounted for their distribution over the time horizon?

Effects and benefits occur during a single school year, so discounting is not necessary.

4. Comparing costs and outcomes

4.1. Is the information on costs and effects used to calculate cost-effectiveness ratios? Are these results used correctly to rank alternatives? Does it appear that errors or omissions in the estimates of costs and outcomes might be sufficient to alter these rankings? In the case of a CB study, are costs and benefits used to calculate cost-benefit ratios, net present values, or internal rates of return? In the case of a CU study, are cost-utility ratios calculated and interpreted?

In their Table 6.2, Harbison and Hanushek present cost-effectiveness ratios for several years and for both measures of effectiveness. (Actually, they present effectiveness-cost ratios, which are interpreted as the units of effectiveness produced by a $1 investment in a given alternative.) The authors note that "the most uniform finding is that software expenditure [e.g., textbooks and writing materials] leads to the largest achievement gains" (p. 141). In other words, these alternatives tend to exhibit the largest effects per dollar of cost. The interpretations appear quite reasonable in light of their results.

In Table 6.4, the authors present the results of a CB analysis. The ratio of benefits to costs is highest for "software" inputs such as textbooks, lending credence to the CE results. That is, greater software in a classroom leads to higher student achievement, which in turn increases the likelihood that students will be promoted to the next grade, which produces cost savings (or benefits) for schools. The CB ratios are next highest for "hardware" inputs like school infrastructure and then for in-service training for teachers. In all these cases, however, even partially measured benefits appear to outweigh costs. This suggests that all investments are worthy from society's point of view; this absolute judgment could not have been made in the CE analysis.

> 4.2. Are the differences in estimates among alternatives large enough that you would have confidence in using them as a basis for decisions? Did the authors present results of a sensitivity analysis? How robust are the results with respect to different assumptions about the ingredient requirements, ingredient values, choice of discount rates, estimates of effectiveness, and the weighting of different dimensions of effectiveness?

The differences between CE ratios are quite substantial in some cases. For example, the ratios for textbooks in the second grade are generally twice as large as other inputs. However, a sensitivity analysis is not conducted to determine how robust these results are to changes in key assumptions. For example, a 95% confidence interval could be constructed for estimates of effectiveness; the high and low estimates could each be used to estimate two CE ratios. Or costing assumptions could be varied one at a time, such as the 10% discount rate used to annualize capital goods. Despite these critiques, it should be emphasized that the authors draw their estimates of effectiveness from multiple samples that span several years. By averaging effects across years (as they do in Table 6.2), one might presume that effects are somewhat more precise than usual.

Magnitudes are also substantial for some benefit-cost ratios. For example, the benefits for software inputs such as textbooks appear to be at least 4 times greater than costs. The robustness of these results is tested with a sensitivity analysis (see pp. 150-153). The authors formulate a pessimistic set of assumptions about the effects of inputs on achievement and the effects of achievement on the likelihood of being promoted. Using these new assumptions, they calculate "lower-bound" estimates of the benefit-cost ratios (see their Table 6.5). In a few cases, the benefit-cost ratios dip below 1, suggesting that "partial" benefits are exceeded by costs. Despite these results, the authors note that "even under these extreme estimation procedures, there is strong evidence of significant offsets to costs of investments in properly selected inputs to primary schooling" (p. 152).

5. Applying the results

> 5.1. How generalizable are the results to the immediate decision context? Are they generalizable to other decision contexts? For example, could they be applied to alternatives for similar populations and environments in other settings? Is it possible to make cost–estimate adjustments that would enable such generalizability?

The large random samples and careful methodological approach suggest that the effectiveness results are generalizable to the states of northeast Brazil. The cost estimates, as noted, were obtained from a single state (Ceará), and using this one source could limit generalizability of cost and cost-effectiveness results if the state's costs are substantially different from the regional levels. In general, this seems unlikely.

The book's title (*Educational Performance of the Poor: Lessons from Rural Northeast Brazil*) suggests that the Brazilian results might be used to better understand educational policy in other poor settings. Some caution is warranted in making these inferences. The results are most easily generalized to contexts where the population, the educational and socioeconomic environment, and the overall implementation and assessment of alternatives are similar. Several points should be considered. First, the authors' own analysis showed that results may differ within Brazil depending on the income level and urban/rural setting (see point 3.5 above). Thus, the results might best be applied to other poor and rural regions in Latin America, although care should be taken to ensure that the populations and settings are similar. Second, the prevailing ingredient costs could be different in other countries; for example, building materials might be cheaper in another setting, implying that "hardware" is relatively more cost-effective. This might be addressed by conducting a simple cost study in another setting. Third, the alternatives in northeast Brazil and elsewhere could differ dramatically in scope and content. There should at least be minimal parallels between Brazilian alternatives and those of another setting.

The Use of League Tables

By now, it should be evident that cost-effectiveness analysis is always a comparative undertaking. We estimate the costs and effectiveness of two or more interventions, and choose that which exhibits the lowest cost per unit of effectiveness. For example, Glewwe (1999) compared the relative costs and effects of three interventions aimed at raising mathematics and reading achievement in Ghana. The interventions included (a) repairing classrooms with leaky roofs, (b) providing classrooms with blackboards, and (c) providing more textbooks to students. In Botswana, a study by Fuller, Hua, and Snyder (1994) compared the cost-effectiveness of three interventions designed to raise mathematics achievement. These included (a) reducing class size, (b) additional teacher in-service training, and (c) providing supplementary math readers.

In making recommendations about the most cost-effective investments, the authors of each study are limited to the range of well-defined alternatives. Nevertheless, in each of the examples presented above, it is certainly possible that other interventions exist, beyond present consideration, that are more cost-effective than any of the others. Within the scope of a single cost study, there is no way to determine this. In search of a broader perspective, it is increasingly common for authors to place their study results in the context of a "league table."

League tables combine the results of many different cost-effectiveness or cost-utility analyses. They are a common feature of CE studies in the health fields. Several examples of health league tables are discussed in Drummond et al. (1997) and Boardman, Greenberg, Vining, and Weimer (1996). For example, one league table compares the cost-effectiveness of numerous government regulations—as diverse as steering column protection legislation and cattle feed regulation—at saving lives (Morrall, 1986). Another combines the results of cost-utility analyses of medical interventions, ranging from cholesterol testing to heart transplantation (Maynard, 1991). The cost-per-QALY of each intervention is compared (Example 8.2 provided a short discussion of Quality-Adjusted Life-Years). The World Bank commissioned a large number of studies in developing country health systems that were used to produce a wide-ranging league table (Jamison et al., 1993; World Bank, 1993).

League tables are much less common in education, perhaps because of the relative scarcity of cost-effectiveness studies. Fletcher, Hawley, and Piele (1990) produced a table that summarizes the results of several cost-effectiveness studies of computer-assisted instruction. The only other example of which we are aware—which summarizes a number of educational CE studies in developing countries—is discussed in Example 9.3 (Lockheed & Hanushek, 1988). As more cost-effectiveness analyses are carried out in education, we can surely expect the number of league tables to grow.

Despite their intuitive appeal, there are many reasons to be cautious in applying the results of league tables. Some of these reasons should already be familiar to readers who have studied the previous chapters or reviewed the checklist for evaluating cost studies. Drummond, Torrance, and Mason (1993) point out a number of caveats to the tables' interpretation, including: (a) the choice of discount rate, (b) the choice of importance weights (in the case of CU studies), (c) the range of costs considered, and (d) the choice of comparison program.

First, each study must choose a discount rate. As we have discussed, this is used to discount the estimated costs or effects to their present values, or it can be used to annualize the costs of buildings or durable goods. If studies use different discount rates, then their cost-effectiveness estimates may differ and interpretations may be skewed. Second, cost-utility studies require the use of utility weights. As we observed in Chapter 8, there are numerous methods for estimating these weights, all of which might turn up varying answers. This critique is most relevant in the health literature, where cost-utility analysis is frequently employed. Third, studies vary in the cost ingredients that are considered and in the care that is taken in placing values on ingredients. For example, some studies may concentrate exclusively on costs to the sponsor, ignoring the opportunity costs of client time. This could severely bias cost comparisons across studies. It is often difficult to assess the likelihood of biases, because many studies provide few details on their costing methodology. Fourth, each intervention in a cost-effectiveness analysis is compared to a baseline, such as the "status quo" or an existing program. Even though baselines might vary widely across studies and contexts, the cost-effectiveness comparisons in league tables implicitly presume a common baseline, which could mislead.

Further concerns arise if cost-effectiveness studies from several countries are compared (Drummond et al., 1993; Levin, 1995). In many health interventions—such as a particular vaccination or drug—estimates of effectiveness might be generally applied to many countries. In education, however, it may be difficult to reasonably extrapolate the estimates of effectiveness from one context to another. For example, "teacher training" or "textbooks" are particular kinds of interventions, but they obviously vary widely in their objectives and content across countries. Thus, evidence of textbooks' cost-effectiveness in one country may not tell us a great deal about how effective textbooks will be elsewhere. Even roughly similar interventions may be less effective in some contexts due to the culturally specific nature of educational production (Fuller & Clarke, 1994).

Cost comparisons across countries are equally challenging. First, the relative prices of cost ingredients—such as teacher salaries or building materials—often differ across countries or even across time periods in the same country. These differing prices could alter their relative cost-effectiveness. For example, if teacher salaries are particularly low in one country, then it might prove more cost-effective to invest in interventions that are labor-intensive (such as class size reduction). The opposite is true where teacher salaries are quite high. Second, costs must be converted into standard currency units. However, frequently utilized nominal exchange rates are less suitable than more sophisticated techniques that should probably be applied.[2] Third, it is often the case that cost studies do not use the ingredients methods, or they provide few details on their methodologies, and the lack of detail makes it difficult to compare their results to those of other studies.

What lessons can be drawn for producers and consumers of league tables? Perhaps most important is the need for included studies to adhere to basic methodological standards (Drummond et al., 1993). Otherwise, it becomes almost impossible to usefully compare their results. There has been some progress in defining methodological standards for cost-effectiveness and cost-utility analyses in health research (Gold, Siegel, Russell, & Weinstein, 1996; Weinstein, Siegel, Gold, Kamlet, & Russell, 1996). The

EXAMPLE 9.3. A Cost-Effectiveness League Table for Developing Countries

Educational resources are scarce and achievement is low in many developing countries. Multilateral organization such as the World Bank or the Inter-American Development Bank frequently make loans worth millions of dollars to these countries in order to contribute to the development of the education systems. Obviously, there are hundreds of possible ways that funds can be invested in the education system. Which investments would yield a given effect on achievement at the lowest cost (or provide the greatest effect for a given cost)? To answer the question, an ideal approach would be to conduct a comprehensive cost-effectiveness analysis in each country and even in particular regions within a country. For example, there are important cost-effectiveness analyses in Brazil (Harbison & Hanushek, 1992), Ghana (Glewwe, 1999), and India (World Bank, 1996).

Unfortunately, CE analyses are still rare. If possible, it would be desirable to apply lessons learned in one context to others where evidence is lacking. Lockheed and Hanushek gathered the results of several cost-effectiveness studies into a league table (summarized in Table 9.2). Almost all estimates pertain to developing countries, although one study from the United States is also included (Levin et al., 1987). Six general categories of education interventions are considered: textbooks, radio education, teacher education, technical-vocational secondary education, cross-age peer tutoring, and cooperative learning.

The authors first assembled the estimates of effectiveness in raising student achievement in many subjects, among them reading, mathematics, and science. Each measure of effectiveness was converted into an "effect size" (measured in standard deviation units) in order to make the diverse estimates comparable. The effect sizes of each intervention in a country were averaged. Thus, the effect size of 0.34 for textbooks in Brazil is an average of four effect sizes,

interested reader is encouraged to consult these sources for further details. A simple but useful guide for educational cost studies is the checklist that was given in Example 9.2. Producers of league tables should exclude (or deemphasize) studies that do not meet minimal standards related to the defi-

EXAMPLE 9.3. continued

drawn from 2 years of data (1981 and 1983) and two measures of effectiveness (reading and mathematics). The per-student cost of applying the intervention was then calculated. In some cases, costs were drawn from the original studies; in others, the authors consulted other sources to derive *ex post* estimates of cost.

The cost-effectiveness ratios indicate the cost for each unit of effectiveness. In examining the league table, one of the authors' general conclusions is that textbooks and radio education appear to be relatively more cost-effective in raising achievement than other kinds of interventions. Given the paucity of evidence, the authors clearly do not intend these results to be used as a strict guide to resource allocation. They observe that the table "only provide[s] examples of how decisions could be informed by such evidence" (Lockheed & Hanushek, 1988, p. 31).

Their reticence is justified by some of the critiques raised earlier. There are few details on the discount rates, ingredients, and costing methodologies used in each study (in some cases, the costs appear to be rough estimates).[3] All the costs are given in dollars, but it is not clear which exchange rates were used to convert from local currencies or whether costs from different time periods were adjusted for inflation. Finally, it is possible that interventions in one country are qualitatively different from those of another (e.g., the content of textbooks or curriculum of teacher training).

SOURCE: Lockheed and Hanushek (1988).

nition of a decision framework and alternatives, the estimation of costs, the estimation of effectiveness, and the proper conduct of a CE analysis (such as applying a sensitivity analysis). Likewise, consumers of league tables are encouraged to retrieve individual studies and subject them to the checklist.

TABLE 9.2 Costs, Effects, and Cost-Effectiveness Ratios of Educational Interventions in Developing Countries

Intervention	Cost Per Student	Effect on Achievement[a]	Cost/Effectiveness Ratio
Textbooks			
Brazil	$1.65	0.34	$4.85
Nicaragua	$1.75	0.36	$4.86
Philippines	$0.27	0.40	$0.68
Thailand	$0.25	0.06	$4.17
Radio education			
Kenya	$0.40	0.53	$0.75
Nicaragua	$1.80	0.55	$3.27
Thailand (northeast)	$0.44	0.58	$0.76
Teacher education			
Brazil (4 years primary)	$2.21	0.21	$10.52
Brazil (Logos II)	$1.84	0.09	$20.44
Brazil (3 years secondary)	$5.55	0.16	$34.69
Thailand (additional semester postsecondary)	$0.09	0.005	$16.67
Technical-vocational secondary			
Colombia (INEM)	$98.00	0.39	$251.28
Colombia (technical-vocational)	$376.00	0.33	$1,139.39
Tanzania (commercial)	$272.00	0.50	$544.00
Tanzania (technical)	$561.00	—	—
Tanzania (agricultural)	$375.00	—	—
Cross-age peer tutoring			
United States	$212.00	0.73	$290.41
Cooperative learning			
Israel	$85.00	1.40	$60.71

SOURCE: Adapted from Lockheed and Hanushek (1988, Table 3).

NOTE: See the original paper for sources of individual estimates. Note that their original table presents effectiveness-cost ratios, rather than the cost–effectiveness ratios presented above.

a. "—" indicates no evidence of positive effect.

Design and Implementation of Studies– Next Steps

As stated in Chapter 1, the purpose of this book is to familiarize the reader with the importance, utilization, conceptualization, and application of cost-analysis approaches to educational evaluations. In this final section, a number of other steps are presented for conducting an analysis, particularly for readers without a strong background in economics.

What Expertise Is Needed?

In most CB or CE evaluations, some expertise will be needed from persons who are specialists in these kinds of analyses. Accordingly, it is important to suggest here what kinds of expertise might be needed and how to assess prospective consultants. The evaluation analyst who requires assistance to develop CB or CE evaluations optimally should select a recognized expert who has done these types of evaluations before and whose work is recognized widely as being of high quality.

Almost any university economics department with a doctoral-level training program will have specialists in economic aspects of evaluation. Cost-benefit analysis, in particular, is a standard component in the study of public finance or government finance. That area addresses itself, in part, to efficiency in government spending and to maximizing social welfare (Musgrave & Musgrave, 1976). For this reason, at least rudiments of cost-benefit analysis will be familiar to virtually all doctoral-level economists who have specialized in government or public finance. In addition, the tool has become increasingly prominent in graduate-level curricula in education and public policy. While students receiving master's degrees in such programs are likely to possess only a consumer's knowledge of the CB and CE tools, some of the doctoral recipients will have specialized in this area of research. Finally, many prominent research organizations in the United States, such as RAND, are heavily engaged in the day-to-day conduct of many cost studies.

In seeking expertise, it is important to ascertain the relevance of the experience of the potential expert to the particular problem that will be raised. One should not assume that every public finance or public policy economist is an expert in CB or CE analysis without scrutinizing articles and reports prepared by that person. If the previous work of the prospective expert looks competent and creative and potentially applicable to the problem of interest, it is likely that the person will provide productive assistance. Above all, one should not confuse expertise in accounting with expertise in CB or CE analysis. While CB and CE analysts must have a good understanding of cost accounting, cost accountants need have no understanding of CB and CE analysis. Often, the correct approaches for cost accounting for business firms are inappropriate for estimating the costs of social projects. In fact, one of the dilemmas of public economics is that, frequently, social costs and benefits differ considerably from private ones. Cost accountants are not usually trained to address social costs and benefits.

Working With the Expert

One of the main purposes of this chapter has been to familiarize administrators and evaluators with the importance and requirements of cost analysis. It is hoped that this familiarity will assist them in working with the cost expert in a number of ways. First, it should assist the evaluator in finding and selecting a consultant on the CB, CE, or CU aspects of the evaluation. Second, it should enable the evaluator to work more productively with cost analysts, by providing an understanding of the basis and overall methodology of the cost-benefit and cost-effectiveness approaches. Normally, when a person is not familiar with a methodology or its terminology, he or she tends to assume that the expert has the answers. However, the premise of this chapter is that there must be an overlap in terms of knowledge among analysts and evaluators in order for productive collaboration to take place.

Finally, a creative collaboration with an expert in economic evaluation requires that the overall evaluation problem be cast in a specific framework that incorporates cost-benefit or cost-effectiveness analysis appropriately. In this respect, the evaluator should be able to conceptualize the nature of the CB, CE, or CU analysis that corresponds to the particular decision problem that is posed. Although expertise may be needed on the precise measurement of costs and benefits, or effects, the actual formulation of the conceptual framework should not be the sole province of the consultant. Rather, the conceptual framework should be based upon an overall understanding by the administrator and evaluator of what is appropriate to the problem. The review of illustrations and concepts from this volume should be of assistance in providing a foundation of knowledge for the evaluator who lacks skills in economic analysis.

Incorporating Cost Analysis Into Evaluation Designs

A final concern is the need to incorporate cost analysis into the evaluation design itself, rather than rely upon the collection of cost data as an afterthought. Clearly, once it has been determined that a CB, CU, or CE study is appropriate, the provision for collecting data on costs is just as important as the provision for data collection on effects. It is much easier to obtain accurate cost estimates when analytic procedures are built into the evaluation design than it is to later collect them on a post hoc basis, because it is possible to account more fully for the resource ingredients that are incorporated into each alternative during the actual functioning of the evaluation. In fact, it is often impossible to ascertain the precise resources that were used after the evaluation of effectiveness has been completed.

Accordingly, an attempt should be made to construct procedures for accounting for ingredients and assessing their costs in the evaluation design itself. Such an effort will provide more accurate and systematic estimates of the costs of the alternatives, and it may also reduce the costs of data collection.

A Final Word

This volume was designed for a wide audience with differing proficiencies in evaluation and economics and with differing expectations for their use of cost analysis. However, those who wish to use the tools provided in this book will wish to read specific studies that have applied the tools to education and other areas. For this purpose, Appendix B contains a bibliography of references that are divided according to specific applications of the methodologies in education. Other readers will wish to seek out studies that apply the tools to their substantive areas of endeavor.

Exercises

1. Assume that you undertake a cost-effectiveness study of alternative ways of improving the mathematics proficiencies of high school students in your state. Your report will be sent to school administrators in all the school districts. What advice would you give them in considering how to apply the results of your report to their districts?

2. Why should secondary audiences be cautious about using CU results that were done for a primary audience?

3. Take a specific CE study, possibly from Appendix B. Use the checklist for evaluating cost analysis reports in order to assess that study.

4. You are a district superintendent who has come across a cost-effectiveness "league table" that summarizes the results of many studies that assessed the costs and effects of interventions to improve reading achievement. Computer-assisted instruction appears to have among the lowest cost-effectiveness ratios of all the alternatives. Is this a compelling enough reason to devote more resources to this intervention?

5. Identify sources of local expertise in cost analysis and in evaluation design. What criteria have you used?

6. What types of assistance would you need in doing a cost evaluation, and what types of expertise could you contribute to the activity?

▶ NOTES

1. See Rossi and Freeman (1993, pp. 443-447) and the citations therein. We have relied on their discussion.

2. For example, purchasing power parity adjustments should be made.

3. One specific example (out of many) in which there might be concern about comparability is the study on cross-age peer tutoring (Levin, Glass, & Meister, 1987). It was conducted in the United States. The costs of personnel in the United States are typically 10 or more times what they are in developing countries.

Appendix A:
Feedback on Exercises

The purpose of this appendix is to provide feedback on the exercises. This will enable you to test your understanding of the material. The nature of the questions in the exercises varies substantially. Some of the questions call for specific answers, while others suggest a discussion of issues. Still others ask you to construct examples for analysis. In some cases there is a single answer or best answer. In others there are many alternatives, but each must be qualified on the basis of the assumptions that you are making. Finally, some answers are spelled out in great detail in the text and require only referring to those sections for review. For these reasons, it is not possible to provide in this section a concise answer to every question in the exercises, for there may not be a single answer for the open questions, and we do not wish to reproduce the lengthy discussions in the text. However, an attempt has been made to provide feedback in each case that should be of assistance in responding to each question.

Chapter 1

1. Choosing the "most effective" alternative—in the absence of cost information—could increase overall costs if the "most effective" alternative were more costly relative to the effects it produces than some other alternative. A hypothetical illustration could show two alternatives in which the higher effectiveness of one alternative was more than offset by higher costs.

2. These studies do not meet the criteria for cost-effectiveness analysis since they do not take account of educational results. They take account

249

only of costs and enrollments, rather than the educational effectiveness of the schools for their enrollments.

3. This information can be found in the explicit descriptions of each approach contained in the chapter (see Table 1.5 in particular).

4 a. This situation fits a CB framework, in which one could compare the earnings of high school graduates in vocational and nonvocational curricula. For each alternative, an estimate would be made of costs and of estimated future earnings based on employment experiences and wages for recent graduates. Since the vocational curriculum is typically more costly than the others, the benefits would have to be higher as well to justify expansion of vocational enrollments.

A CE approach could also be used if an appropriate measure of effectiveness is established. For example, programs could be evaluated on the proportion of recent graduates who found employment within some reasonable period. The costs would be measured in the same way for both CB and CE analyses.

b. In general, this situation suggests a cost-utility strategy, since the results cannot be evaluated in monetary terms and the measures of effectiveness for different courses would differ. The administration can nominate groups of courses that are nonmandatory and susceptible to cuts. These can be evaluated for their enrollments, teaching effectiveness, value to students, and so on, through student, parent, and administrator ratings. Using methods described in Chapter 8, these can be converted to utility scales. These ratings can be related to costs to create CU values. Those with the highest CU ratios would be cut first until the desired reduction was reached.

c. This problem could be addressed with CB analysis. The costs of the program would be the new faculty, staff, and facilities that would be required. The benefits might be viewed as the additional tuition and instructional grants that could be obtained. In this case the new program would be undertaken if costs were less than benefits and if the CB ratio were lower than for other alternatives that might also be considered.

d. This situation suggests a CF study to ascertain what the costs of the new policy would be. This can be compared with available resources.

e. All of these alternatives can be evaluated on the basis of their contribution to student writing. Accordingly, a common measure of effectiveness can be used for the evaluation, and a CE analysis is appropriate.

f. This is a community college version of 4(b), above, and CU analysis would be appropriate.

g. Since both alternatives can be evaluated on a common measure of effectiveness—mathematics competencies—CE analysis can be prescribed.

Chapter 2

1 a. There are many potential causes of declining test scores. These include a changing student composition; changes in curriculum; changes in the test instruments; poorer educational conditions, such as rising class sizes and shorter school days; changes in the home; reduced homework assignments; and so on. Problem identification would require exploring all of these possibilities through interviews and studies of school data.

b. The two leading possibilities for low job placements are a poor job market and a poor training program. The nature of the job market can be assessed by interviewing employers of physics majors in the regions where students usually seek employment. The reputation of the college's program in physics can also be ascertained from such interviews. At the same time, it might be possible to find out from employers how physics graduates' chances for placement might be improved. This information can delineate the specific nature of the problem and where potential interventions should be considered.

c. A budgetary deficit can be resolved through cutting expenditures or raising revenues. Therefore, both areas should be explored to understand the nature of the problem. On the revenue side, one might explore the potential areas of income, including the possibilities of greater funds from state and federal sources, from leasing or selling unused facilities, and from private sources. On the expenditure side, there are many possibilities as well. A preliminary analysis should be made of how the problem arose and how it might be addressed, including a variety of alternatives for both increasing revenues and cutting expenditures.

d. It is important to understand why the university is seeking to replace its mainframe computer. Is the equipment inadequate for the present or projected workload? Is it too expensive to use or maintain relative to more modern equipment? Does it lack the capabilities for meeting certain needs? All of these questions are important for setting out alternatives. For example, if it does not have the capabilities for meeting certain needs, it may be possible to meet these at minimal cost by contracting with outside providers. If there is an overload, it might be useful to consider inexpensive desktop computers to handle some tasks that are presently relegated to the mainframe.

2. There are a great many possibilities. Many of these were referred to above and should be developed more fully here.

3. In each case the primary audience would be composed of those groups that have a direct stake in the decision. The secondary audience would be composed of those groups that have an interest in the evaluation for other purposes. Obviously, the specific answers will depend on your response to the previous question.

4. The answers depend on the nature of the problem and the alternatives that you have selected.

5. Once you have set out the problem and alternatives, it is possible to determine if a formal cost analysis is worthwhile by assessing what might be gained and what the evaluation might cost. The question of what might be gained by the evaluation hinges on the importance of what is at stake. If one is referring to programs with large cost implications, it is more likely that the findings can save substantial resources relative to doing no analysis. Much of this assessment will be intuitive and subjective. If it appears that the decision process will not be responsive to a cost evaluation, it may not be worth doing. The approximate cost of the evaluation can be determined by doing a rough assessment of the resources that will be required.

Chapter 3

1. The term "cost" refers to a sacrifice of some valued resource, whether tangible or intangible.

2 a. A day spent in obtaining a passport is a day lost from other endeavors, such as work or leisure. The value of what was lost might be calculated from

the earnings that one could have obtained by working instead of renewing the passport.

b. At first glance, the cost of your failure to keep records would appear to be the additional amount of tax that had to be paid, which could have been avoided with sufficient documentation. However, we must bear in mind that there is a cost to maintaining records on the pertinent transactions. Therefore, the net cost of the situation is the difference between what would have been saved on taxes and the cost of maintaining the necessary documentation. It is possible that the cost of maintaining records would have been greater than the tax saving for doing so.

c. The costs are determined by the resources required for the party, as well as those required to restore the lawns and shrubbery.

d. The cost to the school of the teacher patrols is what is being given up by using teachers in that way rather than for instruction.

e. The completion of the master's degree has both costs and benefits. Although the benefits of completing the master's degree (such as better employment opportunities or higher earnings) are sacrificed by not completing it, there are also cost savings attached to not diverting time and resources in that direction. Thus the cost can be determined only by ascertaining what benefits are being lost by deferring the master's and what costs are saved by that deferral. The net cost is the difference between the benefits that are lost and the costs that are saved.

3. These details are found in the text under the section "Inadequacy of Budgets for Cost Analysis."

4. The nature of the ingredients approach is also found in the text of this chapter.

5 a. The ingredients include the facility, parent volunteers, tutors, materials, resources for training, and professional staff. Try to describe each of these in more detail on the basis of some hypothetical set of requirements. For example, the facility would include one regular classroom with its share of energy requirements, maintenance, furnishings, and insurance.

b. The ingredients would include the coaches and other personnel, equipment and uniforms, space to practice, insurance, transportation requirements for travel to competitions, and so on. Try to provide more detail.

c. The school district would need to consider such personnel as administrators, teachers, audiologists, health personnel, facilities, equipment, materials and supplies, and so on. Try to develop more details.

d. Ingredients would include those required for the new curriculum and teacher retraining. Curriculum costs would be associated with such ingredients as new materials and equipment. Retraining costs would entail the costs of such ingredients as trainers, space for retraining, additional time commitments from teachers to permit retraining or substitute teachers to allow regular teachers to take retraining during regular school hours, and so on. Try to develop more details.

Chapter 4

1. Market prices refer to prices that are determined in the open and competitive marketplace. A definition can be found in the chapter. They should be used whenever an ingredient is purchased in such a market. Usually there is a reasonably competitive market for teachers in the United States (especially if smaller districts abound that compete for teachers), so teacher salaries and fringe benefits can be viewed as the market price for a teacher with particular characteristics.

2. A shadow price refers to some value that is placed on an ingredient in the absence of a market price. It could be the equivalent of the market price if there were a market for the ingredient. Essentially, it is an attempt to use market-type principles to place a price on an ingredient where that information cannot be obtained directly from the marketplace. An example would be using the leasing cost of equivalent space as the shadow price of an educational facility that has been allotted by the school district for an intervention.

3. The use of market prices assumes that a virtually unlimited amount of a resource or ingredient could be obtained at that price. However, in many

cases, resources may be scarce and may have to be bid away from alternative uses to obtain more of them. In those cases, any increase in demand to meet the needs for future replications may be lead to a rise in price for the ingredient. The problem is that we must make some assessment of how much the price will rise to meet the replication requirements.

4. To the degree that paid personnel are obtained in competitive markets, it is desirable to use their actual salaries and fringe benefits to determine their cost. The value of volunteers can be ascertained by determining what it would cost to obtain similarly qualified personnel to perform the same tasks.

5. The costs of facilities can be ascertained in two ways. The easiest is to take the lease or rental value of the facilities. Of course, if the facility is used for a number of activities, only that portion used for the intervention under scrutiny should be included in the cost. In the case in which the facility is not leased and no lease value can be determined, one can determine the value by knowing the replacement cost, the life of the facility, and the interest rate for this type of investment. Given that information, Table 4.1 can be used to determine the proportion of the replacement cost that is equal to the "annualized" cost of the facility.

6. At an interest rate of 5%, the annualized value would be $71,000; at 10%, it would be $110,200; and at 15%, it would be $154,700.

7. About $98,100.

8. The answer is similar to that for facilities in exercise 5, above.

9. $2,229.

Chapter 5

1. To answer this question, construct worksheets for estimating costs for each alternative. On the basis of the description for the interventions, suggest the ingredients that might be relevant. Follow the procedures set out in

Chapter 4 for ascertaining how costs would be estimated. Remember that the cost of identifying the potential dropouts is common to both programs and should not be charged to either one. Program A will require counseling, facilities, and some clerical and record-keeping activities. Program B would require some placement and clerical functions. Please provide some details.

2. This question requires you to allocate the costs among the various constituencies on the worksheet and to calculate the net costs. The details for doing so are found in the text of this chapter.

3. This question assumes that the cost-effectiveness rankings will be based on the overall costs and effects from a societal perspective. However, the sponsor or other constituencies may face different costs and effects. Differences in costs may be created by cash subsidies or different ingredient allocations from one constituency to another. Differences in effects may be created by particular constituencies valuing effects only for their members. On this basis, the cost-effectiveness ranking for a particular decision maker representing a particular constituency may differ from the overall ranking.

4. Costs are most uncertain for ingredients that are in the developmental stage (e.g., technological applications) and those for which neither market prices nor shadow prices are readily apparent. Provide specific illustrations from your own experience. The procedures for a sensitivity analysis can be found in the text of this chapter.

5. The time pattern of resource deployment is important because resources needed in the present require greater sacrifices than those that will be required in the future. When resource use is deferred, those resources can be used for other purposes until they are needed for the intervention. Accordingly, a sum of annual costs is not adequate in itself. We must also make adjustments for the time pattern of the cost allocations by using present-value calculations for all alternatives.

6. The conceptual basis is that the present-value calculation discounts or reduces the value of future resource requirements relative to present ones. That is, future cost outlays of a particular amount will be weighed less heavily than equivalent outlays at present.

7. The simple summation of costs for the 7 years is $124,300. Their present value at a 5% discount rate is $105,395. Their present value at a 10% discount rate is $90,798.

8. Cost-feasibility is determined by comparing resource availability of a constituency with the costs of each alternative. Since Table 5.1 enables you to determine the costs of each alternative for each constituency, these results can be contrasted with the resource constraints for each constituency. Let us say that a CF calculation is made for a number of alternatives. For at least one of them, the cost to the sponsor exceeds the cost constraint of the sponsor. If this alternative appeared to be particularly attractive, the sponsor might wish to solicit additional resources from other constituencies to bring the alternative within the boundaries of cost-feasibility.

9. The analysis should be based upon marginal costs and effects whenever the interventions are add-ons to existing programs. An example would be the case of alternative programs to increase reading speed, where all the possibilities would provide additional resources while not altering the basic program.

10. The main issue involved here is that the ranking of CE alternatives for small-scale interventions might not be pertinent for large-scale ones. The larger the scale (e.g., enrollment level) of an intervention, the greater the advantages of alternatives with large fixed-cost components. The smaller the scale of an intervention, the greater the advantages of alternatives with larger variable-cost components. Therefore, interventions should be evaluated for variable versus fixed costs and the implications that this will have on cost-effectiveness when shifting interventions from a single school to a school district.

Chapter 6

1. The answer will depend upon which evaluation you choose to address.

2. The answer will depend upon which evaluation you chose in Exercise 1.

3. This could be approached as a CE problem in which the different alternatives are evaluated for their effectiveness in mathematics and science instruction. That is, a common measure of effectiveness, such as a test score, can be used for each instructional domain. The alternatives can be evaluated for their effects on test scores through standard evaluation design. Each alternative should be evaluated for its ingredients requirements and costs. Costs should also be distributed among constituencies. This distribution might show, for example, that the cost to the sponsor of contributed scientists and mathematicians from industry will be low, even though the cost to industry will be high.

4. The approach will probably not be very useful, especially if the meta-analysis considered general categories of interventions (e.g., computer-assisted instruction), rather than a specific variety of intervention that can be recommended to policy makers (e.g., a particular combination of software, hardware, and instructional strategy). Moreover, it will be difficult to place a cost on general categories of interventions, because there is no obvious way to identify the ingredients that make up each intervention. In a meta-analysis, the effect size for a particular intervention is an average of many kinds of programs that probably differ in their ingredients (and costs).

5. The CE study is aided by the fact that effectiveness results already exist for both programs. Thus, it is most important to conduct a cost analysis based on the ingredients method. What are the incremental costs of each program to the university? The evaluator should cast a wide net in searching for ingredients. For example, the upper-level students may be volunteers (or receive minimal payments), but we should endeavor to estimate the opportunity cost of their time.

The effectiveness and cost results can be used to calculate cost-effectiveness ratios. A difference of 10% in the ratios suggests that a sensitivity analysis should be conducted. Are the cost-effectiveness rankings the same when more or less conservative assumptions are made about the potential effectiveness or cost ingredients of each program? (In this case, it seems likely that there is less uncertainty about the effects and costs of the first program, because it has already been implemented on a pilot basis at the university.) If the rankings change, the evaluator may wish to pursue higher-quality information on costs and effects. The evaluator should also consider outside information in her recommendation, such as the attitudes of key stakeholders (see Chapter 9 for a full discussion).

Chapter 7

1. Educational interventions that prepare persons for labor markets and employment often lend themselves to CB analyses. Since a major focus of such projects is to improve employment and wages, the overall results can be viewed in terms of the additional earnings associated with the education or training. Of course, any program could be subjected to a CB analysis, as long as we can monetize the benefits. In some cases (such as preschool programs) this is difficult unless we follow the participants into the labor market over a period of many years or use an alternative method of estimating benefits, such as contingent valuation.

2. The focus of the evaluation would be to compare the costs of each program with its benefits. Costs can be estimated using the ingredients method to obtain a cost per graduate. Costs should include the forgone earnings of the individual while undergoing training. Benefits can be assessed by doing a follow-up on recent graduates to obtain their employment experiences and wages. These can be used to construct estimates of annual earnings per graduate. The overall benefit of each program would be the additional annual earnings per graduate relative to what would have been received without the training. Poor placements will be reflected in unemployment, which will result in low annual earnings for graduates. (A caveat to this approach is that the internal validity of the evaluation design may be low, due to the lack of randomized assignment between treatment and comparison groups.)

Benefit-cost ratios can be calculated for each program (the BC ratio is an appropriate measure because the scales of the programs are similar; however, we might also wish to calculate alternative measures such as net benefits). A necessary condition for retention of a program is that the BC ratio be greater than 1, so that benefits are greater than costs. Of programs that have BC ratios greater than 1, we should rank order the programs and allow the committee to decide whether the lower-ranking programs should be kept or eliminated.

3. The authors of these studies are making an important assumption: that grade-level equivalents of achievement gain are equivalent to additional time spent in school. This assumption may or may not be legitimate. When assumptions like these are made, it is important to present any evidence that may exist to support them (e.g., prior studies). If no evidence exists, then this should be clearly stated, and the results interpreted more cautiously. In either case, a sensitivity analysis should be conducted that explores whether the key findings are robust to more conservative assumptions about the relationship between grade-level equivalents and earnings.

4. "Drop-out prevention" is a rather broad category that could encompass any number of programs. You may first wish to choose a particular program that has been piloted in New Jersey or another state. Without focusing on a particular program, it will be difficult to estimate the program costs. The costs should be estimated via the ingredients method. If the program has not been implemented in New Jersey, you should be careful to adjust the cost analysis to the context of New Jersey. For example, teacher salaries may be higher or lower in New Jersey than other states, and this would affect the costs of programs that rely on additional school personnel.

The method of estimating the benefits will depend on whether any evaluations have already been conducted. Let us assume that another team of evaluators has already conducted an effectiveness evaluation of the drop-out prevention program that you are considering. They assessed the number of dropouts prevented by the program, as well as many other measures of effectiveness (e.g., test score gains and likelihood of getting in trouble with the local authorities). An obvious measure of monetary benefits is the wage gains that accrue to students who stay in school versus those who drop out. You could obtain data on the wages of dropouts and high school graduates in New Jersey, using published census data or another source, and use this to estimate the monetary benefits of the program over the lifetime of students (being careful to discount the benefits for their distribution over time). Of course, it would be even more desirable to actually observe the relative wages of participants and nonparticipants in the program, by observing their success in the labor market over a period of years, but time constraints of your evaluation may not allow for this.

Beyond wage gains, you should consider other potential categories of benefits. For example, the effectiveness evaluation may have revealed that high school graduates are less likely to commit crimes that are costly to the local community. The cost savings of crime reduction can be considered an additional category of benefits. Even if benefits such as these cannot be explicitly estimated, the cost-benefit analysis should discuss their potential magnitudes and how results might be biased by their exclusion.

5. It is first necessary to establish the alternatives that will be considered. Three obvious alternatives would be the programs that were described in the exercise; in addition, one could design other variants on these programs that combined various elements of the three strategies (e.g., job training in addition to child care). One evaluation design that might be pursued would be a randomized experiment. Applicants to the alternatives could be randomly assigned to receive the "treatment" or to serve as a control group. After the treatment is applied, the members of each group would be followed for as long as time and resource constraints would permit, and their outcomes would be compared. In this case, an important benefit would be the wage gains of program participants—or lack thereof—relative to nonparticipants. At least in the initial stages of the evaluation, wages can be observed for only a short period after the program, although we are ultimately interested in lifetime wage gains. Thus, some projections may be required, and the procedures for doing so should be carefully described.

Another category of benefits would be savings in welfare payments (presuming that participants are less likely to receive welfare). For the most part, however, the savings in welfare payments to taxpayers are offset by losses to participants. Thus, they represent a transfer from one group of constituents to another, rather than a net benefit to society (even so, there may be benefits produced by the reduced administrative costs of operating a welfare system).

Chapter 8

1. The advantages of CU in comparison with CE and CB are (a) its use of a variety of existing information on the interventions, including the knowledge, experience, and intuition of the decision makers and (b) its abilities to draw upon the judgments and preferences of stakeholders and to address several outcomes. The disadvantage is that the results are often subjective (especially because of the difficulty of arriving at consistent measures of preferences), so that they are not replicable or generalizable from situation to situation.

2. A CU analysis of which additional language courses to offer would begin by ascertaining the relevant audiences that have a legitimate interest in the outcome (i.e., the stakeholders). Once these are identified, you should indicate the criteria that each might use to set priorities and how you would construct utility scales to measure their preferences. The costs of the alternatives would be measured using the ingredients method. A marginal-cost approach would be pertinent, since you are concerned with the additional costs of providing another year or 2 of instruction in a particular language. Thus, it may be possible that, for some languages, there are teachers on the staff who could simply add a course in the language in place of other duties, whereas for other languages, new teachers would have to be hired. The alternative combinations of languages and their costs should be formulated and compared in the CU evaluation.

3. One way to accomplish this is to separately estimate the effectiveness of interventions for each group that is being considered (e.g., disadvantaged versus advantaged). Then, the evaluator might attempt to elicit the preferences of a group of stakeholders (e.g., the local community, policymakers, or school personnel) for the outcomes of these groups. For example, the stakeholders may place a slightly higher weight on the outcomes of disadvantaged students, or they may weight both groups equally. Using the methods described in the text, the evaluator can obtain a set of importance weights for each group. The effectiveness results for each group can be multiplied by the importance weights and summed in order to arrive at an overall measure of utility for each program. A sensitivity analysis could be conducted by recalculating the results using alternative sets of importance weights.

4. One could conduct a CU analysis by combining the two measures of effectiveness into a single measure of utility. Toward doing so, one needs to estimate importance weights that reflect the relative importance given by stakeholders to each outcome. Depending on the constraints of time and resources, one might attempt to survey a sample of local community members or parents, using some of the preference elicitation methods that were described in the chapter. If time is limited, one might attempt the same exercise

with a smaller group of teachers and other school personnel. The importance weights are used to obtain a single measure of utility for each curriculum, following the procedures described in the chapter. Each measure of utility can be used to construct a single cost-utility ratio for each alternative.

Chapter 9

1. The most important point to stress is that generalizability of a state study to an individual situation is always problematic. You should ascertain the degree to which the state study is based upon students and schools that are representative of those of the specific district in question. A great deal of judgment must be added to the state results to see how they apply in any given situation. This should include various idiosyncratic factors that may or may not support your recommendations in a particular situation. You should try to be specific about which factors a local school district should consider in making this determination.

2. Secondary audiences should be cautious about using CU results that were done for a primary audience because of the nature of the CU methodology and results. For instance, importance weights may vary according to the different populations that are surveyed or according to the method that was employed to elicit preferences. Before applying the CU results, one should look for similarities and differences in the preference structures of stakeholders that were surveyed in the initial study and those to which the study might be applied.

3. This requires a straightforward use of the checklist to evaluate a specific study.

4. Before acting on these results, it is important to obtain more information about the individual studies that were used to construct the league table. What exactly are the alternatives that are being considered (beyond general categories like "computer-assisted instruction")? What were the methodologies used to conduct the studies? For example, did they all follow the ingredients method in obtaining cost estimates, or did they exclude key cost ingredients? To explore these questions, it would be helpful to subject some of the studies to the quality checklist in this chapter. When were these studies conducted (and, if they are quite old, is it likely that costs or effectiveness have changed over time)?

5. The answer will vary according to your situation.

6. The answer will vary according to your situation.

Appendix B:
A Bibliography of Cost Studies in Education

Once you have completed this volume, you may wish to review specific studies using CE, CB, and CU approaches, both to test your understanding of the subject and to see how the techniques have been applied in specific settings. The purpose of this bibliography is to provide references to general methodological readings and to specific ones on cost analysis in education. We have divided the studies into thematic categories and according to whether they are conducted in developed or developing countries (occasionally we have listed a study in two or more categories when it assesses a wide variety of alternatives).

The inclusion of a study should not be interpreted as an endorsement of its methods or conclusions. In fact, the studies vary rather widely in their quality, and a useful exercise would be to test your understanding by applying the checklist in Chapter 9 to some of these studies. In some cases the studies are unclear on their methodologies. For example, many lack detail on the conceptual framework and procedures used to measure costs. Some may fail to make a distinction between the total costs of an intervention and their allocation among different constituencies. Nevertheless, they highlight the enormous range of purposes to which cost analysis can be applied; they also emphasize the great potential for further research to expand our knowledge.

Bilingual Education: Developed Countries

CARPENTER-HUFFMAN, P., & SAMULON, M. (1981). *Case studies of delivery and cost of bilingual education* (N-1684-ED). Santa Monica, CA: RAND.

PARRISH, T. (1994a). A cost analysis of alternative instructional models for Limited English Proficient Students in California. *Journal of Education Finance, 19*(3), 256-278.

PARRISH, T. (1994b). K-12 categorical programs. In W. S. Barnett (Ed.), *Cost analysis for education decisions: Methods and examples* (Vol. 4, pp. 113-144). Greenwich, CT: JAI.

Class Size Reduction: Developed Countries

BETTS, J. R. (1996). Is there a link between school inputs and earnings? Fresh scrutiny of an old literature. In G. Burtless (Ed.), *Does money matter? The effect of school resources on student achievement and adult success* (pp. 141-191). Washington, DC: Brookings Institution.

BREWER, D. J., KROP, C., GILL, B. P., & REICHARDT, R. (1999). Estimating the cost of national class size reductions under different policy alternatives. *Educational Evaluation and Policy Analysis, 21*(2), 179-192.

KRUEGER, A. B., & WHITMORE, D. M. (2000). *The effect of attending a small class in the early grades on college test taking and middle school test results: Evidence from Project STAR.* (National Bureau of Economic Research Working Paper No. 7656). Cambridge, MA: National Bureau of Economic Research.

LEVIN, H. M., GLASS, G. V., & MEISTER, G. R. (1987). Cost-effectiveness of computer-assisted instruction. *Evaluation Review, 11*(1), 50-72.

Class Size Reduction: Developing Countries

BEDI, A. S., & MARSHALL, J. H. (1999). School attendance and student achievement: Evidence from rural Honduras. *Economic Development and Cultural Change, 47*(3), 657-682.

FULLER, B., HUA, H., & SNYDER, C. W. (1994). When girls learn more than boys: The influence of time in school and pedagogy in Botswana. *Comparative Education Review, 38*(3), 347-376.

Compensatory Education: Developed Countries

GARMS, W. I. (1971). A benefit-cost analysis of the Upward Bound program. *Journal of Human Resources, 6*(2), 206-220.

RIBICH, T. (1968). *Education and poverty.* Washington, DC: Brookings Institution.

Computer-Assisted Instruction: Developed Countries

DALGAARD, B. R., LEWIS, D. R., & BOYER, C. M. (1984). Cost and effectiveness considerations in the use of computer-assisted instruction in economics. *Journal of Economic Education, 15*(4), 309-323.

FLETCHER, J. D. (1990). *Effectiveness and costs of interactive videodisc instruction in defense training and education* (IDA Paper P-2372). Alexandria, VA: Institute for Defense Analyses.

FLETCHER, J. D., HAWLEY, D. E., & PIELE, P. K. (1990). Costs, effects, and utility of microcomputer assisted instruction in the classroom. *American Educational Research Journal, 27*(4), 783-806.

JAMISON, D. T., FLETCHER, J. D., SUPPES, P., & ATKINSON, R. C. (1976). Cost and performance of computer-assisted instruction for education of disadvantaged children. In J. T. Froomkin, D. T. Jamison, & R. Radner (Eds.), *Education as an industry* (pp. 201-240). Cambridge, MA: Ballinger Publishing.

KELTNER, B., & ROSS, R. L. (1996). *The cost of school-based educational technology programs.* Santa Monica, CA: RAND.

LEVIN, H. M., GLASS, G. V., & MEISTER, G. R. (1987). Cost-effectiveness of computer-assisted instruction. *Evaluation Review, 11*(1), 50-72.

LEVIN, H. M., LEITNER, D., & MEISTER, G. R. (1986). *Cost-effectiveness of alternative approaches to computer-assisted instruction* (87-CERAS-1). Stanford, CA: Center for Educational Research at Stanford.

LEVIN, H. M., & WOO, L. (1981). An evaluation of the costs of computer-assisted instruction. *Economics of Education Review, 1*(1), 1-25.

LEWIS, D. R., DALGAARD, B. R., & BOYER, C. M. (1985). Cost effectiveness of computer-assisted economics instruction. *American Economic Review, 75*(2), 91-96.

BIBLIOGRAPHY

LEWIS, D. R., STOCKDILL, S. J., & TURNER, T. C. (1990). Cost-effectiveness of micro-computers in adult basic reading. *Adult Literacy and Basic Education, 14*(2), 136-149.

NIEMIEC, R. P., SIKORSKI, M. F., & WALBERG, H. J. (1989). Comparing the cost-effectiveness of tutoring and computer-based instruction. *Journal of Educational Computing Research, 5*(4), 395-407.

SOLMON, L. C. (1999). Afterword. In D. Mann, C. Shakeshaft, J. Becker, & R. Kottkamp (Eds.), *West Virginia story: Achievement gains from a statewide comprehensive instructional technology program* (pp. 43-50). Santa Monica, CA: Milken Family Foundation.

Cost-of-Education Indices: Developed Countries

CHAMBERS, J. (1980). The development of a cost of education index. *Journal of Education Finance, 5*(3), 262-281.

CHAMBERS, J. (1981). The hedonic wage technique as a tool for estimating the costs of school personnel: A theoretical exposition with implications for empirical analysis. *Journal of Education Finance, 6*, 330-354.

CHAMBERS, J., & FOWLER, W. J. (1995). *Public school teacher cost differences across the United States.* Washington, DC: National Center for Education Statistics.

CHAMBERS, J., & PARRISH, T. (1994). State-level education finance. In W. S. Barnett (Ed.), *Cost analysis for education decisions: Methods and examples* (Vol. 4, pp. 45-74). Greenwich, CT: JAI.

DOWNES, T. A., & POGUE, T. F. (1994). Adjusting school aid formulas for the higher cost of educating disadvantaged students. *National Tax Journal, 47*(1), 89-110.

DUNCOMBE, W., RUGGIERO, J., & YINGER, J. (1996). Alternative approaches to measuring the cost of education. In H. F. Ladd (Ed.), *Holding schools accountable: Performance-based reform in education* (pp. 327-356). Washington, DC: Brookings Institution.

Curriculum: Developed Countries

QUINN, B., VAN MONDFRANS, A., & WORTHEN, B. R. (1984). Cost-effectiveness of two math programs as moderated by pupil SES. *Educational Evaluation and Policy Analysis, 6*(1), 39-52.

Delinquency Treatment: Developed Countries

WEINROTT, M. R., JONES, R. R., & HOWARD, J. R. (1982). Cost-effectiveness of teaching family programs for delinquents: Results of a national evaluation. *Evaluation Review, 6*(2), 173-201.

Drop-Outs: Developed Countries

CATTERALL, J. S. (1987). On the social costs of dropping out of school. *The High School Journal, 81*(1), 19-30.

LEVIN, H. M. (1972). *The cost to the nation of inadequate education* [Report prepared for the Select Senate Committee on Equal Educational Opportunity, 92nd Congress, 2nd Session]. Washington, DC: Government Printing Office.

STERN, D., DAYTON, C., PAIK, I. -W., & WEISBERG, A. (1989). Benefits and costs of dropout prevention in a high school program combining academic and vocational education: Third-year results from replications of the California Peninsula Academies. *Educational Evaluation and Policy Analysis, 11*(4), 405-416.

WEISBROD, B. A. (1965). Preventing high school dropouts. In R. Dorfman (Ed.), *Measuring benefits of government investments* (pp. 117-148). Washington, DC: Brookings Institution.

Drop-Outs: Developing Countries

CANN, K. T. (1982). An economic evaluation of elementary education for dropouts in Indonesia. *Economics of Education Review, 2*(1), 67-89.

Early Childhood Education: Developed Countries

BARNETT, W. S. (1985). Benefit-cost analysis of the Perry Preschool Program and its policy implications. *Educational Evaluation and Policy Analysis, 7*(4), 333-342.

BARNETT, W. S. (1985). *The Perry Preschool Program and its long-term effects: A benefit-cost analysis.* Ypsilanti, MI: High/Scope Educational Research Foundation.

BIBLIOGRAPHY

BARNETT, W. S. (1992). Benefits of compensatory preschool education. *Journal of Human Resources, 27*(2), 279-312.

BARNETT, W. S. (1993). Benefit-cost analysis of preschool education: Findings from a 25-year follow-up. *American Journal of Orthopsychiatry, 63*(4), 500-508.

BARNETT, W. S. (1993). Economic evaluation of home visiting programs. *The Future of Children, 3*(3), 93-112.

BARNETT, W. S. (1996). *Lives in the balance: Age-27 benefit-cost analysis of the High/Scope Perry Preschool Program.* Ypsilanti, MI: High/Scope Press.

BARNETT, W. S., & ESCOBAR, C. M. (1987). The economics of early educational intervention: A review. *Review of Educational Research, 57*(4), 387-414.

BARNETT, W. S., ESCOBAR, C. M., & RAVSTEN, M. T. (1988). Parent and clinic early intervention for children with language handicaps: A cost-effectiveness analysis. *Journal of the Division for Early Childhood, 12*(4), 290-298.

BARNETT, W. S., & PEZZINO, J. (1987). Cost-effectiveness analysis for state and local decision making: An application to half-day and full-day preschool special education programs. *Journal of the Division for Early Childhood, 11*(2), 171-179.

EISERMAN, W. D., McCOUN, M., & ESCOBAR, C. M. (1990). A cost-effectiveness analysis of two alternative program models for serving speech-disordered preschoolers. *Journal of Early Intervention, 14*(4), 297-317.

ESCOBAR, C. M., & BARNETT, W. S. (1994). Early childhood special education. In W. S. Barnett (Ed.), *Cost analysis for education decisions: Methods and examples* (Vol. 4, pp. 183-201). Greenwich, CT: JAI.

ESCOBAR, C. M., BARNETT, W. S., & KEITH, J. E. (1988). A contingent valuation approach to measuring the benefits of preschool education. *Educational Evaluation and Policy Analysis, 10*(1), 13-22.

KAROLY, L. A., GREENWOOD, P. W., EVERINGHAM, S. S., HOUBE, J., KILBURN, M. R., RYDELL, C. P., SANDERS, M., & CHIESA, J. (1998). *Investing in our children.* Santa Monica, CA: RAND.

TAYLOR, C., WHITE, K. R., & PEZZINO, J. (1984). Cost-effectiveness analysis of full-day versus half-day intervention programs for handicapped preschoolers. *Journal of the Division for Early Childhood, 9*(1), 76-85.

BIBLIOGRAPHY

WARFIELD, M. E. (1994). A cost-effectiveness analysis of early intervention services in Massachusetts: Implications for policy. *Educational Evaluation and Policy Analysis, 16*(1), 87-99.

Early Childhood Education: Developing Countries

BEDI, A. S., & MARSHALL, J. H. (1999). School attendance and student achievement: Evidence from rural Honduras. *Economic Development and Cultural Change, 47*(3), 657-682.

TAN, J. -P., LANE, J., & COUSTERE, P. (1997). Putting inputs to work in elementary schools: What can be done in the Philippines? *Economic Development and Cultural Change, 45*(4), 857-879.

Educational Media: Developed Countries

LUMSDEN, K., & RITCHIE, C. (1975). The open university: A survey and economic analysis. *Instructional Science, 4*(3/4), 237-292.

WAGNER, L. (1982). *The economics of educational media.* New York: St. Martin's.

Educational Media: Developing Countries

CARNOY, M. (1975). The economic costs and returns to educational television. *Economic Development and Cultural Change, 23,* 207-248.

CARNOY, M., & LEVIN, H. M. (1975). Evaluation of educational media: Some issues. *Instructional Science, 4*(3/4), 385-406.

JAMISON, D. T., KLEES, S. J., & WELLS, S. J. (1978). *The costs of educational media: Guidelines for planning and evaluation.* Beverly Hills, CA: Sage.

JAMISON, D. T., & ORIVEL, F. The cost-effectiveness of distance teaching for school equivalency. In H. Perraton (Ed.), *Alternative routes to formal education: Distance teaching for school equivalency.* Baltimore: Johns Hopkins University Press.

KLEES, S. J. (1995). Economics of educational technology. In M. Carnoy (Ed.), *International encyclopedia of economics of education* (2nd ed., pp. 398-406). Oxford, UK: Pergamon.

MAYO, J., McANANY, E., & KLEES, S. (1975). The Mexican Telesecundaria: A cost-effectiveness analysis. *Instructional Science, 4*(3/4), 197-236.

WAGNER, L. (1982). *The economics of educational media.* New York: St. Martin's.

Employment Training and Vocational Programs: Developed Countries

ASHENFELTER, O. (1978). Estimating the effect of training programs on earnings. *Review of Economics and Statistics, 60*(1), 47-57.

BELL, S. H., & ORR, L. L. (1994). Is subsidized employment cost effective for welfare recipients? *Journal of Human Resources, 29*(1), 42-61.

CHAMBERS, J. (1994). Career oriented high schools. In W. S. Barnett (Ed.), *Cost analysis for education decisions: Methods and examples* (Vol. 4, pp. 75-111). Greenwich, CT: JAI.

CONLEY, R. W. (1969). A benefit-cost analysis of the vocational rehabilitation program. *Journal of Human Resources, 4*(2), 226-252.

HU, T., LEE, M. L., & STROMSDORFER, E. W. (1971). Economic returns to vocational and comprehensive high school graduates. *Journal of Human Resources, 6*(1), 25-50.

HU, T., & STROMSDORFER, E. W. (1979). Cost-benefit analysis of vocational education. In T. Abramson, C. K. Tittle, & L. Cohen (Eds.), *Handbook of Vocational Education.* Beverly Hills, CA: Sage.

LEWIS, D. R. (1989). Use of cost-utility decision models in business education. *Journal of Education for Business, 64*(6), 275-278.

LEWIS, D. R., JOHNSON, D. R., CHEN, T. -H., & ERICKSON, R. N. (1992). The use and reporting of benefit-cost analyses by state vocational rehabilitation agencies. *Evaluation Review, 16*(3), 266-287.

MANSKI, C. F. & GARFINKEL, I. (Eds.). (1992). *Evaluating welfare and training programs.* Cambridge, MA: Harvard University Press.

ORR, L. L., BLOOM, H. S., BELL, S. H., DOOLITTLE, F., LIN, W., & CAVE, G. (1996). *Does job training for the disadvantaged work? Evidence from the National JTPA Study.* Washington, DC: Urban Institute.

RIBICH, T. (1968). *Education and poverty.* Washington, DC: Brookings Institution.

Employment Training and Vocational Programs: Developing Countries

BAS, D. (1988). Cost-effectiveness of training in developing countries. *International Labour Review, 127*(3), 355-369.

BELLEW, R., & MOOCK, P. (1990). Vocational and technical education in Peru. *Economics of Education Review, 9*(4), 365-375.

BENNELL, P. (1993). The cost-effectiveness of alternative training modes: Engineering artisans in Zimbabwe. *Comparative Education Review, 37*(4), 434-453.

TSANG, M. C. (1997). The cost of vocational training. *International Journal of Manpower, 18*(1/2), 63-89.

Higher Education: Developed Countries

CATTERALL, J. S. (1998). A cost-effectiveness model for the assessment of educational productivity. In J. E. Groccia & J. E. Miller (Eds.), *Enhancing productivity: Administrative, instructional, and technological strategies.* San Francisco: Jossey-Bass.

KNAPP, T. R., & KNAPP, L. T. (1990). A benefit-cost analysis of New York State's "Bundy Aid" program. *Economics of Education Review, 9*(1), 31-37.

LEWIS, D. R., & KALLSEN, L. A. (1995). Multiattribute evaluations: An aid in reallocation decisions in higher education. *Review of Higher Education, 18*(4), 437-465.

MASSY, W. F., & WILGER, A. K. (1998). Technology's contribution to higher education productivity. In J. E. Groccia & J. E. Miller (Eds.), *Enhancing productivity: Administrative, instructional, and technological strategies* (pp. 49-59). San Francisco: Jossey-Bass.

BIBLIOGRAPHY

ST. JOHN, E. P., & MASTEN, C. L. (1990). Return on the federal investment in student financial aid: An assessment for the high school class of 1972. *Journal of Student Financial Aid, 20*(3), 4-23.

Methodology and Reviews (Education): Developed Countries

ALKIN, M. C., & SOLMON, L. C. (Eds.). (1983). *The costs of evaluation.* Beverly Hills, CA: Sage.

BARNETT, W. S., FREDE, E. C., COX, J. O., & BLACK, T. (1994). Using cost analysis to improve early childhood programs. In W. S. Barnett (Ed.), *Cost analysis for education decisions: Methods and examples* (Vol. 4, pp. 145-181). Greewich, CT: JAI.

CHAMBERS, J., & PARRISH, T. (1994). Developing a resource cost database. In W. S. Barnett (Ed.), *Cost analysis for education decisions: Methods and examples* (Vol. 4, pp. 23-44). Greenwich, CT: JAI.

CHAMBERS, J., & PARRISH, T. (1994). Modeling resource costs. In W. S. Barnett (Ed.), *Cost analysis for education decisions: Methods and examples* (Vol. 4, pp. 7-21). Greenwich, CT: JAI.

GREENBERG, D. H., & APPENZELLER, U. (1998). *Cost analysis step by step: A how-to guide for planners and providers of welfare-to-work and other employment and training programs.* New York: Manpower Demonstration Research Corporation.

LEVIN, H. M. (1975). Cost-effectiveness in evaluation research. In M. Guttentag & E. Struening (Eds.), *Handbook of evaluation research* (Vol. 2, pp. 89-122). Beverly Hills, CA: Sage.

LEVIN, H. M. (1981). Cost analysis. In N. Smith (Ed.), *New techniques for evaluation.* Beverly Hills, CA: Sage.

LEVIN, H. M. (1988). Cost-effectiveness and educational policy. *Educational Evaluation and Policy Analysis, 10*(1), 51-69.

LEVIN, H. M. (1991). Cost-effectiveness at quarter century. In M. W. McLaughlin & D. C. Phillips (Eds.), *Evaluation and education at quarter century* (pp. 188-209). Chicago: University of Chicago Press.

LEVIN, H. M. (1995). Cost-benefit analysis. In M. Carnoy (Ed.), *International encyclopedia of economics of education* (2nd ed., pp. 360-364). Oxford, UK: Pergamon.

LEVIN, H. M. (1995). Cost-effectiveness analysis. In M. Carnoy (Ed.), *International encyclopedia of economics of education* (2nd ed., pp. 381-386). Oxford, UK: Pergamon.

MONK, D. H., & KING, J. A. (1993). Cost analysis as a tool for education reform. In S. L. Jacobson & R. Berne (Eds.), *Reforming education: The emerging systemic approach* (pp. 131-150). Thousand Oaks, CA: Corwin Press.

RICE, J. K. (1997). Cost analysis in education: Paradox and possibility. *Educational Evaluation and Policy Analysis, 19*(4), 309-317.

ROTHENBERG, J. (1975). Cost-benefit analysis: a methodological exposition. In M. Guttentag & E. Struening (Eds.), *Handbook of evaluation research* (Vol. 2, pp. 89-122). Beverly Hills, CA: Sage.

SMITH, N. L., & SMITH, J. K. (1985). State-level evaluation uses of cost analysis: A national descriptive survey. In J. S. Catterall (Ed.), *Economic evaluation of public programs* (pp. 83-97). San Francisco: Jossey-Bass.

TSANG, M. C. (1995). Cost analysis in education. In M. Carnoy (Ed.), *International encyclopedia of economics of education* (2nd ed., pp. 386-398). Oxford, UK: Pergamon.

Methodology and Reviews (Education): Developing Countries

COOMBS, P. H., & HALLAK, J. (1987). *Cost analysis in education: A tool for policy and planning.* Baltimore: Johns Hopkins University Press.

FULLER, B., & CLARKE, P. (1994). Raising schools effects while ignoring culture? Local conditions and the influence of classroom tools, rules, and pedagogy. *Review of Educational Research, 64*(1), 119-157.

LOCKHEED, M. E., & HANUSHEK, E. (1988). Improving educational efficiency in developing countries: What do we know? *Compare, 18*(1), 21-37.

PSACHAROPOULOS, G., & WOODHALL, M. (1985). *Education for development: An analysis of investment choices.* Oxford, UK: Oxford University Press.

TSANG, M. C. (1988). Cost analysis for educational policymaking: A review of cost studies in education in developing countries. *Review of Educational Research, 58*(2), 181-230.

Methodology and Reviews (General): Developed Countries

BOARDMAN, A. E., GREENBERG, D. H., VINING, A. R., & WEIMER, D. L. (1996). *Cost-benefit analysis: Concepts and practice.* Upper Saddle River, NJ: Prentice Hall.

CLEMEN, R. T. (1996). *Making hard decisions: An introduction to decision analysis.* (2nd ed.). Pacific Grove, CA: Duxbury.

EDWARDS, W., & NEWMAN, J. R. (1982). *Multiattribute evaluation.* Beverly Hills, CA: Sage.

GOLUB, A. L. (1997). *Decision analysis: An integrated approach.* New York: John Wiley.

KEENEY, R. L., & RAIFFA, H. (1993). *Decisions with multiple objectives.* Cambridge, UK: Cambridge University Press.

MISHAN, E. J. (1988). *Cost-benefit analysis: An informal introduction.* (4th ed.). London: Unwin Hyman.

NAS, T. F. (1996). *Cost-benefit analysis: Theory and application.* Thousand Oaks, CA: Sage.

ROSSI, P. H., & FREEMAN, H. E. (1993). *Evaluation: A systematic approach.* Newbury Park, CA: Sage.

STOKEY, E., & ZECKHAUSER, R. (1978). *A primer for policy analysis.* New York: W. W. Norton.

THOMPSON, M. S. (1980). *Benefit-cost analysis for program evaluation.* Beverly Hills, CA: Sage.

VON WINTERFELDT, D., & EDWARDS, W. (1986). *Decision analysis and behavioral research.* Cambridge, UK: Cambridge University Press.

Methodology and Reviews (General): Developing Countries

LITTLE, I. M. D., & MIRRLEES, J. A. (1974). *Project appraisal and planning for developing countries.* London: Heinemann.

SQUIRE, L., & VAN DER TAK, H. G. (1975). *Economic analysis of projects.* Baltimore: Johns Hopkins University Press.

Methodology and Reviews (Health): Developed Countries

DRUMMOND, M. F., O'BRIEN, B., STODDART, G. L., & TORRANCE, G. W. (1997). *Methods for the economic evaluation of health care programmes.* (2nd ed.). Oxford, UK: Oxford University Press.

GERARD, K. (1992). Cost-utility in practice: A policy maker's guide to the state of the art. *Health Policy, 21,* 249-279.

GOLD, M. R., SIEGEL, J. E., RUSSELL, L. B., & WEINSTEIN, M. C. (1996). *Cost-effectiveness in health and medicine.* New York: Oxford University Press.

JOHANNESSON, M. (1996). *Theory and methods of economic evaluation of health care.* Dordrecht, Netherlands: Kluwer Academic.

SLOAN, F. A. (Ed.). (1995). *Valuing health care: Costs, benefits, and effectiveness of pharmaceuticals and other medical technologies.* Cambridge, UK: Cambridge University Press.

UDVARHELYI, I. S., COLDITZ, G. A., RAI, A., & EPSTEIN, A. M. (1992). Cost-effectiveness and cost-benefit analyses in the medical literature: Are the methods being used correctly? *Annals of Internal Medicine, 116,* 238-244.

WEINSTEIN, M. C., SIEGEL, J. E., GOLD, M. R., KAMLET, M. S., & RUSSELL, L. B. (1996). Recommendations of the panel on cost-effectiveness in health and medicine. *Journal of the American Medical Association, 276*(15), 1253-1258.

WEINSTEIN, M. C., & STASON, W. B. (1977). Foundations of cost-effectiveness analysis for health and medical practices. *New England Journal of Medicine, 296,* 716-721.

Methodology and Reviews (Health): Developing Countries

JAMISON, D. T., MOSLEY, W. H., MEASHAM, A. R., & BOBADILLA, J. L. (Eds.). (1993). *Disease control priorities in developing countries.* Oxford, UK: Oxford University Press.

WORLD BANK. (1993). *World development report 1993: Investing in health.* New York: Oxford University Press.

BIBLIOGRAPHY

Miscellaneous School Inputs (Textbooks, Expenditures, Etc.): Developed Countries

BETTS, J. R. (1996). Is there a link between school inputs and earnings? Fresh scrutiny of an old literature. In G. Burtless (Ed.), *Does money matter? The effect of school resources on student achievement and adult success* (pp. 141-191). Washington, DC: Brookings Institution.

LEVIN, H. M., GLASS, G. V., & MEISTER, G. R. (1987). Cost-effectiveness of computer-assisted instruction. *Evaluation Review, 11*(1), 50-72.

Miscellaneous School Inputs (Textbooks, Expenditures, Etc.): Developing Countries

BEDI, A. S., & MARSHALL, J. H. (1999). School attendance and student achievement: Evidence from rural Honduras. *Economic Development and Cultural Change, 47*(3), 657-682.

FULLER, B., HUA, H., & SNYDER, C. W. (1994). When girls learn more than boys: The influence of time in school and pedagogy in Botswana. *Comparative Education Review, 38*(3), 347-376.

GLEWWE, P. (1996). The relevance of standard estimates of rates of return to schooling for education policy: A critical assessment. *Journal of Development Economics, 51,* 267-290.

GLEWWE, P. (1999). *The economics of school quality investments in developing countries: An empirical study of Ghana.* London: St. Martin's.

HARBISON, R. W., & HANUSHEK, E. A. (1992). *Educational performance of the poor: Lessons from rural northeast Brazil.* Oxford, UK: Oxford University Press.

MURPHY, P. (1993). Costs of an alternative form of second-level education in Malawi. *Comparative Education Review, 37*(2), 107-122.

TAN, J. -P., LANE, J., & COUSTERE, P. (1997). Putting inputs to work in elementary schools: What can be done in the Philippines? *Economic Development and Cultural Change, 45*(4), 857-879.

WORLD BANK. (1996). *India: Primary education achievement and challenges* (Report No. 15756-IN). Washington, DC: Author.

Returns to the Quantity of Education: Developed Countries

ASHENFELTER, O., HARMON, C., & OOSTERBEEK, H. (1999). A review of estimates of the schooling/earnings relationship, with tests for publication bias. *Labour Economics, 6*(4), 453-470.

COHN, E., & ADDISON, J. T. (1998). The economic returns to lifelong learning in OECD countries. *Education Economics, 6*(3), 253-307.

McMAHON, W. W. (1998). Conceptual framework for the analysis of the social benefits of lifelong learning. *Education Economics, 6*(3), 309-346.

WILLIS, R. (1986). Wage determinants: A survey and reinterpretation of human capital earnings functions. In O. Ashenfelter & R. Layard (Eds.), *Handbook of labor economics.* Amsterdam: North Holland.

Returns to the Quantity of Education: Developing Countries

PSACHAROPOULOS, G. (1994). Returns to investment in education: A global update. *World Development, 22*(9), 1325-1343.

PSACHAROPOULOS, G., & NG, Y. C. (1994). Earnings and education in Latin America: Assessing priorities for schooling investments. *Education Economics, 2*(2), 187-207.

PSACHAROPOULOS, G., & WOODHALL, M. (1985). *Education for development: An analysis of investment choices.* Oxford, UK: Oxford University Press.

School Choice and Private Education: Developed Countries

BARTELL, E. (1968). *Costs and benefits of Catholic elementary and secondary schools.* Notre Dame, IN: Notre Dame Press.

CHABOTAR, K. J. (1989). Measuring the costs of magnet schools. *Economics of Education Review, 8*(2), 169-183.

GUERRA, M. J. (1995). *Dollars and sense: Catholic high schools and their finances 1994*. Washington, DC: National Catholic Educational Association.

KEALEY, R. J. (1996). *Balance sheet for Catholic elementary schools: 1995 income and expenses*. Washington, DC: National Catholic Educational Association.

LEVIN, H. M., & DRIVER, C. E. (1997). Costs of an educational voucher system. *Education Economics, 5*(3), 265-283.

BIBLIOGRAPHY

School Choice and Private Education: Developing Countries

BRAY, M. (1996). *Counting the full cost: Parental and community financing of education in East Asia*. Washington, DC: World Bank.

JAMES, E., KING, E. M., & SURYADI, A. (1996). Finance, management, and costs of public and private schools in Indonesia. *Economics of Education Review, 15*(4), 387-398.

JIMENEZ, E., LOCKHEED, M. E., COX, D., LUNA, E., PAQUEO, V., DE VERA, M. L., & WATTANAWAHA, N. (1995). *Public and private secondary education in developing countries* (World Bank Discussion Paper No. 309), Washington, DC: World Bank.

KINGDON, G. (1996). The quality and efficiency of private and public education: A case-study of urban India. *Oxford Bulletin of Economics and Statistics, 58*(1), 57-82.

TAN, J. -P. (1985). The private direct costs of secondary schooling in Tanzania. *International Journal of Educational Development, 5*(1), 1-10.

TSANG, M. C. (1994). Government and private schools. In W. S. Barnett (Ed.), *Cost analysis for education decisions: Methods and examples* (Vol. 4, pp. 203-231). Greenwich, CT: JAI.

TSANG, M. C. (1995). Private and public costs of schooling in developing nations. In M. Carnoy (Ed.), *International encyclopedia of economics of education* (2nd ed., pp. 393-398). Oxford, UK: Pergamon.

TSANG, M. C., & TAOKLAM, W. (1992). Comparing the costs of government and private primary education in Thailand. *International Journal of Educational Development, 12*(3), 177-190.

School-Based Health Interventions: Developed Countries

CAULKINS, J. P., RYDELL, C. P., EVERINGHAM, S. S., CHIESA, J., & BUSHWAY, S. (1999). *An ounce of prevention, a pound of uncertainty: The cost-effectiveness of school-based drug prevention programs.* Santa Monica, CA: RAND.

KIM, S., COLETTI, S. D., CRUTCHFIELD, C. C., WILLIAMS, C., & HEPLER, N. (1995). Benefit-cost analysis of drug abuse prevention programs: A macroscopic approach. *Journal of Drug Education, 25*(2), 111-127.

KLEIN, S. P., BOHANNAN, H. M., BELL, R. M., DISNEY, J. A., FOCH, C. B., & GRAVES, R. C. (1985). The cost and effectiveness of school-based preventive dental care. *American Journal of Public Health, 75*(4), 382-391.

Special Education: Developed Countries

BARNETT, W. S., & PEZZINO, J. (1987). Cost-effectiveness analysis for state and local decision making: An application to half-day and full-day preschool special education programs. *Journal of the Division for Early Childhood, 11*(2), 171-179.

BARNETT, W. S., ESCOBAR, C. M., & RAVSTEN, M. T. (1988). Parent and clinic early intervention for children with language handicaps: A cost-effectiveness analysis. *Journal of the Division for Early Childhood, 12*(4), 290-298.

CHAIKIND, S., DANIELSON, L. C., & BRAUEN, M. L. (1993). What do we know about the costs of special education: A selected review. *Journal of Special Education, 26*(4), 344-370.

CHAMBERS, J. G. (1999). The patterns of expenditures on students with disabilities. In T. B. Parrish, J. G. Chambers, & C. M. Guarino (Eds.), *Funding special education* (pp. 89-123). Thousand Oaks, CA: Corwin Press.

CHAMBERS, J. G., & WOLMAN, J. M. (1998). *What can we learn from state data systems about the cost of special education? A case study of Ohio.* Palo Alto, CA: American Institutes for Research, Center for Special Education Finance.

EISERMAN, W. D., McCOUN, M., & ESCOBAR, C. M. (1990). A cost-effectiveness analysis of two alternative program models for serving speech-disordered preschoolers. *Journal of Early Intervention, 14*(4), 297-317.

ESCOBAR, C. M., & BARNETT, W. S. (1994). Early childhood special education. In W. S. Barnett (Ed.), *Cost analysis for education decisions: Methods and examples* (Vol. 4, pp. 183-201). Greenwich, CT: JAI.

ESCOBAR, C. M., BARNETT, W. S., & KEITH, J. E. (1988). A contingent valuation approach to measuring the benefits of preschool education. *Educational Evaluation and Policy Analysis, 10*(1), 13-22.

FRANKLIN, G. S., & SPARKMAN, W. E. (1978). The cost effectiveness of two program delivery systems for exceptional children. *Journal of Education Finance, 3,* 305-314.

HARTMAN, W. T. (1981). Estimating the costs of educating handicapped children: A resource-cost model approach. *Educational Evaluation and Policy Analysis, 3*(4), 33-47.

HARTMAN, W. T., & FAY, T. A. (1996). Cost-effectiveness of instructional support teams in Pennsylvania. *Journal of Education Finance, 21*(4), 555-580.

KAKALIK, J. S., FURRY, W. S., THOMAS, M. A., & CARNEY, W. F. (1981). *The cost of special education.* Santa Monica, CA: RAND.

LEWIS, D. R., BRUININKS, R. H., & THURLOW, M. (1989). Cost analysis for district-level special education planning, budgeting, and administrating. *Journal of Education Finance, 14,* 466-483.

LEWIS, D. R., BRUININKS, R. H., & THURLOW, M. L. (1990). Cost analysis of special schools for students with mental retardation. *Journal of Special Education, 24*(1), 33-50.

LEWIS, D. R., BRUININKS, R. H., THURLOW, M., & McGREW, K. (1988). Using benefit-cost analysis in special education. *Exceptional Children, 55*(3), 203-214.

LEWIS, D. R., JOHNSON, D. R., ERICKSON, R. N., & BRUININKS, R. H. (1994). Multiattribute evaluation of program alternatives within special education. *Journal of Disability Policy Studies, 5*(1), 77-112.

TAYLOR, C., WHITE, K. R., & PEZZINO, J. (1984). Cost-effectiveness analysis of full-day versus half-day intervention programs for handicapped preschoolers. *Journal of the Division for Early Childhood, 9*(1), 76-85.

WARFIELD, M. E. (1994). A cost-effectiveness analysis of early intervention services in Massachusetts: Implications for policy. *Educational Evaluation and Policy Analysis, 16*(1), 87-99.

Student Assessment: Developed Countries

ALKIN, M. C., & SOLMON, L. C. (Eds.). (1983). *The costs of evaluation.* Beverly Hills, CA: Sage.

CATTERALL, J. S. (1990). Estimating the costs and benefits of large-scale assessments: Lessons from recent research. *Journal of Education Finance, 16,* 1-20.

CATTERALL, J. C., & WINTERS, L. (1994). Competency, certification, and "authentic" assessments. In W. S. Barnett (Ed.), *Cost analysis for education decisions: Methods and examples* (Vol. 4, pp. 233-255). Greenwich, CT: JAI.

MONK, D. H. (1995). The costs of pupil performance assessment: A summary report. *Journal of Education Finance, 20,* 363-371.

STECHER, B. M., & KLEIN, S. P. (1997). The cost of science performance assessments in large-scale testing programs. *Educational Evaluation and Policy Analysis, 19*(1), 1-14.

BIBLIOGRAPHY

Teacher Policy: Developed Countries

DENTON, J. J., & SMITH, N. L. (1985). Alternative teacher preparation programs: a cost-effectiveness comparison. *Educational Evaluation and Policy Analysis, 7*(3), 197-205.

LEVIN, H. M. (1970). A cost-effectiveness analysis of teacher selection. *Journal of Human Resources, 5*(1), 24-33.

LEWIS, D. R. (1990). Estimating the economic worth of a 5th-year licensure program for teachers. *Educational Evaluation and Policy Analysis, 12*(1), 25-39.

Teacher Policy: Developing Countries

BEDI, A. S., & MARSHALL, J. H. (1999). School attendance and student achievement: Evidence from rural Honduras. *Economic Development and Cultural Change, 47*(3), 657-682.

FULLER, B., HUA, H., & SNYDER, C. W. (1994). When girls learn more than boys: The influence of time in school and pedagogy in Botswana. *Comparative Education Review, 38*(3), 347-376.

TATTO, M. T., NIELSEN, D., & CUMMINGS, W. (1991). *Comparing the effects and costs of different approaches for educating primary school teachers: The case of Sri Lanka* (BRIDGES Research Report Series No. 10). Cambridge, MA: Harvard University Press.

Whole-School Reform: Developed Countries

BARNETT, W. S. (1996). Economics of school reform: Three promising models. In H. F. Ladd (Ed.), *Holding schools accountable: Performance-based reform in education* (pp. 299-326). Washington, DC: Brookings Institution.

KING, J. A. (1994). Meeting the educational needs of at-risk students: A cost analysis of three models. *Educational Evaluation and Policy Analysis, 16*(1), 1-19.

References

Angrist, J., & Lavy, V. (1999). Using Maimonides' rule to estimate the effect of class size on scholastic achievement. *Quarterly Journal of Economics, 114*(2), 533-576.

Armitage, J., Gomes-Neto, J. B. F., Harbison, R. W., Holsinger, D. B., & Leite, R. H. (1986). *School quality and achievement in rural Brazil* (Education and Training Department Discussion Paper EDT25). Washington, DC: World Bank.

Barker, R. G., & Gump, P. V. (1964). *Big school, small school: High school size and student behavior.* Stanford, CA: Stanford University Press.

Barnett, W. S. (1985a). Benefit-cost analysis of the Perry Preschool Program and its policy implications. *Educational Evaluation and Policy Analysis, 7*(4), 333-342.

Barnett, W. S. (1985b). *The Perry Preschool Program and its long-term effects: A benefit-cost analysis.* Ypsilanti, MI: High/Scope Educational Research Foundation.

Barnett, W. S. (1992). Benefits of compensatory preschool education. *Journal of Human Resources, 27*(2), 279-312.

Barnett, W. S. (1993). Benefit-cost analysis of preschool education: Findings from a 25-year follow-up. *American Journal of Orthopsychiatry, 63*(4), 500-508.

Barnett, W. S. (Ed.). (1994). *Cost analysis for education decisions: Methods and examples.* (Vol. 4). Greenwich, CT: JAI.

Barnett, W. S. (1996). *Lives in the balance: Age-27 benefit-cost analysis of the High/Scope Perry Preschool Program.* Ypsilanti, MI: High/Scope Press.

Barnett, W. S., & Escobar, C. M. (1987). The economics of early educational intervention: A review. *Review of Educational Research, 57*(4), 387-414.

Bartell, E. (1968). *Costs and benefits of Catholic elementary and secondary schools.* Notre Dame, IN: Notre Dame Press.

Berman, P., & McLaughlin, M. (1975). *The findings in review* (Federal Programs Supporting Educational Change, Vol. 4; R-1589/4-HEW). Santa Monica, CA: RAND.

Betts, J. R. (1996). Is there a link between school inputs and earnings? Fresh scrutiny of an old literature. In G. Burtless (Ed.), *Does money matter? The effect of school resources on student achievement and adult success* (pp. 141-191). Washington, DC: Brookings Institution.

Black, S. E. (1998). Measuring the value of better schools. *Federal Reserve Bank of New York Economic Policy Review, 4*(1), 87-94.

Black, S. E. (1999). Do better schools matter? Parental valuation of elementary education. *Quarterly Journal of Economics, 114*(2), 577-599.

Boardman, A. E., Greenberg, D. H., Vining, A. R., & Weimer, D. L. (1996). *Cost-benefit analysis: Concepts and practice.* Upper Saddle River, NJ: Prentice Hall.

Boaz, D., & Barrett, R. M. (1996). *What would a school voucher buy? The real cost of private school* (Cato Briefing Paper No. 25). Washington, DC: Cato Institute.

Bogart, W. T., & Cromwell, B. A. (1997). How much more is a good school district worth? *National Tax Journal, 50*(2), 215-232.

Boozer, M., & Rouse, C. (1995). *Intraschool variation in class size: Patterns and implications* (National Bureau of Economic Research Working Paper No. 5144). Cambridge, MA: National Bureau of Economic Research.

Boruch, R. F. (1997). *Randomized experiments for planning and evaluation: A practical guide.* Thousand Oaks, CA: Sage.

Bray, M. (1987). *Are small schools the answer? Cost-effective strategies for rural school provision.* London: Commonwealth Secretariat.

Bray, M. (1996). *Counting the full cost: Parental and community financing of education in East Asia.* Washington, DC: World Bank.

Brewer, D. J., Krop, C., Gill, B. P., & Reichardt, R. (1999). Estimating the cost of national class size reductions under different policy alternatives. *Educational Evaluation and Policy Analysis, 21*(2), 179-192.

Briggs, A. H., & Sculpher, M. J. (1995). Sensitivity analysis in economic evaluation: A review of published studies. *Health Economics, 4*(5), 355-371.

Bryk, A. S. (Ed.). (1983). *Stakeholder-based evaluation* (New Directions for Program Evaluation, Vol. 17). San Francisco: Jossey-Bass.

Burtless, G. (1995). The case for randomized field trials in economic and policy research. *Journal of Economic Perspectives, 9*(2), 63-84.

Campbell, D. T., & Stanley, J. C. (1966). *Experimental and quasi-experimental designs for research.* Chicago: Rand McNally.

Card, D., & Krueger, A. B. (1992). Does school quality matter? Returns to education and the characteristics of public schools in the United States. *Journal of Political Economy, 100*(1), 1-40.

Card, D., & Krueger, A. B. (1996). Labor market effects of school quality: Theory and evidence. In G. Burtless (Ed.), *Does money matter? The effect of school resources on student achievement and adult success* (pp. 97-140). Washington, DC: Brookings Institution.

Carnoy, M. (1995). Rates of return to education. In M. Carnoy (Ed.), *International encyclopedia of economics of education* (2nd ed., pp. 364-369). Oxford, UK: Pergamon.

Caulkins, J. P., Rydell, C. P., Everingham, S. S., Chiesa, J., & Bushway, S. (1999). *An ounce of prevention, a pound of uncertainty: The cost-effectiveness of school-based drug prevention programs*. Santa Monica, CA: RAND.

Chambers, J. (1980). The development of a cost of education index. *Journal of Education Finance, 5*(3), 262-281.

Chambers, J. (1981). An analysis of school size under a voucher system. *Educational Evaluation and Policy Analysis, 3*(2), 29-40.

Chambers, J. (1999). *Measuring resources in education: From accounting to the resource cost model approach*. Washington, DC: National Center for Education Statistics.

Chambers, J., & Parrish, T. (1994a). Developing a resource cost database. In W. S. Barnett (Ed.), *Cost analysis for education decisions: Methods and examples* (Vol. 4, pp. 23-44). Greenwich, CT: JAI.

Chambers, J., & Parrish, T. (1994b). Modeling resource costs. In W. S. Barnett (Ed.), *Cost analysis for education decisions: Methods and examples* (Vol. 4, pp. 7-21). Greenwich, CT: JAI.

Chaudhary, M. A., & Stearns, S. C. (1996). Estimating confidence intervals for cost-effectiveness ratios: An example from a randomized trial. *Statistics in Medicine, 15,* 1447-1458.

Clemen, R. T. (1996). *Making hard decisions: An introduction to decision analysis.* (2nd ed.). Pacific Grove, CA: Duxbury.

Cohen, D. K. (1970). Politics and research: Evaluation of social action programs. *Review of Educational Research, 40*(2), 213-238.

Coleman, J. S., Campbell, E. Q., Hobson, C. J., McPartland, J., Mood, A. M., Weinfeld, F. D., & York, R. L. (1966). *Equality of educational opportunity.* (Office of Education Publication No. OE-38001). Washington, DC: Government Printing Office.

Coleman, J. S., Hoffer, T., & Kilgore, S. (1982). *High School Achievement: Public, Catholic, and Private Schools Compared.* New York: Basic Books.

Cook, T. D., & Campbell, D. T. (1979). *Quasi-experimentation: Design and analysis for field studies.* Chicago: Rand McNally.

Coombs, P. H., & Hallak, J. (1987). *Cost analysis in education: A tool for policy and planning.* Baltimore, MD: Johns Hopkins University Press.

Cooper, H. M., & Lindsay, J. J. (1998). Research synthesis and meta-analysis. In L. Bickman & D. J. Rog (Eds.), *Handbook of applied social science research methods* (pp. 315-337). Thousand Oaks, CA: Sage.

Crocker, L., & Algina, J. (1986). *Introduction to classical and modern test theory.* Fort Worth: Harcourt Brace Jovanovich College.

Crone, T. M. (1998, September/October). House prices and the quality of public schools? What are we buying? *Federal Reserve Bank of Philadelphia Business Review,* 3-14.

Cummings, R. G., Brookshire, D. S., & Schultze, W. D. (1986). *Valuing environmental goods: An assessment of the contingent valuation method.* Totowa, NJ: Rowman & Allanheld.

Detsky, A. S. (1995). Evidence of effectiveness: Evaluating its quality. In F. A. Sloan (Ed.), *Valuing health care: Costs, benefits, and effectiveness of pharmaceuticals and other medical technologies* (pp. 15-29). Cambridge, UK: Cambridge University Press.

Dorfman, R. (1967). *Prices and markets.* Englewood Cliffs, NJ: Prentice Hall.

Downes, T. A., & Pogue, T. F. (1994). Adjusting school aid formulas for the higher cost of educating disadvantaged students. *National Tax Journal, 47*(1), 89-110.

Dranove, D. (1995). Measuring costs. In F. A. Sloan (Ed.), *Valuing health care: Costs, benefits, and effectiveness of pharmaceuticals and other medical technologies* (pp. 61-75). Cambridge, UK: Cambridge University Press.

Drummond, M., Torrance, G., & Mason, J. (1993). Cost-effectiveness league tables: More harm than good? *Social Science in Medicine, 37*(1), 33-40.

Drummond, M. F., O'Brien, B., Stoddart, G. L., & Torrance, G. W. (1997). *Methods for the economic evaluation of health care programmes.* (2nd ed.). Oxford, UK: Oxford University Press.

Duncombe, W., Ruggiero, J., & Yinger, J. (1996). Alternative approaches to measuring the cost of education. In H. F. Ladd (Ed.), *Holding schools accountable: Performance-based reform in education* (pp. 327-356). Washington, DC: Brookings Institution.

Eddy, D. M. (1991). Oregon's methods: Did cost-effectiveness analysis fail? *Journal of the American Medical Association, 266*(15), 2135-2141.

Edwards, W., & Newman, J. R. (1982). *Multiattribute evaluation.* Beverly Hills, CA: Sage.

Escobar, C. M., Barnett, W. S., & Keith, J. E. (1988). A contingent valuation approach to measuring the benefits of preschool education. *Educational Evaluation and Policy Analysis, 10*(1), 13-22.

Fisher, A., Chestnut, L. G., & Violette, D. M. (1989). The value of reducing risks of death: A note on new evidence. *Journal of Policy and Management, 8,* 88-100.

Fletcher, J. D., Hawley, D. E., & Piele, P. K. (1990). Costs, effects, and utility of microcomputer assisted instruction in the classroom. *American Educational Research Journal, 27*(4), 783-806.

Fuller, B., & Clarke, P. (1994). Raising schools effects while ignoring culture? Local conditions and the influence of classroom tools, rules, and pedagogy. *Review of Educational Research, 64*(1), 119-157.

Fuller, B., Hua, H., & Snyder, C. W. (1994). When girls learn more than boys: The influence of time in school and pedagogy in Botswana. *Comparative Education Review, 38*(3), 347-376.

Garber, A. M., & Phelps, C. E. (1997). Economic foundations of cost-effectiveness analysis. *Journal of Health Economics, 16*, 1-31.

Garber, A. M., Weinstein, M. C., Torrance, G. W., & Kamlet, M. S. (1996). Theoretical foundations of cost-effectiveness analysis. In M. R. Gold, L. B. Russell, J. E. Siegel, & M. C. Weinstein (Eds.), *Cost-effectiveness in health and medicine* (pp. 25-53). New York: Oxford University Press.

Gerard, K. (1992). Cost-utility in practice: A policy maker's guide to the state of the art. *Health Policy, 21*, 249-279.

Glass, G. V. (1984). *The effectiveness of four educational interventions* (Project Report No. 84-A19). Stanford, CA: Stanford University, Institute for Research on Educational Finance and Governance.

Glass, G. V., Cohen, L., Smith, M. L., & Filby, N. (1982). *School class size.* Beverly Hills, CA: Sage.

Glewwe, P. (1999). *The economics of school quality investments in developing countries: An empirical study of Ghana.* London: St. Martin's.

Gold, M. R., Patrick, D. L., Torrance, G. W., Fryback, D. G., Hadorn, D. C., Kamlet, M. S., Daniels, N., & Weinstein, M. C. (1996). Identifying and valuing outcomes. In M. R. Gold, L. B. Russell, J. E. Siegel, & M. C. Weinstein (Eds.), *Cost-effectiveness in health and medicine* (pp. 82-134). New York: Oxford University Press.

Gold, M. R., Siegel, J. E., Russell, L. B., & Weinstein, M. C. (1996). *Cost-effectiveness in health and medicine.* New York: Oxford University Press.

Golub, A. L. (1997). *Decision analysis: An integrated approach.* New York: John Wiley.

Greenberg, D. H., & Appenzeller, U. (1998). *Cost analysis step by step: A how-to guide for planners and providers of welfare-to-work and other employment and training programs.* New York: Manpower Demonstration Research Corporation.

Greene, W. H. (1997). *Econometric analysis* (3rd ed.). Upper Saddle River, NJ: Prentice Hall.

Greenwald, R., Hedges, L. V., & Laine, R. D. (1996). The effect of school resources on student achievement. *Review of Educational Research, 66*(3), 361-396.

Grissmer, D. (1999). Class size effects: Assessing the evidence, its policy implications, and future research agenda. *Educational Evaluation and Policy Analysis, 21*(2), 231-248.

Hanushek, E. A. (1986). The economics of schooling: Production and efficiency in public schools. *Journal of Economic Literature, 24*(3), 1141-1177.

Hanushek, E. A. (1997). Assessing the effect of school resources on student performance: An update. *Educational Evaluation and Policy Analysis, 19*(2), 141-164.

Hanushek, E. A. (1999). Some findings from an independent investigation of the Tennessee STAR experiment and from other investigations of class size effects. *Educational Evaluation and Policy Analysis, 21*(2), 143-164.

Harbison, R. W., & Hanushek, E. A. (1992). *Educational performance of the poor: Lessons from rural northeast Brazil.* Oxford, UK: Oxford University Press.

Hartman, W. T. (1981). Estimating the costs of educating handicapped children: A resource-cost model approach. *Educational Evaluation and Policy Analysis, 3*(4), 33-47.

Hartman, W. T., & Fay, T. A. (1996). Cost-effectiveness of instructional support teams in Pennsylvania. *Journal of Education Finance, 21*(4), 555-580.

Heckman, J. J. (1979). Sample selection bias as a specification error. *Econometrica, 47*(1), 153-161.

Heckman, J. J., Layne-Farrar, A., & Todd, P. (1996). Does measured school quality really matter? An examination of the earnings-quality relationship. In G. Burtless (Ed.), *Does money matter? The effect of school resources on student achievement and adult success* (pp. 192-289). Washington, DC: Brookings Institution.

Heckman, J. J., & Smith, J. A. (1995). Assessing the case for social experiments. *Journal of Economic Perspectives, 9*(2), 85-110.

Hedges, L. V., & Olkin, I. (1985). *Statistical methods for meta-analysis.* Orlando, FL: Academic Press.

Hopfenberg, W. S., Levin, H. M., Chase, C., Christensen, S. G., Moore, M., Soler, P., Brunner, I., Keller, B., & Rodriguez, G. (1993). *The accelerated schools resource guide.* San Francisco: Jossey-Bass.

Hoxby, C. M. (1998). What do America's "traditional" forms of school choice teach us about school choice reforms? *Federal Reserve Bank of New York Economic Policy Review, 4*(1), 47-59.

Independent School District of Boise City. (1983). *1982-83 evaluation report* (Project Instruct, Chapter 1 Program). Boise, ID: Author.

Jamison, D. T., Klees, S. J., & Wells, S. J. (1978). *The costs of educational media: Guidelines for planning and evaluation.* Beverly Hills, CA: Sage.

Jamison, D. T., Mosley, W. H., Measham, A. R., & Bobadilla, J. L. (Eds.). (1993). *Disease control priorities in developing countries.* Oxford, UK: Oxford University Press.

Jimenez, E., Lockheed, M. E., Cox, D., Luna, E., Paqueo, V., de Vera, M. L., & Wattanawaha, N. (1995). *Public and private secondary education in developing countries* (World Bank Discussion Paper No. 309), Washington, DC: World Bank.

Johannesson, M. (1996). *Theory and methods of economic evaluation of health care.* Dordrecht, Netherlands: Kluwer Academic.

Jones-Lee, M. W. (1989). *The economics of safety and risk.* Oxford, UK: Basil Blackwell.

Kaplan, R. M. (1995). Utility assessment for estimating quality-adjusted life years. In F. A. Sloan (Ed.), *Valuing health care: Costs, benefits, and effectiveness of pharmaceuticals and other medical technologies* (pp. 31-60). Cambridge, UK: Cambridge University Press.

Kealey, R. J. (1996). *Balance sheet for Catholic elementary schools: 1995 income and expenses.* Washington, DC: National Catholic Educational Association.

Keeler, E. (1995). Decision trees and Markov models in cost-effectiveness research. In F. A. Sloan (Ed.), *Valuing health care: Costs, benefits, and effectiveness of pharmaceuticals and other medical technologies* (pp. 185-205). Cambridge, UK: Cambridge University Press.

Keeler, E. B., & Cretin, S. (1983). Discounting of life-saving and other nonmonetary effects. *Management Science, 29,* 300-306.

Keeney, R. L., & Raiffa, H. (1976). *Decisions with multiple objectives.* New York: Wiley.

Keeney, R. L., & Raiffa, H. (1993). *Decisions with multiple objectives.* Cambridge, UK: Cambridge University Press.

Kenny, L. W. (1982). Economies of scale in schooling. *Economics of Education Review, 2*(1), 1-24.

Krueger, A. (1999). Experimental estimates of education production functions. *Quarterly Journal of Economics, 114*(2), 497-532.

Laska, E. M., Meisner, M., & Siegel, C. (1997). Statistical inference for cost-effectiveness ratios. *Health Economics, 6,* 229-242.

Layard, P. R. G., & Walters, A. A. (1978). *Microeconomic theory.* New York: McGraw-Hill.

Lee, V. E., & Smith, J. B. (1997). High school size: Which works best and for whom? *Educational Evaluation and Policy Analysis, 19*(3), 205-227.

Levin, H. M. (1975). Cost-effectiveness in evaluation research. In M. Guttentag & E. Struening (Eds.), *Handbook of evaluation research* (Vol. 2, pp. 89-122). Beverly Hills, CA: Sage.

Levin, H. M. (1981). Cost analysis. In N. Smith (Ed.), *New techniques for evaluation*. Beverly Hills, CA: Sage.

Levin, H. M. (1988). Cost-effectiveness and educational policy. *Educational Evaluation and Policy Analysis, 10*(1), 51-69.

Levin, H. M. (1991). Cost-effectiveness at quarter century. In M. W. McLaughlin & D. C. Phillips (Eds.), *Evaluation and education at quarter century* (pp. 188-209). Chicago: University of Chicago Press.

Levin, H. M. (1995). Cost-effectiveness analysis. In M. Carnoy (Ed.), *International encyclopedia of economics of education* (2nd ed., pp. 381-386). Oxford, UK: Pergamon.

Levin, H. M. (1998). Educational vouchers: Effectiveness, choice, and costs. *Journal of Policy Analysis and Management, 17*(3), 373-391.

Levin, H. M., & Driver, C. E. (1996). Estimating the costs of an educational voucher system. In W. J. Fowler (Ed.), *Selected papers in school finance 1994* (pp. 67-87). Washington, DC: National Center for Education Statistics.

Levin, H. M., & Driver, C. E. (1997). Costs of an educational voucher system. *Education Economics, 5*(3), 265-283.

Levin, H. M., Glass, G. V., & Meister, G. R. (1987). Cost-effectiveness of computer-assisted instruction. *Evaluation Review, 11*(1), 50-72.

Levin, J., & Plug, E. J. S. (1999). Instrumenting education and the returns to schooling in the Netherlands. *Labour Economics, 6*(4), 521-534.

Lewis, D. R. (1989). Use of cost-utility decision models in business education. *Journal of Education for Business, 64*(6), 275-278.

Lewis, D. R., Johnson, D. R., Chen, T. -H., & Erickson, R. N. (1992). The use and reporting of benefit-cost analyses by state vocational rehabilitation agencies. *Evaluation Review, 16*(3), 266-287.

Lewis, D. R., Johnson, D. R., Erickson, R. N., & Bruininks, R. H. (1994). Multiattribute evaluation of program alternatives within special education. *Journal of Disability Policy Studies, 5*(1), 77-112.

Lewis, D. R., & Kallsen, L. A. (1995). Multiattribute evaluations: An aid in reallocation decisions in higher education. *The Review of Higher Education, 18*(4), 437-465.

Lewis, D. R., Stockdill, S. J., & Turner, T. C. (1990). Cost-effectiveness of microcomputers in adult basic reading. *Adult Literacy and Basic Education, 14*(2), 136-149.

Light, R. J., Singer, J. D., & Willett, J. B. (1990). *By design: Planning research on higher education*. Cambridge, MA: Harvard University Press.

Lipscomb, J., Weinstein, M. C., & Torrance, G. W. (1996). Time preference. In M. R. Gold, L. B. Russell, J. E. Siegel, & M. C. Weinstein (Eds.), *Cost-effectiveness in health and medicine* (pp. 214-246). New York: Oxford University Press.

Lockheed, M. E., & Hanushek, E. (1988). Improving educational efficiency in developing countries: What do we know? *Compare, 18*(1), 21-37.

Lou, Y., Abrami, P. C., Spence, J. C., Poulsen, C., Chambers, B., & d'Apollonia, S. (1996). Within-class grouping: A meta-analysis. *Review of Educational Research, 66*(4), 423-458.

Luce, B. R., Manning, W. G., Siegel, J. E., & Lipscomb, J. (1996). Estimating costs in cost-effectiveness analysis. In M. R. Gold, L. B. Russell, J. E. Siegel, & M. C. Weinstein (Eds.), *Cost-effectiveness in health and medicine* (pp. 176-213). New York: Oxford University Press.

Maddala, G. S. (1983). *Limited-dependent and qualitative variables in econometrics.* Cambridge, UK: Cambridge University Press.

Mandelblatt, J. S., Fryback, D. G., Weinstein, M. C., Russell, L. B., Gold, M. R., & Hadorn, D. C. (1996). Assessing the effectiveness of health interventions. In M. R. Gold, L. B. Russell, J. E. Siegel, & M. C. Weinstein (Eds.), *Cost-effectiveness in health and medicine* (pp. 135-175). New York: Oxford University Press.

Manning, W. G., Fryback, D. G., & Weinstein, M. C. (1996). Reflecting uncertainty in cost-effectiveness analysis. In M. R. Gold, L. B. Russell, J. E. Siegel, & M. C. Weinstein (Eds.), *Cost-effectiveness in health and medicine* (pp. 247-275). New York: Oxford University Press.

Maynard, A. K. (1991). Developing the health care market. *Economic Journal, 101,* 1277-1286.

McEwan, P. J. (1999). Private costs and the rate of return to primary education. *Applied Economics Letters, 6*(11), 759-760.

Mehrotra, S., & Delamonica, E. (1998). Household costs and public expenditure on primary education in five low income countries: A comparative analysis. *International Journal of Educational Development, 18*(1), 41-61.

Mishan, E. J. (1988). *Cost-benefit analysis: An informal introduction.* (4th ed.). London: Unwin Hyman.

Mitchell, R. C., & Carson, R. T. (1989). *Using surveys to value public goods: The contingent valuation method.* Washington, DC: Resources for the Future.

Moffitt, R. (1991). Program evaluation with nonexperimental data. *Evaluation Review, 15*(3), 291-314.

Mohr, L. B. (1995). *Impact analysis for program evaluation.* (2nd ed.). Thousand Oaks, CA: Sage.

Molnar, A., Smith, P., Zahorik, J., Palmer, A., Halbach, A., & Ehrle, K. (1999). Evaluating the SAGE program: A pilot program in targeted pupil-teacher reduction in Wisconsin. *Educational Evaluation and Policy Analysis, 21*(2), 165-177.

Monk, D. H., & King, J. A. (1993). Cost analysis as a tool for education reform. In S. L. Jacobson & R. Berne (Eds.), *Reforming education: The emerging systemic approach* (pp. 131-150). Thousand Oaks, CA: Corwin Press.

Morrall, J. F. (1986). A review of the record. *Regulation, 10*(2), 25-34.

Mosteller, F. (1995). The Tennessee study of class size in the early school grades. *The Future of Children, 5*(2), 113-127.

Mullahy, J., & Manning, W. (1995). Statistical issues in cost-effectiveness analysis. In F. A. Sloan (Ed.), *Valuing health care: Costs, benefits, and effectiveness of pharmaceuticals and other medical technologies* (pp. 149-184). Cambridge, UK: Cambridge University Press.

Murnane, R. J., Newstead, S., & Olsen, R. J. (1985). Comparing public and private schools: The puzzling role of selection bias. *Journal of Business and Economic Statistics, 3*(1), 23-35.

Murphy, P. (1993). Costs of an alternative form of second-level education in Malawi. *Comparative Education Review, 37*(2), 107-122.

Musgrave, R. A., & Musgrave, P. B. (1976). *Public finance in theory and practice.* New York: McGraw-Hill.

Nas, T. F. (1996). *Cost-benefit analysis: Theory and application.* Thousand Oaks, CA: Sage.

Orr, L. L. (1999). *Social experiments.* Thousand Oaks, CA: Sage.

Orr, L. L., Bloom, H. S., Bell, S. H., Doolittle, F., Lin, W., & Cave, G. (1996). *Does job training for the disadvantaged work? Evidence from the National JTPA Study.* Washington, DC: Urban Institute.

Oster, G., & Epstein, A. M. (1987). Cost-effectiveness of antihyperlipidemic therapy in the prevention of coronary heart disease: The case of cholestyramine. *Journal of the American Medical Association, 258*, 2381-2387.

Pauly, M. V. (1995). Valuing health care benefits in money terms. In F. A. Sloan (Ed.), *Valuing health care: Costs, benefits, and effectiveness of pharmaceuticals and other medical technologies* (pp. 99-124). Cambridge, UK: Cambridge University Press.

Peterson, P. E., Myers, D., & Howell, W. G. (1998). *An evaluation of the New York City School Choice Scholarships Program: The first year.* Unpublished manuscript.

Pitz, G. F., & McKillip, J. (1984). *Decision analysis for program evaluators.* Beverly Hills, CA: Sage.

Psacharopoulos, G. (1994). Returns to investment in education: A global update. *World Development, 22*(9), 1325-1343.

Psacharopoulos, G., & Ng, Y. C. (1994). Earnings and education in Latin America: Assessing priorities for schooling investments. *Education Economics, 2*(2), 187-207.

Psacharopoulos, G., & Woodhall, M. (1985). *Education for development: An analysis of investment choices.* Oxford, UK: Oxford University Press.

Quinn, B., Van Mondfrans, A., & Worthen, B. R. (1984). Cost-effectiveness of two math programs as moderated by pupil SES. *Educational Evaluation and Policy Analysis, 6*(1), 39-52.

Ragosta, M., Holland, P. W., & Jamison, D. T. (1982). *Computer-assisted instruction and compensatory education: The ETS/LAUSD study* (Final Report, Project Report No. 19). Princeton, NJ: Educational Testing Service.

Ribich, T. (1968). *Education and poverty.* Washington, DC: Brookings Institution.

Rice, J. K. (1997). Cost analysis in education: Paradox and possibility. *Educational Evaluation and Policy Analysis, 19*(4), 309-317.

Rossi, P. H., & Freeman, H. E. (1993). *Evaluation: A systematic approach* (5th ed.). Newbury Park, CA: Sage.

Rouse, C. E. (1998). Schools and student achievement: More evidence from the Milwaukee Parental Choice Program. *Federal Reserve Bank of New York Economic Policy Review, 4*(1), 61-76.

Saint, S., Veenstra, D. L., & Sullivan, S. D. (1999). The use of meta-analysis in cost-effectiveness analysis. *Pharmacoeconomics, 15*(1), 1-8.

Salkeld, G., Davey, P., & Arnolda, G. (1995). A critical review of health-related economic evaluations in Australia: Implications for health policy. *Health Policy, 31*(2), 111-125.

Scriven, M. (1974). Evaluation perspectives and procedures. In J. W. Popham (Ed.), *Evaluation in education: Current applications.* Berkeley, CA: McCutchan.

Slavin, R. E. (1984). Meta-analysis in education: How has it been used? *Educational Researcher, 13*(8), 6-15, 24-27.

Slavin, R. E. (1986). Best-evidence synthesis: An alternative to meta-analytic and traditional reviews. *Educational Researcher, 15*(9), 5-11.

Sloan, F. A. (Ed.). (1995). *Valuing health care: Costs, benefits, and effectiveness of pharmaceuticals and other medical technologies.* Cambridge, UK: Cambridge University Press.

Sloan, F. A., & Conover, C. J. (1995). The use of cost-effectiveness/cost-benefit analysis in actual decision making: Current status and prospects. In F. A. Sloan (Ed.), *Valuing health care: Costs, benefits, and effectiveness of pharmaceuticals and other medical technologies* (pp. 207-232). Cambridge, UK: Cambridge University Press.

Smith, M. L., & Glass, G. V. (1987). *Research and evaluation in education and the social sciences.* Englewood Cliffs, NJ: Prentice Hall.

Smith, N. L., & Smith, J. K. (1985). State-level evaluation uses of cost analysis: A national descriptive survey. In J. S. Catterall (Ed.), *Economic evaluation of public programs* (pp. 83-97). San Francisco: Jossey-Bass.

Stern, D., Dayton, C., Paik, I. -W., & Weisberg, A. (1989). Benefits and costs of dropout prevention in a high school program combining academic and vocational education: Third-year results from replications of the California Peninsula Academies. *Educational Evaluation and Policy Analysis, 11*(4), 405-416.

Stokey, E., & Zeckhauser, R. (1978). *A primer for policy analysis.* New York: W. W. Norton.

Tatto, M. T., Nielsen, D., & Cummings, W. (1991). *Comparing the effects and costs of different approaches for educating primary school teachers: The case of Sri Lanka* (BRIDGES Research Report Series No. 10). Cambridge, MA: Harvard University Press.

Tsang, M. C. (1988). Cost analysis for educational policymaking: A review of cost studies in education in developing countries. *Review of Educational Research, 58*(2), 181-230.

Tsang, M. C. (1995). Private and public costs of schooling in developing nations. In M. Carnoy (Ed.), *International encyclopedia of economics of education* (2nd ed., pp. 393-398). Oxford, UK: Pergamon.

Tsang, M. C., & Taoklam, W. (1992). Comparing the costs of government and private primary education in Thailand. *International Journal of Educational Development, 12*(3), 177-190.

Udvarhelyi, I. S., Colditz, G. A., Rai, A., & Epstein, A. M. (1992). Cost-effectiveness and cost-benefit analyses in the medical literature: Are the methods being used correctly? *Annals of Internal Medicine, 116*, 238-244.

Viscusi, W. K. (1992). *Fatal trade-offs.* Oxford, UK: Oxford University Press.

Viscusi, W. K. (1995). Discounting health effects for medical decisions. In F. A. Sloan (Ed.), *Valuing health care: Costs, benefits, and effectiveness of pharmaceuticals and other medical technologies* (pp. 125-147). Cambridge, UK: Cambridge University Press.

von Winterfeldt, D., & Edwards, W. (1986). *Decision analysis and behavioral research.* Cambridge, UK: Cambridge University Press.

Walberg, H. J. (1984). Improving the productivity of America's schools. *Educational Leadership, 41*(8), 19-27.

Warfield, M. E. (1994). A cost-effectiveness analysis of early intervention services in Massachusetts: Implications for policy. *Educational Evaluation and Policy Analysis, 16*(1), 87-99.

Weinstein, M. C., Siegel, J. E., Gold, M. R., Kamlet, M. S., & Russell, L. B. (1996). Recommendations of the panel on cost-effectiveness in health and medicine. *Journal of the American Medical Association, 276*(15), 1253-1258.

Weinstein, M. C., & Stason, W. B. (1977). Foundations of cost-effectiveness analysis for health and medical practices. *New England Journal of Medicine, 296*, 716-721.

Weisbrod, B. A. (1965). Preventing high school dropouts. In R. Dorfman (Ed.), *Measuring benefits of government investments* (pp. 117-148). Washington, DC: Brookings Institution.

Weiss, C. H. (1975). Evaluation research in the political context. In E. L. Struening & M. Guttentag (Eds.), *Handbook of evaluation research* (Vol. 1, pp. 13-26). Beverly Hills, CA: Sage.

Weiss, C. H. (1998). *Evaluation* (2nd ed.). Upper Saddle River, NJ: Prentice Hall.

Willis, R. J., & Rosen, S. (1979). Education and self-selection. *Journal of Political Economy, 87*(5), S7-S36.

Witte, J. F. (1992). Private school versus public school achievement: Are there findings that should affect the educational choice debate? *Economics of Education Review, 11*(4), 371-394.

Witte, J. F. (1996). School choice and student performance. In H. F. Ladd (Ed.), *Holding schools accountable: Performance-based reform in education* (pp. 149-176). Washington, DC: Brookings Institution.

Witte, J. F. (1998). The Milwaukee voucher experiment. *Educational Evaluation and Policy Analysis, 20*(4), 229-251.

Wolfe, B. L. (1995). External benefits of education. In M. Carnoy (Ed.), *International encyclopedia of economics of education* (2nd ed., pp. 159-163). Oxford, UK: Pergamon.

Woolridge, J. M. (2000). *Introductory econometrics: A modern approach*. Florence, KY: Southwestern College Publishing.

World Bank. (1993). *World development report 1993: Investing in health*. New York: Oxford University Press.

World Bank. (1996). *India: Primary education achievement and challenges* (Report No. 15756-IN). Washington, DC: Author.

Index

About the Authors

HENRY M. LEVIN is the William Heard Kilpatrick Professor of Economics and Education at Teachers College, Columbia University, and Director of the National Center for the Study of Privatization in Education, a nonpartisan entity. He is also the David Jacks Professor Emeritus of Higher Education and Economics at Stanford University, where he served from 1968 to 1999. He is a specialist in the economics of education and has published 14 books and almost 300 articles in this and related fields. He is the recipient of numerous awards, including the Gunnar Myrdal Prize for Contributions to the Field of Evaluation. For the last 14 years, Levin has dedicated himself to the establishment and development of the Accelerated Schools Project, a national school reform project for accelerating the education of at-risk youngsters.

PATRICK J. MCEWAN is currently at the University of Illinois at Urbana-Champaign. Formerly, he was Assistant Director for Research at the National Center for the Study of Privatization in Education at Teachers College, Columbia University. He completed his Ph.D. in education at Stanford University, in addition to master's degrees in economics and international development. He has consulted on education policy and evaluation at numerous institutions, including the Inter-American Development Bank, UNESCO, and the ministries of education of several countries. His most recent research, with Martin Carnoy, evaluated the impact of Chile's national voucher plan on the effectiveness and efficiency of primary education.